BUCK BARRY

Lawerence T. Jones III collection, Austin, Texas

BUCK BARRY
TEXAS RANGER
and
FRONTIERSMAN

Editor—Biographer
JAMES K. GREER

University of Nebraska Press
Lincoln and London

First Bison Book printing: October 1984

Library of Congress Cataloging in Publication Data
Barry, James Buckner, 1821–1906.
  Buck Barry, Texas ranger and frontiersman.
  Reprint. Originally published: New ed. Waco, Tex. :
Friends of the Moody Texas Ranger Library, c1978.
  Includes index.
  1. Barry, James Buckner, 1821–1906. 2. Pioneers—
Texas—Biography. 3. Texas Rangers—Biography.
4. Frontier and pioneer life—Texas. 5. Texas—History—
1845–1950. 6. Indians of North America—Texas—Wars—
1815–1875. I. Greer, James K. II. Title.
F391.B28 1984   976.4'05'0924 [B]   84-11863
ISBN 0-8032-2119-3
ISBN 0-8032-7013-5 (pbk.)

To
P.M.G.H.

THE RANGER

Once along the border, like the drift of autumn leaves,
Thronged the Indians, desperadoes and the cattle-lifting
    thieves
Until there came swift-riding over the valley, hill and flat
The Law in dirk and derringer and tall—white—hat.

Rip Ford and old Buck Barry—there is glamor in the names
Of the men who made the Rangers, as the record still
    proclaims:
The lifter left the cattle and the outlaw hid his gat
When they thought about the rider in the tall—white—hat.

As tall as he his story from the borderland uncouth—
Some of it is legend but most of it is truth . . .
For fact stands out of hard fought fight, or years of stand-up
    strife—
The Ranger rode the border and the outlaw rode for life.

His is a tale unended. Still riding down the years
Come the hoofbeats of the Ranger and his stalwart form
    appears . . .
Though dark may be the danger, he has no care for that,
Riding on into the future in his tall—white—hat.

William B. Ruggles, Dallas
Trails of Texas (San Antonio, 1972)

FOREWORD TO THE FIRST EDITION

A GENERATION ago the historian, George P. Garrison, said that, "the greatness of Texas lies, not so much in its vast extent of territory and its abundance of natural resources, as in the character of its people, which is a composite—with the good predominant—of qualities peculiar to many lands, whence the citizenship of the State has been recruited."

Even before the fall of the Alamo and the Battle of San Jacinto, pioneers of Texas, led by the immortal statesman, diplomat, and greatest of impresarios, Stephen F. Austin, dreamed of a great future for the southwest. These same pioneers blazed the way for the Lone Star State's accomplishment with daring, faith, and resolute labor. Perhaps it was their vision which gave them strength to carry on when less resolute men would have given up because of the apparently overwhelming odds.

One man who was attracted by the gleaming star of the southwest and who answered its appeal before the Republic of Texas had ceased to use its original flag, was James Buckner Barry of North Carolina, a descendant of men who had fought for independence in both hemispheres. He was to serve in three of her armies and do such deeds as become traditions. Not quite early enough to meet Travis and Bowie, he knew Houston and Johnston, Hays and the McCullochs, Throckmorton and Mills, Chief Placidio of the friendly Tonkawas and Iron Jacket of the raiding Comanches. As a Ranger with Hays he met the Mexican, as a sheriff he encountered outlaws, as a frontiersman he fought Indians, as a stockfarmer he was the Nemesis of horse thieves, as a ranchman he experienced the annoyance of fence cutting, and as a Texan and southerner he saw four years of the most gruelling, the most undesirable type of military service. On the other hand, he served as a faithful county civil officer, legislator, and village postmaster. Nor did life in the great period of adventure before, during, and after the Civil War prevent his frequent attendance on the services of the circuit rider and the occasional camp meeting in his section of the State. No writer of western stories has created better fiction of adventure than this quiet, unassuming, early settler lived, although he does not meticulously detail it. But, perhaps, by its very simplicity—this commendable restraint—his story gains in force.

Following the Mexican War, settlers flocked to Texas in even greater numbers than before; and their rapidly moving line of settlement westward angered the Indian, who slipped into the settlements, made his attack with arms and torch—at times kidnaping women and children—herded together the horses of his victim as booty, and rode rapidly on his return by trails he well knew. Unorganized, the frontiersmen had to fend off the raiders as best they could, gather volunteer bands and pursue at once. Out of these experiences grew such organizations as the Texas Rangers and the Texas Frontier Regiment of which last Wooten's *History of Texas* records that, "the service rendered is said to have been the most efficient ever given the frontier [of Texas], and that during the two years of its service more stolen property was recaptured and more marauding Indians killed than were recaptured and killed by the United States troops from Annexation to 1861." The same source states that:

> The members of this regiment shared few of the honors of the war, but the dangers which they encountered were exceeded by few others, and the numerous unmarked graves which excite the curiosity of the settlers in the section of country covered by them, attest many a bloody encounter with hostile savages. No flowers are strewn upon their graves on Decoration Day, no monuments are erected to their memory, but the vast extent of country then depending upon them solely for protection suffered none of

the horrors and few of the privations of war; and its brave defenders are still held in grateful remembrance by the early settlers upon the Texas Frontier.

Barry and his wife owned slaves and these, together with his stock and lands, had enabled him to get on the road to prosperity as a prominent frontier stockfarmer before the war. But the losses occasioned by Indian raids, by the Civil War, and by enforced neglect of his private interests while in public service were heavier than he could afterwards overcome. But apparently he was happy. Perhaps his life was a good example of the maxims on service and happiness.

The old lure of the frontier lives still in the popular craving for its story. Despite the successes of hundreds of writers of western fiction, the most satisfactory accounts are those of the frontiersmen themselves. Simple and modest though these narratives often are, they bear the stamp of genuine experience; we can never have too many of them.

Colonel Barry himself has stated how he came to write his reminiscences. He had retained his military papers and military post order book; his diary, covering several years previous to the middle of 1862, and his official and personal correspondence. As he wrote he was thus enabled to refer to these data. The task was interrupted by blindness a few years before his death, and although relatives planned to secure a stenographer to take the remainder of his narrative, it was never done.

When, in December, 1906, he died at his home in Walnut Springs, Texas, he left these papers to his son, Mr. Kossuth Barry. The son presented them to the Archives of the University of Texas in February, 1927.

As Barry was a man of action rather than a student of composition and never set down his experiences with publication in mind, the editor has made certain minor corrections in the reminiscences that the author would have no doubt made had the opportunity of proof reading been his. Several pages of the reminiscences irrelevant to the narrative and of no permanent historical value have been eliminated; for instance, Barry's views on natural history. A few explanatory statements, taken largely from the diary, which runs concurrently from 1855 to 1862, inclusive, and is a repetition of much of the reminiscences and was no doubt frequently consulted by the narrator, have been added. Care was taken, however, not to modify the style of the narrator nor his meaning. The chief function of the editor has been to complete the story, using the Barry papers not only as a source but weaving them together so that they complete the tale. Only the central thread of the narrative was extended so that much interesting material has been discarded. But this is in keeping with Barry's method, and is as he would have had it, since he was unobtrusive in manner and had the military disinclination toward garrulity. Long hours in the saddle on the trail of the wary Comanche was conducive to the development of reticence and terseness rather than volubility. It was deemed proper to add a casual epilogue.

It is trite but true to say that the cosmopolitan Texas of today was made possible by the activities of our pioneers. And the last word of the preceding statement is a much abused one. Men, it has been frequently said, are worth more than money. It is to be hoped that the present volume may suggest studies of other somewhat unusual personalities among our leaders and frontiersmen, especially of the type who were modest about their own achievements.

Grateful acknowledgments are due Miss Winnie Allen, Assistant Archivist, University of Texas, who freely placed the Barry papers at my disposal, and Charles W. Ramsdell, Professor of American History, University of Texas, who helpfully read the completed manuscript.

JAMES K. GREER

Birmingham, Alabama
March, 1932

PREFACE TO THE 1978 EDITION

The first edition of BUCK BARRY is now rare. Entitled A TEXAS RANGER AND FRONTIERSMAN: THE DAYS OF BUCK BARRY IN TEXAS, it was published in 1932 by The Southwest Press. Though no new chapters have been added, it was deemed highly desirable to reissue this book. The narrative is Barry's, yet the editor-biographer felt compelled to complete the memoir by composing, chiefly from Barry's sources, the last six chapters in the first edition. Changes have been made in the preliminaries, but this edition is essentially a reprint.

The *New York Times* (July 10, 1932) stated; "Very much of a man Colonel James Buckner Barry, whose modest story of his experiences in the pioneer days of Texas makes this book." And the *New York Herald Tribune* (July 17, 1932) declared Barry "was absolutely fearless," yet "His fame rests not upon flaming deeds but upon being a solid citizen, one of the substantial pioneers who kept their word, worked hard, fought Indians, loved their families and their state." The *Boston Evening Transcript* (July 9, 1932) affirmed that Barry's adventures constitute "a real epic of personal adventure. . . ." "To his uncommon knowledge of human nature and Indian character Barry added the characteristic of self-possession and promptness in action so essential to a frontier leader."

Allen Peden wrote (*See* the *Houston Gargoyle,* July 3, 1932): "Readers such books as this (BUCK BARRY) one is again reminded that the alleged troubles of this soft age of ours would have seemed puny to the he-men who fought the battles of the wilderness." However, Americans now are engaged in a struggle to preserve their principles and ideals. Past experience will perform a primary part in the making of our future. Perhaps today's youth will see in Buck Barry their present problems in their right historical perspective.

James K. Greer

Waco, Texas
October 1978

CONTENTS

ILLUSTRATIONS

MAPS

BARRY'S PREFACE

MY CHILDREN have urged me for years to write up short sketches and reminiscences of my journey through life, and numerous other individuals have also manifested an interest in my experiences. I shall endeavor to comply with their request by giving them some idea of my origin, or ancestry; reminiscences of my boyhood, my departure from my North Carolina home and the subsequent voyage to Texas; a narration of the happenings in my life in Texas up to the date of my marriage, my life in the Trinity River country; and later, on the Bosque, some experiences as a settler before, during and after the Civil War, and of my later life up to the present time.

Though many incidents and experiences through life may be overlooked or forgotten that would be of some interest to my children, I will promise them that there shall be no fictitious stories of my own put in this book for them to waste time in reading. But there are many reminiscences which I have gathered from old pioneers and comrades that have never found their way into history, and there can be, at this time, no better material produced than the words of these old pioneers. I will perhaps refer to them as told to myself. Occasionally, I will endeavor to present my ideas, also, on religion and politics, as politics is said to be good for our bodies while we live, and it is pleasant to have the hope, while we live, that religion will comfort our souls after we die. It appears to me that every man who has not the moral courage to proclaim to the world individually and independently both his religion and politics, is a moth to society.[1]

J. B. BARRY

---

[1]Preface to Barry's reminiscences, one of the sources of this volume.

CHAPTER I

BOYHOOD IN NORTH CAROLINA

MY GREAT-GRANDFATHER, James Buckner Barry, whose name I bear, was born in Ireland. Some time during the early part of the seventeenth century there was a rebellion in Ireland in which he took an active part. When the rebellion was quelled he fled the country to save his neck from a British halter. He shipped to America, disguised as an emigrant. To make more perfect the disguise, he brought my grandfather who was only four years old at that time. I have no information of his ever hearing from his family after he left Ireland. He stopped in the upper part of Cartwright County, North Carolina, near the line of Jones County, where he died, leaving my grandfather (Bryant Buckner Barry) to battle through life the best he could.

My grandfather grew to manhood and married an Irish girl whose maiden name was Nobles. She bore twelve children, of whom my father was the youngest and named for my grandfather. My two oldest uncles, Mark and David Barry, bore arms in the Revolutionary War. My father was seven years old when the British army made its forced march through North Carolina from Charleston, South Carolina, to Yorktown, Virginia. As this army, in three divisions, had to forage all the way from Charleston to Yorktown, it, together with the Tories, caused much distress among the Whig families. As my father was the youngest of twelve children and I next to the youngest in his family, my uncles and aunts were old people before I was born and I have no recollection of ever seeing any of them.

The widows of Mark and David Barry moved to Tennessee, at an early date, to make their homes. The government was not able to pay the Revolutionary soldiers except in wild lands. My father often spoke of his two older brothers. On one occasion, they were with a company hunting Tories and British who were camped near a man's house whose name was Love, a Whig. Love took his saddle upstairs with him, thinking if the enemy should come and find his saddle gone they would believe he was not at home and would make no search for him. But not so; they started upstairs in search of him. He knew that the Tories would give no quarter, so he held his saddle before him and sold out at dear price to them. He fought his way downstairs and into the yard before they killed him. He killed three of them and wounded several others.

My father was in his seventy-eighth year when he died of typhoid fever. My mother died of congestive chills at fifty-eight. My mother's ancestors were perhaps among the first settlers of Maryland. My grandfather, William Murrill, and two of my granduncles, Kemp and Henry Murrill, came from Maryland when young men and settled in Onslow County, North Carolina, where my grandfather married Susan Brinson, whose mother's maiden name was Marshburn. They had four children born to them, my mother, Mary, being the oldest; John, Susan, and Elijah were the other three, and all of them raised families. To my parents were born twelve children, namely, William, Bryant, Bazel, Brinson, Mary, Rachel, Athelia, Augustus, Claudius, and myself, James Buckner Barry. Ten of us raised families, the other two having died in childhood.

My grandfather, William Murrill, and his two brothers, Kemp and Henry, like my two uncles on my father's side, participated in the war of 1776. Their principal field of operation was in the Carolinas against the Tories, some of whom were their neighbors.

I must here remember Uncle Tony who lived out his full century, five score years, and whose mother I well recollect. He was brought from Africa by a slave trader and sold to my grandfather. Uncle Tony, who was grown when peace was declared, might also be classed as a Revolutionary soldier. He often accompanied my grandfather and his brothers on their expeditions against the British and Tories. When the Tories were too strong for the Whigs, the Commander of the Colonial forces would send troops and drive the Tories out of the country. When the Whigs were too strong for the Tories the British commander would send British troops and make the Whigs hunt their hiding places. I have sat up late of nights with Uncle Tony in his cabin and listened to him tell us boys many stories of the Revolutionary War, two of which I here relate.

The Colonial government, not yet established, had no credit abroad and but little at home. Therefore, the Colonial soldiers had to furnish their commissary, quartermaster, and ordnance stores the best they could. Small detachments, with no transportation other than pack horses, or their own manly shoulders, often had to travel byways to and from home to get clothing, provisions, etc. Here is where Uncle Tony's services came in: to help with the pack horses and to bring them back home.

On one of these trips some fifteen or twenty soldiers were traveling on foot, as their horses were packed with supplies. Through the woods they came to a body of water, which they supposed to be a mill pond, where they stopped to rest and get dinner. About the time they had unpacked the horses, a sharp firing commenced on the other side of the pond, whereupon, all gathered their guns and ran around the pond. My grandfather said, "Tony, stay with the horses until we come back." They were gone some hours. About the time the shooting stopped, Tony looked across the pond and saw two Britishers, as he called them, swimming right toward him. His first thought was that his friends were killed and that they were coming across the pond after him and the horses. He hid behind a tree, covered his face with a bush, and kept close watch on them. He had picketed his horse in order to have him near to make his escape. When they came within gunshot of the shore and saw the pack horses, they swam up behind a floating log and hid themselves.

When my grandfather and his squads came back, they brought some of the spoils of the Tory and British camp with them, among which was some whiskey of which Master Kemp Murrill had taken too much. Uncle Tony told my grandfather about the "Britishers" hiding behind the log, whereupon, he ordered them to come ashore. When they came out of the water, Master Kemp and another man were going to shoot them, but my grandfather took their guns from them and prevented the shooting. If Uncle Tony knew what was done with the prisoners he never told, only that they took them along for a day or two.

Another very interesting incident of the Revolutionary War, as told by Uncle Tony, and contradicted by none of the old people of that day, concerned two Whig soldiers, Franks and Blackshear. They were at home on furlough to get supplies. Some Tories waylaid and killed them just before peace was made. Three of these Tories were captured and sentenced by a court-martial to be hanged. Two of them, young men, were said to have been engaged to Whig girls. Just at this time, peace was declared. Some of the Whig soldiers thought it wrong to hang them after peace was declared, although the crime was committed and the court-martial decision announced before the peace was known. They sent an express to the commanding general of that department, asking if the sentence should be carried into execution. His reply and order was to carry the sentence into execution on every man who could not get a Whig girl to marry him under the gallows.

When the order was made known, the day set, and the order read to the culprits on the scaffold, two Whig girls stepped to the front and saved the necks of two of them—young White and young George. The other poor fellow, whose name I've forgotten, could get no Whig girl to marry him and had to hang. Perhaps this is the only instance wherein a hanging and a marriage took place under the same gallows, on the same day, with every male spectator bearing a gun in his hand except Uncle Tony.

I have seen David White and George White, brothers to the Tory the girl saved, but who were little children during the war. Robert White, son of George White and nephew of the Tory of that name, lived neighbors to my father, their farms adjoining.

And now I will speak of myself. I was born December 16, 1821, in a farmhouse, built before the Revolutionary War by a man named Scott. It was a frame house of two stories, with brick chimney, built before sawmills, nails, window glass, etc., came into use in that country. Every sill, sleeper, rafter, joist, and studding was hewn with broadaxe. The outside boards were heart of white oak, riven out with a frow, and nailed on with rough nails, forged and shaped by a country blacksmith. It was sealed and floored with plank sawed with a whipsaw and covered with rich heart of pine shingles, without a solitary nail being driven into them or the lathing, all fastened on with wooden pegs.

I helped tear this house down after it had been used for nearly a century. It was then in a good state of preservation. The roof had never been known to leak a drop. This house and farm were situated on a creek named Bachelor's Delight, about halfway between the great desert from which it had its source and New River into which it emptied.

There was but one public road in the country and necessarily there was much travel on it. It was located on the upland between the solid farms on the riverside and the scattered farms on the desert side. Each farm had its own private road leading out to the public road.

I received a very fair English education at country schools. The farmers who were able employed good teachers. I walked nearly two miles to recite my lessons and to get my whippings like all other boys. I thought it good trading to have my sports and pastime and pay out nothing and get a whipping thrown in.

My first experience with school was with an old Revolutionary soldier named Grantham, who took my jacktar knife from me. My older brother, Brinson, gave it to me upon promise that I would go to school. I suppose he wanted me to keep out of the way at home.

My next experience was with another soldier named Odom who went on crutches, having been wounded in the hip by a splinter from a ship's mast when it was carried away by a cannon ball. I had many experiences with other teachers, but my last was with James M. Sprout, a Scotchman, educated in Edinburgh for the ministry. He taught all branches generally taught in college.

While school was kept by a man named Villard, I overheard the larger boys agree to steal watermelons from a neighbor Pitman's field. This suited me exactly, but they would not allow the smaller boys to go with them or tell where they were going. I slyly followed them until they got over the fence, where I overtook them. By promising never to tell on them, they allowed me to go with them.

After we had each secured a melon, they suggested that I pull off my breeches, fill the legs and take enough to do us next day. All agreed to this, but when we started back, we heard Pitman cough and clear up his throat in a patch of corn, near-by. We broke into a run for the woods, one of the boys carrying my breeches full of melons. When we got to the fence he threw my breeches across the fence and tore them in two, one leg falling on the inside, the other falling outside of the fence.

All of the boys except one ran and left me in this horrible fix. The one who stayed helped me into the brush, where we pinned my breeches together with wood pins, the best we could. Of course, I stayed away from school that evening. My comrade promised that if any inquiry was made about my absence he would tell the teacher I was sick and maybe had gone home.

My mother knew of my practice of climbing after young birds and squirrels and whipped me for climbing. The teacher whipped me the next morning for not being sick and whipped my comrade for telling him I was sick. The other boys got no whipping as I stood to my promise never to tell on them.

This was my last experience in stealing and I have been careful about making promises to others that I would keep their secrets. I learned one lesson from this incident that is not taught in every school. If a boy or a man steals he will tell a lie, also. If a boy or man lies, he will also steal. If you find a man guilty of one of these crimes he only lacks the opportunity to commit the other.

I will now give a few sketches of my experience among the wild animals, birds, snakes, fish, etc., in the swamps of North Carolina.

The last panther seen in these regions was killed by a man named Key. The last wolf was caught in a steel trap in the lower end of the county near where one of my sisters lived. She and perhaps a hundred others went to see it. There are lots of bear, deer, fox, and smaller animals in and around this big desert yet. Bears are very bad about killing hogs, and the wild cat, called by some catamount, is bad after the pigs. The people have to hunt them in self-defense.

I spent many of my youthful days hunting these animals and killed many of them, all except the bear. I was with my brother, Bryant, one day when he killed one and shot and wounded another. My father had a neighbor, named Hackett, who raised his own bread and vegetables. He spent most of his time hunting.

One night he was fire hunting for deer near the desert of which I have spoken. He heard something up a gum tree and, turning his light, he saw two pairs of eyes up the tree. He thought it was coons after gum berries and fired at them, but it proved to be young bear. He said one fell to the ground, squealing for his mother. The other one up the tree, thought to be wounded, was also squalling for its mother. He heard her coming through the brush. His gun was empty. She saw the fire and, thinking that her cubs were being murdered, made for the scene. In the fight in the dark, he lost his gun, hatchet and knife, but held to the fire pan which was red hot. He slapped that over her head and face to push her off himself, whereupon, she grabbed the pan with both paws. He broke and ran, leaving the bear holding the hot pan on her head.

As my father's house was the nearest place where dogs were kept, he went there without hat or weapons. After listening to Hackett's tale, my father told him to lie down and take a nap. He said they would have some fun in the morning. He sent one of my older brothers to Jimmy Parker's, who lived three miles distant, with a message to be there early next morning with his dogs.

Upon Parker's arrival next morning, they all put out to the battleground. They found Hackett's hat, pan, hatchet, and knife, and one of the cubs lying dead under the gum tree. The dogs followed the old bear about a mile into the desert where she was killed. She, or Hackett, or both, had held the hot pan over her head until her ears, nose, paws, and the skin over her eyes were crisp. Her eyes were so swollen she could not see.

Another incident as told by Benjamin Brock, a well-to-do bachelor, who lived in another settlement just across the line in Jones County, may be related here. He had a neighbor, named Jones, who did not care anything about hunting. Brock kept a yard full of dogs and put in most of his time training and hunting with them. One day Jones went over to Brock's house, saying, "Neighbor Brock, the coons are eating up my corn. Will you come over tonight with your dogs and catch them?"

"Yes," said Brock, "it will be fun for me and the dogs." Night found Brock at Jones' as he had promised. They went down on the farther side where the coons, as Jones thought, were destroying his corn. The dogs took track over the fence into a muddy swamp where they barked up a tree. Jones and Brock had torch lights but could find no eyes up the tree.

Brock said, "My dogs seldom bark up the wrong tree. I will climb the tree and find out whether they have made a mistake." He climbed the tree and announced to Jones that there were two coons.

"Shake out the rascals," said Jones. "The dogs and I can kill them both." They proved to be cub bears. When Brock commenced shaking the limb the cubs began to cry out for their mother, as Hackett's cubs had done. Brock said he heard the old bear coming through the mud and brush. She made for the torch light and knocked Jones down. She and the dogs fought over Jones and kept him in the mud until he was like a hog just out of his wallow.

The old bear finally whipped the dogs and went up the tree where Brock and her cubs were sitting. This change of section left Jones free to flee from the battleground, leaving Brock and all the bears up the same tree. Brock was expecting the bear to come up the tree as soon as the dogs, which were afraid of her, went away. He climbed down part of the way and went out on a limb of the tree. The bear passed by him to where her cubs were. Brock came down but it was so dark he had to feel his way out of the swamp. He could not find his shoes that he had pulled off when he climbed the tree. He made his way back to Jones', where he found Jones lying in the door offering up his lamentations over the sad fate he thought Brock had suffered.

Next morning Brock took his dogs back to the tree. The dogs tracked up the old bear and cubs and brought them to bay and killed them. Although these are second-hand bear stories, no old experienced hunter will doubt the struggles, for a mother bear will fight to the finish to protect her young ones.

This desert I mentioned above covers an area equal to the average county in the state and many interesting hunting stories can be told by the old hunters who yet live there.

When I was a boy, I considered myself an expert in capturing birds, especially young birds, as I was a good hand to climb trees. I found it difficult to get at the humming birds' nests, as they invariably build on limbs of trees over the water. Yet, I succeeded on several occasions in bringing them in with their eggs.[2]

The most interesting thing I saw among birds was the fish hawk, which, after having captured his fish, would start with it to the nest to feed its young. Whereupon, the eagle perched in the boughs of some tall tree, watching the movements, would go after the hawk at bullet-speed, making the hawk turn loose its fish. The eagle often catches the fish in its own claws before it gets to the ground, carrying it to its own young ones.

My experience, as a boy, among the snake tribe was oftentimes interesting. On one occasion, I saw a snake charming a bird, as it is called. I had often been told that when a snake gets its eyes fastened squarely on the eyes of a bird or anything else, the victim loses all its power and reason to control itself or ability to escape. But upon this occasion I learned that this information was not wholly correct.

I saw a bird flipping around in the brush and it seemed to be very disturbed. I cautiously approached and found that it was the snake's tongue and not its eyes it was using to charm the bird. It lay partly hid under the leaves with its forked

---

[2]Here, several pages of Barry's reminiscences of his boyhood which have to do with his experiences and observations on subjects pertaining to natural history, have been eliminated as of no particular historical importance.

tongue extending out over an inch and a half. One prong was of a dark color, the other yellow or reddish, both looking like long different colored worms, moving gently to and fro, thus decoying the bird. This attracted the bird several times to within a few inches of the snake's mouth. The snake was patiently waiting for the bird to grasp its tongue with its beak before attempting to seize the bird. Seeing what was going to happen, I scared the bird off and killed the snake. Here I learned why the deceptive and fraudulent man has always been compared to the serpent, because he has a forked tongue to deceive those whom he wishes to devour.

There was a great variety of snakes in the swamps of North Carolina. There was one species called by some the "stinging snake," others called it the "horn snake." Another species, called the "King snake," was harmless, and we boys were given orders not to kill them, as they were held by the old farmers to be a friend to man and beast. They had no weapon of defense whatever. When approached they would make no sign of defense or escape. They grew to a length of six or seven feet. Then there was the "chicken snake," which was nearly the size of the "king snake." They were expert climbers. They could climb any tree with rough bark and would swallow the young birds and squirrels they found.

But the snake most expert in capturing grown squirrels and rabbits which I have observed was the rattlesnake, which used some mysterious charm or secret maneuver of its own. Its appetite was great. I killed one, in Bosque County, Texas, that had swallowed three rabbits, one of which he had swallowed within the last few hours, apparently. One had been digested to the skeleton and the other had left only a few loose bones in an advanced state of decomposition. Also, I have always derived pleasure from watching the habits of the opossum.

A part of the history of my boyhood experiences has to do with the alligator and other animals which lived in or about the water. The alligator, many of which we killed both in

Carolina and Texas, never went very far from the water. They lived principally in rivers whose banks were shaded by large timber. Then there were the otter, the beaver, ducks, geese, etc., whose habits are familiar to most of the boys of this country.

There are few boys living, however, except those near the ocean, who are familiar with the customs of the salt water fish. Nearly all that hovered near the coast in spawning went up the rivers into fresh water to lay their eggs. I have seen them in such quantities that when they got where the river was narrow they were very thick. For miles they would be so thick they hardly had room to swim.

On one occasion I knew them to come up New River in such solid bulk that they raised the water in the river two or more feet on the banks. The bulk of these fish was herring, shad, and rockfish. The last named follow and live upon the herring. Every year, in the early spring, all the farmers near the rivers would get together and build what they called a wire trap across the river to catch these fish. Two men were required to watch the trap every night to gather the fish in, taking turns about during the spawning season.

Once, when the night came for my father and the widow Parker, who had two sons, to sit up and watch the trap, I was detailed by my father from our family and Benjamin Parker was detailed by his mother from her family. We were both about sixteen years old.

When we reached the river where the trap was laid, an hour or more before sunset, we found the fish so thick below the trap, trying to get up the river, that there was no necessity of fishing the trap, as we could stand on the bank of the river or in a boat and dip and scoop up with our nets as many, or more, than we could lift into our boats. We worked all night or, at least, as long as we could stand and about daybreak one of the neighbors came down. He looked at the pile of fish and said, "Boys, I will go back and send word to all the neighbors to bring their wagons and carts." By ten o'clock they were all there, dividing the fish by counting them. When they finished they reported fourteen thousand herring and many other varieties of fish, and the river was still full of fish. The only compliment we received for our night's work was from an old farmer who said to us, "Boys, this is wasteful. You have caught too many. I fear that we will not be able to take care of them all." But I did not hear of any going to waste.

The most delicious fish that came up our rivers from the ocean was the white shad and rockfish. The rockfish grew to weigh fifty or sixty pounds. They lived and fattened on the herring. We caught them by putting a live herring on the hook. The first one I caught was a ten-pounder. It made me feel like I was a grown man.

I shall now tell a shark story. My first wife's grandfather, John Matticks, was a man who was well-to-do. He had plenty of sail and rowboats, and one vessel, a schooner, that he used to take his products to northern markets. My wife's father, William Matticks, was captain of the schooner. On one occasion, when he was returning home from one of these voyages, round ballast and heavy seas caused the vessel to sink about sixty miles offshore. The captain was the only one of the crew to reach land.

But to old John Matticks again; he would invite the young people from the interior to come down on pleasure trips and to help him fish every fall, with both seines and hooks. On one occasion, a shark took hold of the old man's hook. He had his line fastened to the buttonhole of his vest, and when he found that the shark was about to take him to sea he hallooed for help. Help came slowly but was near enough to hear him shout a statement. The breakers were bursting over his head and he jerked out his fishing knife from his belt, reached out as far as he could, saying, "Darn you! I'll save a bag string!" After which to "save a bag string" became prominent to designate an act of economy. I have been present at the capture of a porpoise but never saw a whale captured.

CHAPTER II

"GONE TO TEXAS!"

When I quit school, I was over twenty years old. I then set up for myself and taught the first free school ever taught in Onslow County. I taught a second term and then concluded that I would go to Texas. I sold a negro woman I had heired from my grandfather's estate for three hundred and seventy dollars. I shipped for New York, at a town named Swansboro, aboard a sailing vessel loaded with naval stores. The pilot, Daniel Helty, refused to put the vessel across the bar at Bear Inlet. We were detained there two weeks, waiting for flood tide. I spent the days hunting, fishing, etc. The old pilot gave us pastime at night.

On one occasion, the young folks had a candy pulling which was soon turned into a dance. As I was the only one who could play the violin, I got in one corner of the room on a yellow stool chair. The dance soon stopped temporarily for refreshments. Some one put cake-candy in my chair and dimmed the light in my corner. I had on a seven dollar pair of new pants. As the candy was the color of the chair, I sat down without noticing it and sawed away on the violin for nearly an hour. When I got up, the chair stuck fast to my pants, and I saw the sell-out. I walked around as though nothing was out of order until the chair was pointed out to me, whereupon, I took a scare at it, and ran off with both the chair and the violin and went aboard the vessel. This broke up the dance.

When Captain Helty got flood tide he put us over the bar into deep water. The wind was fair, and we made Sandy Hook (New York Inlet) in about three days. I had to wait about two weeks for a large bark to load for New Orleans. I had never seen much of city life. Therefore, I wandered more or less over the city every day.

One day I was slowly wandering along the sidewalk and when opposite what seemed a jewelry store, heard someone inside exclaim, "Going! gone! good gold watch for thirty dollars." I walked in. One watch after another was put up but hardly any were sold for want of bidders. While I was there eight or ten men walked in who were, apparently, sailors. Some of them bid for the watches at four dollars. I also bid for one. I saw that I had only bought a shell. The sailors went out. After a little I started out and met the sailors coming back. I heard one say, "Boys, we will have our money back or have blood."

I went back with them to see what would happen. We walked in. Some of them went straight to the back door and locked it and others at the same time locked the front door. That is, they locked themselves, the auctioneer and me all in together. The spokesman told them to give back the money or he would shed their blood. Some took the money, some paid four dollars more and took good watches. I, for one, took a good watch, brought it to Texas and traded it for the land on the forks of the Bosque, where my farm is now located.

As I was coming back from the theatre late one night I passed a saloon where they were rolling tenpins. I walked in, as I had never seen much tenpin rolling. The barkeeper asked me, "What will you drink?" I replied that I wanted nothing and walked on to the alley room door, where one man played drunk, staggered against me and tried to push me into the alley room. At the same time, the barkeeper locked the front door. Seeing the desperate situation, I jerked out my pistol, pointed it at the man who had locked the door and told him to unlock it.

He opened it just in time to save his blood. By this time, the drunken man had become sober and the lights were blown out. As I stepped out on the street, everything was as quiet as a graveyard.

When the vessel got all her cargo on board, the captain hoisted sail for New Orleans. We came out of Sandy Hook in a snowstorm that lasted over three days. To avoid all danger of being driven ashore, the captain steered a little north of east, until the sun showed again, the quadrant being worthless to navigators in cloudy weather, and the log uncertain in rough, cloudy seas. We found ourselves a thousand miles offshore when the sun shone out. The quadrant worked now and we steered for New Orleans.

When we steered south we met several whales going north, one passing within two hundred yards of us. It was swimming leisurely along, skimming the blubber off the water, swallowing the grease and spouting the water collected with the grease through the top of its head. (Whalers have told me the whale has something where its gills ought to be, like a horse's mane, which separates the blubber from the water, taken in with the grease.)

We kept our course south to the Bermuda Islands, where the captain reported to the United States consul and laid in a good supply of turtles and turtle's eggs. We then steered for the Bahama Islands where the captain reported again. Then we steered for Key West, where we harbored for two days, because a gale was blowing. I saw an English ship, loaded with cotton from New Orleans, go ashore. There I saw my first tropical fruits growing.

We then steered for the mouth of the Mississippi River, having been on the ocean and gulf twenty-nine days before we entered the river. We were towed up to New Orleans where I had to wait nearly a week before I caught a boat going up Red River. It not only went up Red River but made its way through Soda and Caddo Lakes into Texas to a landing then and now called Jefferson. There were a hundred and thirty-odd passengers aboard.

This was the second boat that made its way to Jefferson. A majority of the passengers, like myself, were going to Texas. Many of them had their guns with them and put in much time shooting alligators on Red River and the lakes. We had eaten all the provisions on board and might have gone hungry had we not struck an Indian camp, on the bank of the river just before we entered the lakes, that furnished the captain with wild game.

Upon arriving at Jefferson, the captain notified us that we would have to look out for our own breakfast, as we had eaten all the rations on board. Going ashore next morning, I inquired where to get my breakfast. I was pointed to where a smoke was coming up out of the brush nearly two hundred yards distant. In company with a young Tennessean I made my way through the brush to the smoke where a man served us with meat, bread, and black coffee, using a very large pine log for a table. This was my first meal on Texas soil.

There were several houses under construction but there was only one finished. It was a log cabin built without a nail in it. It was covered with split boards and they were weighted down and held in place by small logs on top of them. It had a puncheon floor and a stick and mud chimney.

There was a farmer there by the name of Steward, who lived some twenty miles away. I climbed aboard his wagon and went home with him. It was timber country all the way, with very few settlers. Next day I heard wild turkeys gobble and I asked Steward to let me have his gun to try my hand at killing one.

I soon reached them and fired at a large gobbler, while he was strutting. I cut off the tip end of both wings. He could fly but little. I chased him over the hills and hollows through the woods until my bottom wind was gone. I threw down the heavy rifle gun and renewed my determination to catch him, which I did. But the chase was so long through the woods and brush that I could not find Steward's gun. I shouldered the gobbler and went back to the house.

The first question asked was, "Where is my gun?" I told my story but imagined I could read in his countenance that he thought I had hidden his gun and would take it with me when I went away. He told me to eat breakfast and that he would go with me to find the gun. I took him to where I had shot the turkey and also to the place where I caught it, but the race had been long, and I had no idea where I had thrown the gun down. After a tedious hunt, we found it and went back to the house well pleased, especially Steward, for a man's gun was then his biggest aid toward gaining his living.

He charged me nothing for a week's board, but paid me to help him two days to chop blown-down logs on his new corn land. The balance of the week I killed more game than his family could eat.

Next, I struck a Baptist preacher named Cherry. I helped drive his hogs from his farm to the white oak prairies where he had moved his family the fall before. His was the outside house, there being no settlement west of him and only three near him on the east. I aimed to go to San Antonio the first chance.

Mr. Cherry told me he had a friend on Red River, at Clarksville, who was wanting to travel to San Antonio and that he was going to attend preaching there. This friend, he said, could come by his house and accompany me. I stopped with the parson a month and put in my time hunting deer, turkeys, and wild cattle in the canebrakes of White Oak bottom. He had a fine slow track dog that would follow me when I had his master's gun, yet seemed to have but little use for me.

One day I shot and wounded a wolf. The dog thought it his business to finish him. Though the dog was large, the wolf was holding a bloody battle with him. I struck the wolf on the head with the heavy rifle (stocked to the muzzle) shattering part of the stock and bending the barrel. After killing the wolf I went sorrowfully home with the parson's ruined gun.

He said for me to get on an old mare and take the gun to the shop and have the barrel straightened and the stock mended. I asked where I would find the shop. He replied that it was in the Keith settlement, on the Sulphurs, about twenty-five miles toward the north, and a little to the west. I asked if there was any road, but he said I could not miss the way, for there were only two roads from the Keith settlement, one going to Shreveport, Louisiana, and the other to Saline on the Kickapoo, a branch of the Neches River. He stated that if I would bear to the right that I would come to the Shreveport road and that if I bore too far to the left I would strike the Saline road.

I had had some experience as a woodsman in the swamps of North Carolina and had no fear of getting lost. I started out and was bothered some in getting through the canebrakes in White Oak bottom. I camped out that night. The next morning the old mare seemed to think she was going to preaching in the Keith settlement again. Consequently, I hit no road until I got to Keith's shop where the road forked. When I returned the parson put up a target and shot three times at it, which satisfied him that his gun was all right.

I had arrived in Texas and experimented among the outside settlers who made the first marks of civilization in that section of the country. They were a self-reliant and self-sustaining people. They dealt and acted on the plan that necessity makes no mistakes. If they needed any clothes, household, or agricultural implements, they made them or traded work with some mechanic who could make them. Learning their necessities, habits, and customs, I began to prepare for my trip across the Lone Star Republic.

So when Parson Cherry's two friends,' spoken of previously, arrived, I was ready to start, but I had no saddle. I traded my trunk for a pair of saddle bags, bought a good horse, traded for a gun, camp blankets, etc. The parson told his friends to lay over for a day and he would finish up my saddle, which he already had under way. There was no other chance to get a saddle nearer than Shreveport, Louisiana, a hundred and fifty miles away. I played around, mainly, and did chores while the parson worked on my saddle. He made it of linden wood, a timber I had never seen before. Its leaves were said to never stop rustling and waving, no matter how dead the calm might be; its leaves were alive and rustling while the rest of the forest hung in dead silence. In the absence of nails and wood screws, he fastened the horn and cantle to the sideboards with wooden pins and rawhide strings. He turned me out the skeleton of a light, stout, and pleasant riding saddle, when my camp blanket was thrown over it.

Next morning we started traveling more by a pocket compass than by a road. The first settlement we struck was the outside settlement on the waters of the Sabine River. The next settlers we found were on the Trinity River where the buffalo hunters had made a crossing and a road through the Trinity bottom to get to the prairies west of the river where there were a great many buffaloes. This settlement was about seven miles above Bazette Bluff, where there was another settlement. We encountered but three settlements and one Indian trading house between the Trinity River and the falls of the Brazos River. But we passed several camps of buffalo hunters who were killing the animals for their hides and tallow.

Captain Hagler had quite a number of hands hired to kill and skin the buffaloes. He was camped on Chambers Creek, ten miles below where Corsicana has since been built. All the country between the Trinity and the Brazos Rivers was then the territory of Robertson County. We came to Captain

---

'The second friend is not mentioned previous to this point in the manuscript.

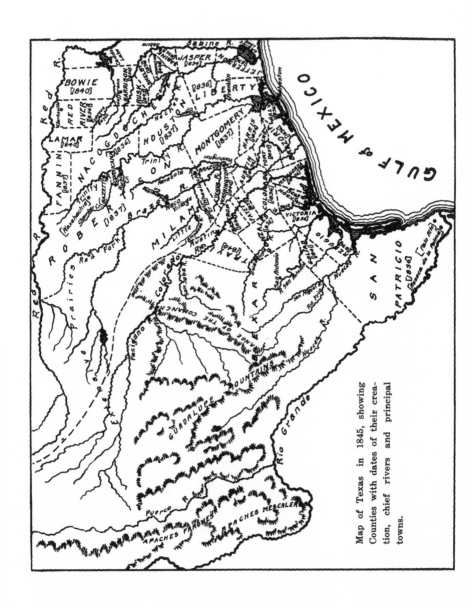

Map of Texas in 1845, showing Counties with dates of their creation, chief rivers and principal towns.

Youree's camp on Richland Creek. He had a company of men killing buffaloes. The buffaloes were in greater numbers there, betwen Richland and Chambers Creeks, than anywhere else on our route of travel. We shot buffaloes until it was neither pastime nor profit to us.

Our guns were our smokehouse. Game, all the way, was plentiful and fat. When we could get no bread we fared just as well without. These outside settlers ground their meal, as a majority of all the Texans did at that time, on a steel mill turned by hand.

We crossed the Brazos River just above the falls. This was the upper and outside settlement on the Brazos River. We had a trail to follow all the way to Austin made by a company of Rangers. We found but two settlers between the Brazos and Colorado Rivers, one of whom was Colonel Bryant, on Little River, who had forty mustang colts and buffalo calves. He had plenty of cattle and many negro boys to milk them and feed the colts and calves. The other settler, named Merrill, lived in the outside house on Brushy Creek. He looked sad and lonesome. The Indians had killed and taken all his family and his negroes when he happened to be away one day. Merrill and one negro man had been after bread-stuff to the lower settlements at the time. This incident occurred several months before we reached there.

Austin, the capital of the Republic of Texas, had only a few houses built of logs, clapboards, whipsawed lumber, etc. The capitol building, where the congress met, was large enough for the purpose. All of its heaviest timbers were hewn out by broadaxes, its flooring sawed with whipsaws, and it was covered with split, drawn shingles. This, the capital, was also the outside settlement on the Colorado River. I recollect seeing only one white woman in the town, if it could be called a town. There were a good many men, besides the officials and a company of Rangers to guard the archives between Austin and San Antonio.

We saw but one settlement, quite a settlement, too, of Germans on the Guadalupe River. They were all living in tents and grass-covered shanties. They were working like bees to build themselves houses. Here it was that I saw the first woman sawing with a crosscut saw. The women were anxious to have a house to live in and they were helping their husbands and brothers the best they could.

The day after my arrival at San Antonio it was reported that the Mexican army had crossed the Rio Grande. We joined the independent company of Rangers to help drive them back. When we reached the Medina we learned the Mexicans had recrossed the Rio Grande. Their object was to take San Antonio by surprise, but they failed to keep their plot secret and so had to retire. Major Jack Hays kept a spy in their camp all the time. There were many patriotic Mexicans in Texas.

Having failed to get in a fight, my comrade, Baker, and I (the other men having gone back home) went up the Medina to a German settlement. They were just from Germany and seemed ahead of their brethren on the Guadalupe. Most of them had their houses built with posts set in the ground and thatched with grass on the sides and roof, which made a pleasant shelter, both summer and winter. They had built a large church on the same plan, without the use of a nail or the sound of a hammer. The braces and every stay were tied with rawhide. This finished our visit to all the outside settlements from the Red River to the Rio Grande.

We returned to San Antonio and spent the fourth of July, 1845. I had been from the 12th of April, the time I ate my first meal on the pine log at Jefferson, to the latter part of June, making my way across the frontier of Texas.

We returned east pretty much the same way we traveled west. When we got back to Austin, Congress, or rather a convention, had met there to consider the propriety of annexing to the United States. The members were camping out, sleeping on their blankets. There was a company of Rangers there to keep the Indians from scalping the delegates to the convention, although each member was heavily armed and a first-class Ranger himself. I took a trip up the Colorado, and to the head of the Lampasas with a company of Rangers, where a spy company was kept during the sitting of the convention.

CHAPTER III

ENLISTING WITH HAY'S RANGERS

When I returned to the falls of the Brazos, I joined the little army of the Republic of Texas, numbering two hundred and fifty men, commanded by Major Jack Hays. I was placed in Captain Thomas J. Smith's company that was assigned to the protection of that portion of the frontier between the Brazos and the Trinity Rivers, a day's ride above the settlements.

There were only thirty men in Smith's company, and he divided his company into three squads. One squad of ten men had its headquarters near the Brazos River on Tehuacana Creek, some ten miles below the Waco village where the city of Waco is now located. No white persons lived above our line of operation and none below it, nearer than the falls of the Brazos. One squad of ten had their headquarters on the Trinity River, something like halfway between where Dallas and Fort Worth have since grown to be cities. The squad I was with had its rendezvous on the head of Richland's Creek, commanded by Sergeant James Sanford, who settled and died in Hill County. He was loved and respected by all the early settlers of the county.

We had but two positive orders from our captain. One was that each squad should patrol its section of our line every day, running near and along the lower edge of the Cross Timbers, and to see that no Indians took the settlements by surprise. In case we discovered Indians or their trail going toward the settlements, it was our business to beat them there and notify the minutemen of their coming. Every settler was a minuteman. In fact, every man in Texas was a soldier, organized into minute-companies and required to keep forty rounds of ammunition and to be ready to start at a moment's warning. These minutemen were really the army of Texas, as Hays' Battalion was composed of only spy companies to watch after the enemy and report to the minutemen.

The other special order we had from Captain Smith was to get in no fight or conflict with Indians, as he truly said no dead man could make a report to the minutemen. Never more than three of us went on one patrol at the same time, and sometimes only one was sent. We had certain places to meet the patrol, or spies, from the other camps.

On one occasion when three of us were on patrol, we rose out of a prairie hollow and saw two Indians after a lone buffalo, coming toward us. One of the Indians ran his pony close to the buffalo, jerked out an arrow and shot it back into the buffalo again. This was evidence that he had no more arrows; the buffalo had them all. When they saw us, they jabbered and motioned to us to shoot the buffalo. One of my companions, John Covington, ran on to it and killed it. The Indians claimed to be friends to Texas and said that they were hungry. One cut out a marrowbone, the other cut out the manifold. We rode on, leaving them eating the raw meat and getting back all their arrows they had shot into the buffalo.

During the time of my service in Captain Smith's company, the United States and Texas invited all the Indians, that is, those who were friendly and also those that were hostile to Texas, to meet in a grand peace council on Tehuacana Creek, some ten or twelve miles below Waco village. Treaties with such wild and warlike tribes as the Comanches, Kiowas and Wichitas would insure peace on the frontier, pending trouble with Mexico. The Indians were informed that Texas and the United States were good friends and that they had to be friendly to Texas, or enemies to the United States.

Several months later, after many delays, a great treaty council was held with eight or ten tribes of Indians, and about that many thousand, for the whole of the tribes, except those who did not want peace, came to the meeting, because they did not believe in representative government, but wanted the voice of the whole tribe on questions touching their tribal interests. The United States had sent Commissioners P. M. Butler and M. G. Lewis to make the treaty with the Texas Indians, and they did not seem to understand Indian character, as these reminiscences will show.

The tribe of Lipans who had befriended Texas in all her struggles was there. This tribe had no sins to atone for when Texas was annexed, for the Lipans were annexed, also. But there were two Lipans, young warriors, who had come across two Germans on the head of the Medina, getting timber. As they could not talk English, Spanish, or the Indian language, they took them to be intruders on Texas soil and killed them, which act they did not deny. So General Butler told the Lipan chief to bring these two young warriors up to be tried for the murder and that he would hold him responsible for the act if he failed to bring up the culprits. The chief told the agent, Butler, that these Germans were not good Texans, as they could not talk like Texans, their clothing was not like that of the Texans, and they wore wooden shoes. That night the whole tribe ran away and went to Mexico. There were but five of us Rangers and we made no attempt to follow them.

Another tribe present, the Wacoes, had said that they had some prisoners and stolen horses which they would release. But a part of their tribe, especially some of the old squaws, who had raised the prisoners from childhood and had therefore become attached to them, were deemed untrustworthy. So it was decided that we had better send a showing of soldiers to intimidate them.

Two days after the treaty was over, Captain Smith started sixteen of us to their village with a Delaware Indian, Jack Harry, to act as interpreter for us. We followed the trail up on the east side of the Brazos River for perhaps a hundred

miles and crossed the divide on to the Trinity, near where
now stands the city of Weatherford. A blizzard struck us, together with a snow storm. It was bitterly cold and some of
the boys became faint-hearted and talked of going back. But
our guide and interpreter, the Delaware Indian, who, in the
absence of our experienced captain (Thomas J. Smith), had
very naturally become our acting captain, assisted by Sergeant
Sanford, said no. They declared that the snow would help us
find them; that they would not travel their women and children through a snow storm, and that we would overtake them.
The snow had covered their trail. Acting Captain Jack Harry
thought it made no difference that their trail was hidden by
the snow, as we could keep the course they were traveling, and
if we missed them we would eventually find their horse tracks.
He said they turned all their horses loose to get their living and
that there would be lots of horse tracks after it quit snowing,
since the Wacoes would be out hunting them.

So we kept our course the best we could, having nothing
to guide us but the north wind and the drifting snow. So well
did our Delaware Indian keep his course that we rode right
into their camps with the snow falling so thick it hid the smoke,
and their wigwams were covered, looking like the surrounding
hills and rocks. The first I knew of being in their camp was
when I saw the little naked children running from one of their
snow hills (wigwams) to the others, giving the alarm of our
approach.

While our interpreter was talking to the chief we rolled
some logs into a ravine and started a fire. The chief was the
only Indian who showed himself at that time. I suppose the
warriors were inside preparing their weapons of war.

We stayed right there among them two nights. They could
neither move their women and children nor find their ponies
while it snowed. We were in but little better fix. The grass was
covered with snow. There was nothing but brush for our horses
to eat. They were tired and hungry.

Next day, their young warriors, principally, (the older ones were holding themselves in reserve in their tents) came out, advanced toward us, warpainted and with their bows strung. Our interpreter told them to go back or they would get into a fight. They laughed at him and asked where his men were who were going to fight. Sergeant Sanford told him to tell them that we had come after the prisoners and horses and we were not going back without them, and that if they did not have the prisoners and horses there when the sun rose the next morning we would sell out. We knew we could kill two of them to one of us and we would kill their women and children also.

Next morning, at sunrise, they brought up one prisoner and five head of horses. We did not ask further questions, for we well knew we would all have left our hair among them if the weather had been favorable enough to have removed their women and children to a place of safety. We supposed they had some sixty or seventy warriors at this camp, and they told us there were as many Wichitas, their good friends, at another camp three leagues away, who would help them fight.

We got away with our horses and prisoner and rode one day altogether. That evening late, our Delaware Indian killed a deer. We agreed not to eat it until morning, when the eighteen of us devoured it, even to the soft bones. The cause of our being hungry was that the thousands of Indians, who came down between the Trinity and Brazos Rivers to the treaty line and returned the same way, had driven the buffaloes out of this section of the country. The extreme cold weather had driven the smaller game into the timber and we had no time to stop and hunt them. The grass was still covered with snow, and our horses were growing weak for want of feed.

Such conditions were partly the cause of a falling out among ourselves and a division of our little squad into two groups. Seven of us contended that the nearest settlements were on the Trinity, the others thinking the falls of the Brazos was the nearest, so we separated without a good-bye. Late that evening one of us, Caps, killed a wild goose and next morning one of the boys killed a hawk. We divided this food into seven parcels. After each man had hidden his rations in his stomach, we resumed our course. The snow had commenced melting and we went through the Cross Timbers near the headwaters of Mountain Creek.

In the edge of the timber, we saw an Indian butchering a buffalo. Well out on the prairie Sergeant Sanford ordered us to form a V on him, which we did. He mounted his pony and tried to make his escape. But we ran him down and caught him. Then he saw himself surrounded by seven men with loaded guns, and his gun was empty, for he had used his shot to kill the buffalo. After talking to him with signs and otherwise, he made us understand that he was a Choctaw, that a good many Choctaws had come across Red River to kill buffaloes and were camped on the Trinity River. We turned him loose, went back to his buffalo, got plenty of meat, found a place in the timber where the snow had melted, built a fire, roasted our meat, and filled up the vacuum inside us.

We pursued our course and came upon a camp of buffalo hunters on Trinity River from Arkansas. As I now recall it, they were directly across and opposite where the city of Dallas now stands. We lay over here two or three days, until our horses filled up on the winter grass in Trinity bottom. We then struck out for the falls of the Brazos River. There was no road and only one settlement of four families between this point on the Trinity and the Brazos, near where I think is now Ash Creek in Hill County. A dry blizzard hit us, but we found enough brush on this creek to keep us from freezing. To keep warm next morning we walked and led our horses.

When we were within six or eight miles of the settlement on the Brazos, we saw a horse at a distance standing still with a saddle on. We steered toward the horse and found his rider frozen to death with a noose of the bridle reins around one wrist. As it was too cold for an inquest, we hastened to the settlement and reported the scene. A party of men started out to bring the man in. When they found him, the horse had frozen also. On arriving at this settlement we learned that our captain had orders to muster his company out.

CHAPTER IV

WITH THE TEXAS RANGERS TO MEXICO

AFTER I had been mustered out of the army of the Lone Star Republic, I joined a company of surveyors going out to locate headrights and headrights certificate land, with which I worked until April. Our work was in Navarro, Hill, and Ellis Counties, which were then in Robertson County land district. Robertson County, at that time, covered all the territory between the Brazos and Trinity Rivers, from the old San Antonio and Nachitoches road to Santa Fé. Franklin was the county site and is now in the confines of Brazos County. Buffalo hunters and land locaters were our principal associates. I carried the chain around the survey where Waxahachie now stands; carried it around the survey in which is now Milford and other towns that have since sprung up. I carried it around the survey where Corsicana with its oil treasure has since been developed.

When we established the northwest corner there were three buffalo hunters with us. While we were in the timber resting and waiting for the surveyor to make out his field notes, a drove of buffaloes ran by within fifty steps of us. We did not shoot or kill any game except when we wanted meat. But the buffalo hunters shot down one apiece. They had a large dog with them. He, too, ran in and caught one himself. The buffalo was not able to carry the dog and keep up with the herd, so it was soon left alone. I became much interested in the dog and buffalo fight. I ran along through the timber, enjoying the scene until I was out of sight of my comrades. I saw the dog had his eyes shut and was holding to the jaws of the buffalo with a death grip. I ran up on the off-side and drove my knife into the vital parts, the dog never opening its eyes or loosening its grip until the buffalo was still in death. Then he looked up to me and spoke in what seemed to me plain English. He wagged his tail and appeared to be thanking me for my assistance. However, he excused himself and went off to see about his master, leaving me in full possession of the game.

I took out the buffalo's tongue and hurried back to the crowd that had paid no attention to the dog and but little heed to my absence. I told the crowd that I had killed a fatter buffalo than those the hunters had killed, and that we had better get some meat from it. They knew I had taken no gun and that they had not heard the report of a gun, but the tongue was proof that I had killed it. The surveyor asked me how I had killed it without a gun. I told the crowd that I had just outrun it and had killed it with my knife. But I did not tell them that the buffalo was carrying the weight of the dog on the side of its jaw.

The tongue was not satisfactory evidence, so all hands went to see the proof of the mystery. They turned the buffalo over and over but could see no wound except the one my bowie knife had made. In cutting out the tongue the wounds of the dog's teeth had been spoiled out, so I was champion hunter of that day.

We worked up Chambers and Brier Creeks to ten or twelve miles above where Corsicana now stands. We made a habit of shooting off signal guns every evening and morning to notify anyone wanting to locate certificates where to find us. One morning we fired our signal and who should ride into our camp but the old veteran, Colonel Nail, who was wounded by a Mexican lance thrown from the top of a house during the siege of San Antonio. While our distinguished visitor was eating his breakfast he told us the United States troops had landed in Texas, and the Mexican army had been surrounded near the mouth of the Rio Grande. He said that General Taylor, commanding, had appealed to the people of Texas through their governor for immediate help.

All the boys began saddling their horses to go to the rescue of General Taylor. The surveyors said, "Boys, are you going to leave me here with my pack mule and my Jacob's-staff? You must help me get to the settlement." We helped him to the settlement. Captain Eli Chandler had been authorized by the governor to raise a company. We made haste to the county site, Franklin, gathering recruits as we went. We organized at a little place called Wheelock, killed two large beeves, barbecued them, and set out for the scene of action, swimming every stream but the Colorado, which we crossed by ferry. This was in April, 1846.

When our bread and coffee gave out we fattened on meat alone. When we arrived at the battle grounds of Resaca de la Palma and Palo Alto the fight had been over ten days, and the Mexicans had retired across the Rio Grande. We organized into a regiment on the battlefield of Palo Alto, electing Captain Jack Hays as Colonel, Walker, Lieutenant Colonel, and Zavala, Major. We crossed the river at Matamoras, but Taylor had taken possession of this city before we arrived.

Eight companies of our regiment were ordered to reconnoiter the country to find out where the Mexican army was located. We found that the Mexican army was concentrating at Monterey. Taylor was notified and he started his march at once up the San Juan River. Our eight companies fell in with the main army. We did a day and a half march before we got to Monterey. In this day and a half, General Taylor worked us in the advance of his army. My recollection is that it was Saturday evening when we arrived in sight of the city of Monterey, which was in a bend of the San Juan River, a tributary of the Rio Grande. The Sierra mountains were to the south and west while to the north were woods. It was there at the Black Fort that the Mexicans opened fire on us with shell and round shot. Sunday we went on foraging raids, and there was some firing kept up during the day.

Next morning we were ordered to reconnoiter the upper portion of the city to the road running up the river to Saltillo. It was yet dark when we came to the road, having started from camp several hours before day to get back to the Black Fort while it was dark. We had dismounted near this road to rest and wait for daylight. Some of the boys fell into deep sleep, some had unsaddled to let their horses cool. This was the disorganized condition we were in when day revealed to us a regiment of lancers approaching us.

They formed a line about two hundred yards away, each man had the Mexican flag waving from his lance, making the most beautiful spectacle of mounted men I ever expect to see. Although everything was silent, these little flags told us in plain language they were after our blood. Our colonel, seeing our situation, with some of the boys barely yet awake, tried to gain a little time to better prepare us to receive the charge. He rode out front with his saber in his hand and challenged the colonel of the lancers to meet him halfway between the lines to fight a saber fight. Our colonel talked good Spanish, in which the challenge was made. For a moment the burden of suspense and anxiety was very great, while waiting for the conflict between our noble Jack Hays and the commander of the Mexican lancers.

Hays knew no more about saber fighting than I did, but his object was for the light companies of his regiment to become prepared for the charge of the lancers. So, as soon as the Mexican colonel could divest himself of all encumbrances, he advanced waving his saber, while his horse seemed to dance rather than prance. Within a few feet of the Mexican, Hays pulled a pistol and shot him dead from his horse. This relieved all suspense and anxiety; they charged us like mad hornets. The colonel hallooed to us as he came back to our line to dismount and take shelter behind our horses. This order saved us much blood. By the time, and even before, all were dismounted, they were among us. They fought through our line, formed in our rear and charged through the line again, formed in our front and charged through our line a third time. I have never called a Mexican a coward since.

They left many of their dead among us. We had but one man killed but many wounded. They would have ruined us if we had not dismounted. We killed about eighty, but we should have done better, as we only had to shoot them but a few feet from behind our horses. We had shot our muzzle-loading guns empty, and they had charged us so fast that we had no time to load again.

There was one Mexican battery on a height across the river, one on the height below us; both commenced firing round shot at us as soon as their friends retired from their attack upon us. The Mexicans commanding these two batteries on the heights witnessed the cavalry fight we had in the valley. I looked down the road, or rather suburban street, and the Mexican infantry was coming on the double-quick in solid columns. Just at this time, General Worth, with our flying artillery and some infantry, came up and opened fire on the approaching columns of infantry and drove them back into the city. But we were under fire from two batteries. General Worth, seeing the situation, ordered Colonel Hays to dismount his regiment and take the battery across the river.

I tied my horse to a fence and cut a turn of green corn for him. I did not see my horse again until the fight was over—five days later. A company of Louisiana volunteers was attached to our regiment. We commenced our advance on the battery, through the cornfield and crossed the San Juan River, which was hip deep and ran so strong it washed some of our men down. When we reached the foot of the mountain on which the battery was located, there was another river, waist deep, but the current was not so strong; here the musketry opened fire upon us. We advanced up the side of the mountain, which was so rough with hills, hollows, rock, and brush we could not keep up any system. Every man had to assume the right to be his own commanding officer.

When we drove them from the battery that had been firing on us all the forenoon, three or four hundred yards off there was another battery, of which we knew nothing, that opened fire upon us. Without orders or system, we bore down on it, well knowing that we had to capture it or lose all the ground we had taken. Our loss up to this time had been light, but in capturing this second battery our loss was equal to what we had sustained during all the earlier part of the day.

We turned the artillery we had captured at these batteries against a strong fortress across the river, called the Bishop's Castle. It, in return, opened fire upon us. It was at the storming of this battery, that a Mexican ball gave me a discharge from further service. When we dismounted to capture these batteries, I took my holster pistols and stuck them in my saber belt; they stuck out exactly in the right place, the ball hitting it plumb. The force and weight against my pistol broke my ribs and marked up my lungs so that I did not get a good natural breath for three months.

When I was shot down, our first Lieutenant, Thomas Bell, ran to me and asked me some questions, but I could not talk as all my breath was knocked out of me. He was a large, stout, active man (it was a hot day) and, with his gun in one hand, he caught me by the coat collar and dragged me to the shade of a bush. He ran on toward the battery from which the Mexicans were soon to flee down the mountains toward the Bishop's Castle. A line of forts with strong masonry buildings at intervals, such as the "Citadel" and the "Bishop's Palace" on Independence Hill, was the chief defense of the Mexicans.

The detail that was left to take care of the wounded and to bury the dead placed me in a position that commanded a view of the city. The boom of cannons and musketry we could hear at the lower portion of the city, told us that General Zack

Taylor (who commanded the first division) was having a hot time and was causing much blood to be spilled down there. I did not see Lieutenant Bell, my company, or my horse for about a week. Lieutenant Bell reported me killed to the New Orleans *Picayune,* so the report went through all the papers.

There was yet the Bishop's Castle, a stone building, with twelve guns, and another battery that commanded the entrance to the city which had to be captured before our troops could enter the city without great loss. Next morning by sunrise, the battery on the height above the Bishop's Castle was taken, where our regiment lost its major and one captain. Some others were killed who belonged to other troops. This battery was four or five hundred yards above the castle, uphill, but there was smooth road on the backbone of this mountain to the battery. Our men turned the cannon they had captured on the castle. The detail left at the battery across the river, where I was, kept up a fire with the guns we had captured on the castle, which continued to keep up fire on our troops. But it was upgrade, while our guns shot downward at the castle. I was where every move could been seen, but my breath was too short to fully enjoy it.

About nine o'clock a solid column of Mexican cavalry came out of the city; it looked as if it was a brigade. It advanced upward by the castle, to the backbone of the mountain which was too narrow for them to form in line, so they charged the battery we had taken in columns. The dismounted rifles were prepared for them. The cross fire from the riflemen dismounted them so fast that they were thrown into confusion. As the first of the column retreated, they mixed up with the rear of their column that was making haste to the attack on the battery that clogged the road to the castle. Our regiment, led by Lieutenant Colonel Walker, followed up the retreating rear of the confusion, right to the walls of the castle.

The troops in the castle became panic-stricken and vacated the castle with its twelve guns, which our dismounted men took possession of without losing a drop of blood. That evening all the wounded, both American and Mexican, were gathered together in the Bishop's Castle but with no doctor to give them attention. It is rather remarkable that there were no wounded sent to the rear, nor any prisoner taken by either side, unless he was wounded.

During the five days' fight our regiment, the First Texas Mounted Rifles, lived on raw green corn. We were too busily engaged in the daytime to cook it, and if we had built up a fire at night a bombshell would have paid us a visit. It seemed that we did as well on raw green corn as if we had beefsteak and flour bread. When the castle was in our possession, it gave us an open way into the city, but every inch of ground was obstinately contended for by the Mexicans from the house tops, on which were stone parapets, and from barricades and deep ditches across the streets; every block of the city had an impassable ditch, making it next to impossible to advance. Every house had a flat cement roof, the walls extending from two to four feet above the roof, which made every house a fortress and every street a plain road to death.

This timely precaution on the part of the Mexicans made our advance into the city very slow and hazardous. Inch by inch, we drove them to the center of the city; often the Mexicans were on one side of the street and the dismounted riflemen of the First Texas Rangers on the other side, shooting through doors and windows. Often the Texans were in the lower story of the houses and the Mexicans in the upper story and on top of the houses.

The only means of our advance into the city was through holes picked with crowbars, sledges, etc., in the walls of concrete and rock houses. Often there was only a single wall between the Texans and Mexicans, so as soon as the Texans battered a hole through the wall the Mexicans would commence shooting at random through it. It was nothing strange for the muzzles of the Texans' and Mexicans' guns to clash together, both intending to shoot through the hole at the same time.

While this scene was going on in the lower stories, the Mexicans in the upper stories and on top of the houses were also disputing every inch against a part of our regiment, who were going to the tops after the enemy.

Reader, don't forget it; those Mexicans were good shots. When one of the boys would put his hat on his ramrod and hold it over the wall or window sill, as though he were peeping over for an enemy to shoot, he was sure to get one or two holes made in it. Very seldom did either the Texans or the Mexicans have anything to shoot at except the face of their enemy over the wall. When the report of a Texas rifle was heard it was safe to bet a bullet had been bloodied.

Don't forget; I was not in the house top fight, but my messmates and company comrades, whose veracity I can vouch for, told it to me just as I have written it at this time. I was lying in the Bishop's Castle, living on very short breaths. I could hear reports of guns all day and the boom of mortars all night pitching shell into the city and the Black Fort, and the Black Fort pitching shells at us.

General Worth's division, led by the first regiment of dismounted riflemen of Texas, drove the Mexicans a mile and a half down the streets and along the housetops into the city. The first division of the army, however, under General Taylor, had only driven them two and a half blocks into the lower end of the city, and had lost over ten men to Worth's one, but General Taylor had the fire from the Black Fort to contend with all the time. His whole army of nearly seven thousand men could not have taken it, if they had assaulted it at the same time. It had a ten-foot ditch surrounding it with dirt thrown up on the inside, making an embankment high and wide enough for safe protection, while the fort itself was made on the blockhouse plan.

The Mexican army was reported at twenty-one or -two

thousand, but was about half that strength when it surrendered to seven thousand Americans. The Mexicans fought bravely, but numbers did not count much in street and housetop fighting since only so many as limited space would admit could be brought effectively to bear against us. When the Mexicans surrendered, the wounded in Worth's division were moved from the Bishop's Castle half a mile down the city to the Bishop's Palace, which was being used as a hospital when I left.

In two weeks I began to breathe better. The doctor told me to walk around when I felt like it, as it would be better for me than medicine. I visited the Black Fort and inspected many of the houses where my regiment had such close combat with the Mexicans from their house tops and through the holes my comrades had battered through the walls.

During the five days fight, or before, the women and children evacuated the city and retired to the mountains across the San Juan River. Of course, the dogs all went with the women and children, who must have been on short rations. The dogs came back after the surrender so hungry and starved that they ate the dead men who were overlooked or buried in shallow graves. I saw these dogs eating on the carcasses of men who were killed where General Taylor had his first engagement outside the city. My breath was short and the stench was bad; I did not examine them to see if they were Mexicans or Americans.

Our regiment, First Texas Mounted Rifles, was composed of three months volunteers. Our time was served out over two weeks before the fight, but some of us had traveled six hundred miles to kill a Mexican and refused to accept a discharge until we got to Monterey where a fight was awaiting our arrival. This victory was so complete that there was no probability of another fight for months. Therefore, most of the regiment went back home; the rest reorganized and stayed with Taylor.

My messmates promised to see me back to the Rio Grande, so I sold my horse to the artillery service for $90.00, bought a Mexican pony for $3.00 and paid $2.00 to get it shod. I sold it in Carmargo for $5.00, boarded a little steamer and started home.

When about to leave Monterey, General Worth told Colonel Hays to march his regiment through his quarters in single file so he could look us all in the face and shake every man's hand, saying, "It was the untiring vigilance, bravery, and unerring shots of your regiment that saved my division from defeat." After this battle the "Texas Rangers" became famous and ever since have received praise and glory for their achievements.

Here I'll give a reminiscence of one man who was a member of our company only three days. His name was Crooks—Jim, I believe. He was red-headed and freckled faced. He came to our camp near the Guadalupe River when we were on our way to Mexico. He was a stranger to us, but our captain, Eli Chandler, knew him. He said he wished to join our company. Our captain had his company to parade in double file, saying he wished to introduce us to Mr. Crooks, who wished to join our company, and, as he had been acquainted with Mr. Crooks a long time, he felt it his duty to give us Mr. Crooks' general character before he enrolled him. Then, he said, he would leave it to a vote whether he should muster Mr. Crooks into service. His introduction was about as follows, "I have known Mr. Crooks for a long time and have never known but one good thing he has done. He helped whip the Mexicans at San Jacinto. He has committed every crime known in the catalogue of crimes and is the d—est rascal that is now going unhanged. But there is no counterfeit in his being a fighter." Lieutenant Bell spoke, "Boys, in a few days we will need fighting men. What need we care about Mr. Crooks' other qualifications? Let us vote for the captain to put his name on our muster roll." So we voted.

When between the San Antonio and Nueces Rivers we came to a ranch kept by an Irishman and his wife. Other men were there, Mexicans and Americans. It was the last and only ranch we saw for a day's ride back. We camped near this ranch. This Irishman told us that he had plenty of cows and if we wanted milk, to go milk them. Some of the cows were wild but it made no difference, we roped them and milked them just the same. Next morning the Irishman came into our camp and said his wife's clothesline was gone. The captain said, "Parade here, boys!" He appointed a detail to search every man's baggage, but said to search Mr. Crooks' first. So they did and found the woman's clothesline, many of the boys' knives, spurs, etc., that he had stolen during the three days he had been with us. The captain said, "Shall we keep him or drum him out?" A unanimous voice went up, "Drum him out!" Which we did.

This man made his way way to the Rio Grande, joined another company and was in the thickest of the fight at the battle of Monterey. That night, while in camp, Captain Chandler gave us a more detailed account of Mr. Crooks. He said that it was probable that this man Crooks had caused the tide to turn at San Jacinto in favor of the little band of Texas patriots and veterans, commanded by General Sam Houston. As Houston had fallen back before Santa Anna's army he had sent word of the approach and helped all he could to get the women and children to go east out of the way of the Mexican army.

This man Crooks was one of the detail to notify and help the fleeing women and children. While among them and helping them he committed a rape. The outraged woman came into Houston's camp and pointed out the criminal to him, whereupon, Houston summonsed a court-martial that tried Crooks and sentenced him to the death penalty. There were several other prisoners under penalty, but the captain only told of Crooks' crime. When Houston reviewed his little army and found more men were leaving him than recruits were coming in, he determined to hazard a fight. He rode to where these prisoners were and told them, addressing himself principally to Crooks, "I am going to fight the Mexicans. The sentence of death will be executed on you unless you promise to go into the thickest of the fight and stay in it until the fight is ended. I will reprieve you." All the prisoners agreed to this.

When a charge was ordered on the Mexican line of battle, Crooks fired his gun one time, threw it down and ran through the Mexican line. (Perhaps they thought he had surrendered to them). He went down the line in the rear, drove his bowie knife into every Mexican who was in the rear line, while their attention was fixed on the charging line of Texans. Others of the prisoners and daring men followed Crooks' action, which threw the Mexicans into confusion and then into flight. Captain Chandler said that when the fight was over, Crooks was the bloodiest man he ever saw and did not have a scratch on him. Crooks was a stout, active man and may have killed at least a hundred or more Mexicans in the short time the battle lasted. Crooks' story after the fight was that he took down the rear of the Mexicans' line and killed them or drove his knife into them nearly as fast as he could count. About the time he got to the end of the line, he said the other end of the line was fleeing. There was a general rout in a few minutes, but he kept up his part of the fight and killed all he could outrun.

The captain never told us, but we naturally came to the conclusion that he and the majority of the Texas army never took time to load their guns after the first fire, for he told us that out of the several hundred Mexicans killed, three-fourths of them were killed with bowie knives. Houston lost seven men who were killed. He and others were wounded, while his little army killed twice its numbers, took as many prisoners as he had men, and drove the other division of Santa Anna's army back across the Rio Grande.

There are some even today who doubt General Houston's good generalship for detailing Deaf Smith with a posse to destroy the bridge across the river, thus cutting off all chances of escape in case his little army was defeated. But our captain said that his principal object was, in case of defeat, to retard the Mexican army, and to keep it from taking the great multitude of women, children, and negroes; and to seek other stock and valuables, easily carried, before they crossed the Sabine River and landed on United States territory; and that when the last of the fleeing women and children were across, the bridge was to be destroyed.

There were many men who thought it better to lead the van of these fleeing families into Louisiana than to risk their chance in battle. But the little band that remained with Houston, covering the retreat of the fleeing families, had made up their minds to neither run on to strange soil for protection nor to surrender to an imperialistic tyrant. Their battle cry was "Remember Goliad and the fate of Fannin! Remember the Alamo and its brave defenders!" And they carried out the words of Patrick Henry, "This day we will have our liberty or death." Said our Captain Chandler, "Perhaps every man in the battle of San Jacinto, like myself, had a wife, a mother, a sister, or friend in the fleeing army of non-combatants, and the Mexican army would have had to kill every man before Santa Anna could have claimed a victory."

These men, through the influence of Austin, and what they considered best for their own interests, had sworn allegiance to the Bustamante government. But when Santa Anna came into power, to rule the people with imperialistic tyranny, not only Texas, but other states also revolted. But when Santa Anna marched his army into them they submitted to his rule until he came into Texas, where he was resisted by such means of warfare as the people had on hand. The most efficient weapons they had were hammered barrel, muzzle-loading rifles, such as were used in the battle of New Orleans.

None doubted Santa Anna's motives to drive every man across the Sabine River and kill all who refused to swear allegiance to his imperial and tyrannical government.

I have diverged far from my own reminiscences and have dwelt on reminiscences as told by others, whom I believed to be men of truthful character. Will now go back to Monterey for one more item there. When my regimental comrades were battering holes through the walls of one house to another from one block of the city to another, they got into business houses of all varieties, one of which was a jewelry store. The most valuable of its goods were, of course, taken out. We had a yearling boy in our company, son of one of our captain's neighbors and friends. Of course, he was the captain's pet. When he got into the jewelry store he thought he had found all he had been fighting for, so he gathered up a turn, and when the fight was over he took it to his quarters. All laughed at his sudden fortune so much that he threw it away.

Our men picked their way through the walls of every kind of business house, as I have said. The most important thing they captured was quite a lot of soldiers' uniforms and officers' clothing, which we needed badly. Many of us had only a part of the suit we had worn from home, and they were more rags than clothes. When we had time to wash them in the creek or river, we would wait in the shade of a tree for them to dry. My messmates brought me two pairs of pants, one soldier's coat, one officer's coat, a linen shirt, and a hat, all of which I needed very much. I rolled up my Mexican uniforms in a handmade Mexican blanket and started for home. When I got to Brazos-Santiago at the mouth of the Rio Grande, I dressed up in Mexican uniform. Here, about five hundred sick and discharged boarded the steamship, the McKinney, for Galveston and New Orleans. Before we got out of sight of land, it semed to me that four hundred men became seasick and were all vomiting at the same time. All who could, got to the side of the ship and cast their bile into the gulf. While I was vomiting over the side of the ship, another man vomited into my fine Mexican hat I had left on a coil of rope to keep from losing it overboard.

When we reached New Orleans I bought a trunk and filled it with clothes to my notion. I wore one of my Mexican uniform suits from there to my home. I buckled my Mexican blankets on to the trunk and ran my Mexican sword-spear under the straps, which made it the center of attraction at hotels, on board ship, and all the way home. From New Orleans, I shipped to Wilmington, North Carolina, then made my way out to Onslow County where I spent the winter and until March, among my relatives and old friends. I made my home at my father's house while there.

CHAPTER V

PANTHER, BEAR, AND DEER HUNTING

I was married February 24, 1847, to Sarah Anapolis Matticks. In a short time, I started back to Texas, accompanied by my wife and her brother, William Curtis Matticks. My brother, Augustus, was to start to Texas, traveling overland, early in 1848 and bring servants belonging to me and my wife. Claudius, my youngest brother, had emigrated in January, 1848, with some neighbors, and a few months later, A. B., an older brother, came to Texas. August and A. B. bought lands in neighboring counties to mine but Claudius went to California in the gold rush of 'forty-nine. Nothing of any importance happened on our way to Texas. From Charleston, South Carolina, to Galveston there were but three families as passengers on board, one Catholic, one Protestant and one Jew family. We had quite a gale one day. I was on deck looking at the worst of it. When I returned to the cabin, the Catholic and the Jew ladies were on their knees praying. I asked why all were not praying. The Protestant lady replied, "I was taught that in time of peace to prepare for war, so we will be better prepared to fight the enemy successfully when attacked."

We ran up to Houston on a bayou boat, where I hired two ox wagoners to haul us to Bazette bluff, on the Trinity River, not that my family had so much to haul, but they were afraid of Indians in the upper country. One would not go alone, so I gave them a load of salt and some other merchandise, and bought a horse and saddle for my wife to ride. My

47

wife's brother, the negro boys, Caesar, Strutham, and the
teamster's young friends, who went with them, took it afoot,
a distance of two hundred and fifty miles. I'll mention only
two incidents on our journey. Some forty or fifty miles from
Houston, some of the boys, rambling away from the road,
found an alligator's nest (a hot bed), tore it open and found
forty-odd eggs, with which they amused themselves several days by playing ball with them. Their tough leathery
skin is not very easily burst. When in Leon County, late one
evening, we heard some buffaloes grunting a sort of a bellow.
I told the teamsters to strike camp and that I would go kill
them some meat. I found the buffaloes in the timber, pawing
and wallowing in the sand. There were about forty in the
drove. I shot one down and the others were not alarmed at it.
The others were down rolling in the sand and seemed to
think the dead one had laid down to roll again. One was more
meat than we wanted so I ran the others off, took out the
tongue and marrow bones, and struck for camp. Next morning the teamsters got all the meat they wanted. It was no
trouble to kill meat through the section of the country we were
passing, as there was every variety of game at that date.

We finally arrived at Bazette bluff, where I helped make
the first sign of civilization. There was one family there, but
they were in but a very little better condition than myself.
The first thing to do was to build a house. The next was to
get some land in cultivation to make my bread. We managed
to get bread until we could make it. We ground it with a
hand mill until a Mr. Sperlin settled eight miles above me.
He put up a hand mill, with one horse to pull it. The band was
a rawhide rope. His son, William Sperlin, married John H.
Reagan's sister, the first white woman, or rather girl, I
ever heard make a talk from the public rostrum. Her subject was "Education." As for meat we had a choice of all the
wild game, which was abundant, because it had not as yet

been hunted and killed out, and was unafraid of man. I often killed game within gunshot of the house.

I bought my start of hogs from Owen Humphrey, who had driven his hogs when he moved in from Arkansas. I soon had more than I could use, for the range was fresh, and they were no trouble to keep, except to protect them from the bears, panthers, etc. This made it necessary to keep a yard full of dogs. The dogs were a source of pleasure as well as profit, as I trained them to hunt with me.

I only killed one buffalo while I lived on the Trinity River. But Humphrey, his boys and I killed fourteen panthers one fall, winter, and spring, and we kept an abundance of bear bacon, and dried venison hams in our smokehouses, while wild turkey and fish were no rarity. When fresh pork was sold at all, it could be bought at one and a half cents per pound. When the river was up, we caught fish with hooks; when down we would kill them with a rifle, which was the fastest way to get them. We would go to the shoals in the early morning, pick out the ones we wanted for breakfast and kill them. On one occasion, alligators were numerous in the river, and some other young men and I were swimming when a man on the bank warned us that one was approaching us. We looked up the river and could see him steadily coming toward us, with his eyes the only part of him we could see. We kept in the water until we tolled him down opposite the man on the bank, who shot him. He floated a minute, then sank in about three feet of water. The bloody water and the bubbles made us believe he was dead. We formed a line and began searching for him. A stout young man, John O'Neil, stepped on him and said, "Here he is! I'm standing on him. I'll dive down and bring him up!" He dived, but the alligator was very much alive and there was a lively fight until the shore was reached, with first O'Neil and then the alligator on top. The ball had broken the alligator's jaw, otherwise, he would have drowned O'Neil. The 'gator was then in full possession of the battle ground, swimming around and seeming to dare us to intrude again on his premises, until the man on the bank shot him again. We knew the shot was fatal, for he sank without a struggle. We formed another line, found him dead, and brought him ashore.

At another time I was sitting on the bank of a river at a deer lick, two or more miles from the house, and as I happened to look up the river, I saw a bear coming out of a cave in the bluff bank. He scratched himself like a dog does, went to the edge of the water and drank, then commenced to swim across the river. I saw at once that I could run around the bend of the river and be within twenty steps of him when he landed. But when the bear neared the bank, and I had just secured my position, an alligator took charge of him and pulled him under the water. In a minute or two the bear rose to the surface, apparently badly strangled, only to be pulled under again. I supposed the bear would bite and scratch the alligator while under water to make it turn loose. By this time I had lost all desire to kill the bear, as all my inclination was to kill the alligator. The bear finally crawled to the bank within twenty feet of me, but was again pulled into the water and was taken under the hollow bank, as evinced by the bubbles coming out from under it. The alligators were so deadly to our dogs that we never let one escape if we had a chance to kill it.

To illustrate the quality, grit, and ferocity of our dogs, I shall relate how they behaved in a fight. One morning, early, one of Mr. Humphrey's boys went out to hunt the horses and our dogs went with him. After the boy brought in the horses he went to look for the dogs, which had taken track and run off, but he could not find them. Next morning, which was Saturday, the younger dogs were home, which fact told us that the older dogs were staying with either a bear or a panther. In the forenoon we hunted down the river bottom and after dinner we went up the bottom. Just before the sun set we heard one of the dogs bark. The young dogs had followed us and had gone to where they had left the old dogs the night before. The old dogs had a bear up a tree. We killed it and fed the dogs, for they had not been fed for forty-eight hours. Judging from the signs on the tree, the bear had come down a dozen or more times and the dogs had fought him so furiously that he had to go back up to get out of their way. There were many signs to show that there had been hard-fought battles.

There was a little pond of water two hundred yards from the house toward which my hogs had made a trail on their trips to get a drink. When my hogs would come home looking frightened and disturbed, I would put my dogs on their back track. By the time I would find a dead hog, the dogs would have a panther or a bear up a tree ready for me to kill.

Time and space will permit me to tell only a few of my experiences as a hunter. Here is one where my wife's brother, a half-grown boy, eleven dogs and I battled with one lone panther. He was an unusually big one and was well experienced in warfare. My dogs loved a fight and would go hunting alone if they had to. One morning I heard them out on the post oak hills. I tried to get my brother-in-law to go make the coon, cat, or fox, jump out of the tree and let the dogs kill it, but he said, "I'll get my breakfast first." After breakfast we both went, believing it to be only a wild cat or a coon, and we did not bother to take a gun. When on our way, we found that whatever the dogs were fighting, it was traveling on the ground. I said, "Curtis, they are fighting either a bear, panther, or straggling buffalo, and I insist that you go back after a gun."

But he wanted to see first what it was they were after. When we finally overtook the dogs, they had run a very large panther up a tree. I again insisted that he go back for a gun, but like all boys, he was after fun, as well as the panther. He said, "Let us chunk him out! If he can whip us and all the dogs, then I'll go after the gun."

We threw a stick at the panther, and he jumped out of the tree but he climbed another one before the dogs could get hold of him. We threw sticks and rocks at him, but he seemed to dread the fight. Panthers are very cowardly when attacked, but when they bring on the assault, they will fight to the finish. After arming ourselves with green hickory clubs, my brother-in-law started up the tree. As soon as the panther saw him coming, he jumped out of the tree. He leaped out and the dogs covered him. But when they would pull him down he would roll over on his back and with one frantic effort, slash right and left with his claws, liberate himself and get back on to his feet. But he would get only a short distance until the dogs would pull him down again. We used our clubs on his head but with little effect. He would only shut his eyes. He looked more like a lion than a panther and was what some are pleased to call a Mexican lion. After fighting him uphill and down for about three hundred yards, he acknowledged himself whipped and went up another tree to get away from us and take a rest before renewing the fight. When he started to climb the tree, three of the dogs had hold of his hind legs. When he had his legs clear of the ground, two of the dogs turned loose, but the other, a big heavy dog, braced his feet against the tree and tried to jerk the panther down but failed to do so. I ran up and grabbed the other leg but we failed to pull him down. I had to turn loose my hold or be taken up the tree with him. We threw chunks and rocks at him, but he refused to come down, as he dreaded another charge of his combined enemy. He had gone out on a limb with his head toward the trunk of the tree. The fight had become so interesting by this time that neither of us was willing to stop to go after a gun. Our only chance was to climb the tree and scare him out again, but he wouldn't scare. He would walk the limb to the trunk of the tree, snarling at me, reaching his paw down at me, and telling me in so many words, that if I came any nearer he would hurt me. And I knew he was telling me the truth, so I climbed back down.

I next cut a four-foot stick, tied my bowie knife on one end of it with my suspenders, went back up the tree and climbed out on a limb below the one the animal was on. I viewed the situation and concluded that the surest way to win the fight was to cut his bowels out. I slashed down his underside. The second jump he made on the ground I saw his entrails wind around him. The dogs covered him, but the victory was not yet won. The bloodiest part of the fight had just begun. As he was badly wounded, he depended more on fighting than running. I hurried down the tree and found my bowie knife and the stick which I intended to pitch down, lodged in the tree. I heard the battle raging down the ravine, over a hundred yards off. When I reached the scene, the panther had the head of my favorite dog in his mouth. My brother-in-law had hold of one of his hind legs, and it was so large that it took both hands to reach around. As I now had no knife, I ran my hand into Curtis' pocket and found a four-bladed Congress knife. The blades were short, but the force of the blow I gave him with the knife, pressed his sides in, and after a dozen or more stabs, the short blade reached his heart and my dog was released.

We all, man, boy, and dogs carried back home the bloody signs of battle. I had to climb the tree to get my knife, with which I skinned the animal. His hide nearly covered one end of a log cabin we stretched it on. He was nine and a half feet from tip to tip and was the largest panther killed on the Trinity. John Pillow, then only a boy, who now lives near Bazette was at my house when we came home with the hide and the wounded dogs.

My brother and family came in from North Carolina and brought three fine fox hounds with them. I had a log house built for him by this time, but it lacked floors, doors, and gables being finished. We soon sawed lumber with a whip-saw for the floors, and my brother moved out of his tent into it. The negroes had two tents about fifty yards in front of the house. One night as the negroes were eating their supper, they were throwing the scraps to five pigs my brother had brought. A panther came right among the little negroes, caught up one of the pigs and ran off with it. His dogs were up at my house, and he sent two negro boys after me and the dogs. After quite a round, making it jump out of two trees, we finally killed it in the third tree, without any of the dogs getting hurt. The night was very dark and we had no torch lights to help us see our way through the timber.

Just a few nights later, or rather, just before day one foggy morning, a panther came and picked up a pig within fifty feet of the house. There was not a dog on the prem-ises, as I had loaned them to a Mr. Coburn to help him catch a panther that was eating his pigs. I noticed the course the panther took from the squealing of the pig, called my broth-er's Tar Heel dogs, put them on the trail, and they soon brought it to bay on the ground by a pit. I blundered along through the timber, feeling my way for about half a mile. When I came up to where the dogs were, I could tell when I was near the varmint by the dogs getting behind me. When I would back off, the dogs would get in front of me. I could hear the pig's dying breaths, but I could see nothing to shoot at. I felt around with my feet until I found a piece of rotten limb. I picked it up, advanced quickly with a shout of en-couragement to the dogs and threw the stick at the dying pig. I heard the panther make two jumps up a tree. I leveled my gun the best I could at the place where I guessed the panther was from the noise it made by its second jump up the tree. My gun was a big bore gun, and the ball happened to cut it across the abdomen making a hole large enough for its guts to come out of, but I did not know at that time that I had hit it at all. It jumped to the ground and ran through the brush into the Trinity bottom, about half a mile away, and ran up an ash tree.

By the time I had felt my way through the dark and reached the dogs, it was becoming daylight. My brother had never killed a panther, so I holloed to him, for I wanted him to kill it. By the time he reached me with his shotgun it was good daylight. I insisted that he shoot it with my gun, but, no, he said he could kill it with his gun. The negro boys had been squirrel hunting the day before with his gun and it was loaded with squirrel shot, which only stimulated the panther to take refuge under a tree top that lay over the roots of a blown down tree. While my brother was looking for a chance to shoot him under the brush, one of his dogs got too near the panther, which pulled him under the cover with his paw and chewed him up so badly that he died the next day. When we skinned the panther we found all his entrails had been torn out by the brush and briers through the hole my ball had made in his abdomen, and only the stomach remained. Yet he had lived to kill one dog before he was shot again.

One cold day when the limbs of the trees were being crushed off by the weight of sleet, my neighbor, Humphrey, proposed that he, his three boys, and I go hunting. In about an hour's time we had killed one panther and three wild cats. Humphrey said, "This panther's stomach looks full. Believe I'll cut it open and see if he has been eating my pigs." He found no pigs, but the stomach was packed full of large wood rats. He had swallowed them whole, after one crunch or two with his jaws. We next examined the wild cats' stomachs and found that they had been dealing in the rat business also. The rats were about all they could find for food, as all the other animals were sheltered from the cold.

In writing a few of the reminiscences of my life, I have confined myself to facts and have written of the incidents as told to me by others that I had every reason to believe were truths. I shall now puppy down as a coward because I fear readers will believe the following incidents to be fiction, when I tell that I killed two panthers and one deer with the same bullet. "Hold! It is not fair! It is not honest!" For a man to condemn or endorse any question until he gives that question an honest consideration and unbiased thought is to judge before all the evidence is in.

At this time it took one deer hide to buy a pound of lead, about three hides to buy a pound of powder, without the caps, and we husbanded our ammunition as we did our money. Our nearest markets were Shreveport, Louisiana, and Houston, Texas, and it was over two hundred miles to either city. We used muzzle-loading, flintlock guns. The old Harper's Ferry Jaeger was used principally for large game.

As I have said before, if our dogs became anxious for a hunt, they took it if they had to go by themselves. One morning I heard them across the river. I crossed over to them and they had a panther up a forked ash tree. It was standing in the forks. I walked near, in front of it, and shot it through the neck, breaking it. The bullet lodged against its thick skin, and when I took the skin off, I found it, somewhat battered from hitting the neck bone, and saved it.

Sometime afterward I was hunting my hogs in the river bottom. I shot off my gun at a buffalo across the river. When I commenced reloading, I found there were no bullets in my shot pouch except the battered one I had killed the panther with. Not caring to go back home, two miles, with an empty gun, I loaded up with the battered bullet. On my way home, I had a good chance for a shot at a buck and killed it. I got my bullet back again, which was lodged against the buck's hide, and it was badly battered this time.

One Sunday morning I heard the dogs about half a mile off. I told a couple of negro boys, who were fond of hunting, to go and make whatever the dogs had jumped get out of the tree and let them kill it. Directly, one of the boys came back, saying that it was a panther and he was afraid that if he made it jump out it would hurt some of the dogs. I took down my gun, found it empty, and no bullets in my shot pouch but the battered one. I shaped it up and ran it down my gun, saying to the negro boy, "If I can get close enough, this piece of bullet will kill it."

When I went up with the gun, it gave new life to the dogs, which made the panther restless, and he commenced coming down the tree. This gave me my chance to shoot it not more than eight or ten feet from the muzzle of the gun. With this same bullet, I had killed another panther and an old buck, which I have above related.

I will tell another incident. One of my neighbors took his axe, bucket, and ten-year-old son one evening and went to the river bottom to cut a bee tree. After he had felled the tree he heard a panther scream in the distance. For pastime, he mocked, or imitated it, but he quit this when he heard the panther getting nearer. But the sound of his axe cutting out the honey, guided the panther to the man, as he told it, and the animal came by the stump of the tree, mounted the butt end of the log, and made for the man. The man related the fight thus: "I thought I would kill it with my axe, but it sprang so far and so quick upon me that my axe was of no avail. Instead of getting me through the throat, it caught me through the shoulder and commenced trying to tear me to pieces with its hind claws. I had one hand and arm unincumbered. I jerked my bowie knife from its scabbard, and made my licks with the knife, as fast as it made its licks with its claws. It soon turned me loose and ran off around the top of the fallen tree. I hurried home, half naked, badly scratched, badly bitten, and bleeding. Next morning I rode to the battle ground with a neighbor and our dogs and found the panther fifty feet away, dead. Got the honey all right, but concluded I would never mock another panther, unless I had a gun."

During the six years' stay in Corsicana, the professional and business men, and others, were often wanting me to go hunting with them. One night, Doctor Dixon, Doctor Leach, and another man, went on Rush Creek, fire hunting. They put it on me to carry the light and do the shooting. I shot twice and killed four deer. I killed three at one shot, an old doe and two six-months-old fawns. Their eyes all seemed to be in a cluster. We had a deer for each of us, so we went home.

Another night Doctor Dixon and another man were with me when I killed five deer, a wild cat, and a whip-poor-will, never missing a shot. I was at a friend's house on the Brazos, Ned Franks by name, with whom I had hunted on the Trinity River. After supper he said, "Buck, let us take a fire hunt." We went and, as usual, he had me to carry the light and do the shooting. I had a heavy rifle, shot six times and killed five large bucks and a cat. I killed four of the bucks inside his field. These were my best night hunts, but I seldom failed to kill one or more.

I was hunting one day with John Street. He had some good deer dogs, and they brought something to bay in the brush. We concluded it must be a bear, but when we reached the scene it was two large bucks which had been fighting and had their horns locked together. We killed them, opened their stomachs, which were filled with acorns and vegetation, which evidenced that their horns had not been locked over two hours. We carried their heads into Corsicana and no two men could pull them apart. I have found two other pairs with locked horns, but they were dead. Of one pair, one seemed to have had its neck broken, or had died at least ten days before the other one did. It was in a state of decomposition while the other one had drug it around until it starved for food and water. It had died so recently that it was not even swollen.

This scene reminded me of a tale I read when I was a boy about a band of people, or a tribe, who had made a law that if one of them killed his fellowman they would confine him to his victim and leave him to die of starvation in the stench of his victim.

I was once returning from a trip to the lower Brazos when night overtook me when I was between two settlements. I put my horse to grass, ate a cold snack, spread my blanket and went to sleep in the edge of a prairie. Next morning I heard a clashing noise and looked to see ten or a dozen deer coming out of the timber onto the prairie. Among them were two bucks, fighting. They were warding off the blows of each other with their horns. They were within gunshot, but I had no use for meat, so I sat and watched them fight. Soon they locked their horns and spun around and around, while the other deer grazed slowly across the little prairie into the timber. The locked-horn bucks tried to follow the others, but made a very poor out of traveling. Although I was amused, I felt sorry for their inevitable fate. I finally concluded to take my rope off my horse, rope them and try to relieve them. When they saw me coming they exerted themselves more. When within a few feet of them, they seemed to make an extraordinary exertion and pulled themselves apart.

One evening Joe Garner and I went down near the mouth of Brier Creek, turkey hunting. I had a dog that would find and bark at a turkey at night as he would in the daytime. We had killed one apiece and had scattered the others. My dog commenced barking in the creek bottom. Garner said, "You kill the one the dog's found. I'll go down where I heard one light in a tree."

I probed my way through vine, brush, briers and the darkness, looking at the tree tops, but could see nothing that looked like a turkey. I found that the dog was barking at something on the ground. I pulled through the vines and briers toward the dog. I came to a large log that had fallen, carrying the vines and briers from the other trees with it, making quite a dense thicket on both sides of the fallen tree. I pulled the brush apart to look over the dog, and there lay a bear within two feet of my face. I could have put my hand on her face, I was no near.

The dog closed on her, which caused her to move and to prepare for a fight. This caused her young ones to commence crying and me to retreat, as I well knew what would happen next. Garner heard the crying of the cubs and came running until he struck the dense thicket. He asked me if the old bear was there. I told him she was and that one of us would have to hold the vines out of the way while the other shot her. "Well," he said, "you do the shooting." He looked over the log and asked me if the black bulk against the log was the bear. I could not see where her head was, but I gave her both barrels. We had to get the help of a limb and make a lifting tackle to help us hoist her to my horse's back. Five or six miles from home, Garner took three turkeys and my gun on his horse, and I had myself and four bears on my horse, which load almost broke him down. The largest cub was dead. They did not have their eyes open and had no hair and weighed only about a pound and a half each, but they knew something was wrong. I had their mother in front, thrown over the saddle, and the cubs kept climbing out of my saddle pockets, whining and crying. All the boys and half the girls wanted the cubs, so it was no trouble getting them off my hands.

I brought my bear dogs with me when I moved to Corsicana and loaned all except two to the Rankin boys, with whom I often hunted. On one occasion we killed eight bears, principally "yearling" size, in the Trinity bottom near the mouth of Red Oak Creek. We organized another hunting party and went back, thinking we would make a big haul, but, lo the first one we struck was an old coaster, perhaps from Arkansas. Our dogs could not force him to climb. He ran into a dense thicket, and he chewed up our dogs horribly before we could kill him, and this broke up our hunt. We had to carry some of our dogs home.

CHAPTER VI

SHERIFF OF NAVARRO COUNTY

WHEN annexation had been accomplished, settlers came in thick and fast. We were constantly writing to relatives and friends in North Carolina, urging them to come and cast their lot with ours. Corn sold readily to new settlers and pork rose from one and a half to three cents a pound. I got along finely with all my neighbors. One of my neighbors, who was also one of the earliest settlers, and I were the only ones who had any corn to sell. But someone set fire to my crib, which contained nearly five hundred bushels of corn, and it would have burned if a heavy sleet and rain had not come up. There was no roof to the crib, so the rain put out the fire. Only the shucks were burned off some of the corn. There was no thunder or lightning during the sleet storm which was evidence that someone had set the crib on fire.

Soon after this occurred, the other man, William Ladd, from Arkansas, who also had corn for sale, had a family row with his mother-in-law. As her tongue was her only available weapon, she turned it loose and shelled all the woods in range. She reminded him of his criminality in Arkansas and bitterly accused him of having tried to burn my corn so he could get two prices for his. He asked me if I believed that he had tried to burn my corn crib. I answered that it was hard for me to believe a thing I knew nothing about. He got mad and told me in the presence of several others that he would make me say it or he would dance over my liver. I told him in a good-humored tone that if he did, not to have any friends help him dance but that it was all right with me for him to dance.

It was eighteen miles from Corsicana to my house and fifteen miles to his. We had to pass through an eight-mile-wide prairie. I saw that his horse was inferior to mine. When he got out of sight in the timber, I rode slowly until he got well out on the prairie, then I galloped until I overtook him. When he heard my horse's feet he started to run, but I headed him off. He got back in the road, pulled out a bottle and said, "Hello! I'm glad to see you. Come have a drink." I did not drink but rode along with him about six miles to his house, where he invited me to stop. I excused myself and rode home.

Some time after this, district court met at Corsicana. I had no business at court, but it was a sort of show in that section. The grand jury was in session. I was one of those summoned to appear before it. After asking me some questions, the foreman said, "We did not expect much information from you, but we wanted to inform you that this grand jury has dissolved as a grand jury, and you are now in a nominating convention." He told me they had examined records and sheriff returns and felt that it was their duty as grand jurors to nominate a candidate for sheriff.

"Then, why select me, living eighteen miles away?" I asked.

"We have had witnesses before us to testify in yours and O'Neil's racket. We have heard of you and Bill Ladd making friends on the eight-mile prairie. That is the reason why we have selected you. Our first sheriff, Allen Johnson, resigned because he could not arrest the criminals who have stopped at this place. Stokes, who is filling out the unexpired term, has returned two writs against Ladd, and could not serve them on account of resistance."

I remarked that this was a desperate state of affairs and that I would give my decision the next day. I then told the jurors I would accept the nomination if they would promise to back me in my official acts. After much hesitation they all promised, except one.

In the pending canvass my opponent was William Stokes, who was then serving out the unexpired term. This man Ladd canvassed the county for Stokes. On several occasions he told me in the presence of a crowd that if I was elected I would have to make the same returns that Stokes made. I told him that I was such a cursed fool that I never knew what I could do until I tried, and if I failed, I would try again. During the canvass he sold his farm and moved to Corsicana, the county seat, where he seemed to be the commander-in-chief of the criminals and outlaws.

I was elected and moved to Corsicana in 1849-50. I got a man named Boone, who claimed to be, and perhaps was, a great grandson of Daniel Boone to take charge of my place at Bazette. He was to take care of the stock, bees, hogs, and nine pet deer we had left there. And he took care of the bees, hogs, and deer especially well, so that at the end of three years all had left, and their tracks were too cold to follow.

Well, the second writ put in my hands was from East Texas against Ladd; one of those that could not be served. I gave two active young men a special deputation and told them to go down to the tenpin alley; one was to get in a game with Ladd, while the other one was to signal me from the door when to come up. The sign was made and I walked in on the tenpin floor saying, "Well, Ladd, here is the same old writ we used in the canvass." He replied, "Damn the old writ! It's a bailable case." And it was. "Write out a bond and I'll give security," he said.

I had taken the two young deputies' pistols away from them and had armed them with slingshots. (I was a little afraid those boys might shoot somebody if they were allowed to carry their pistols.) Ladd never knew but that I went into his own den of friends and arrested him by myself. He did not know that those boys were fairly itching for an excuse to burst his skull with their slingshots. I had no more trouble with Mr. Ladd, although I served writs on him afterwards.

The last act of his life was to spit in his wife's face. His last words were, "I'd give fifty dollars for a good breath," and with the last word, went his last breath. My brother Bryant was an eyewitness at this scene at Waco, where they both lived at that time. I have spent more space and time writing up Mr. Ladd than the interest of his case warrants. It is merely to show that a sheriff has all the criminals of his county to deal with, and there were many in Navarro County when it was a part of the frontier.

The county, as a part of the frontier, covered all the territory between the Brazos and the Trinity Rivers, west to New Mexico. Court was held in a log cabin. We had no jail, consequently, I had to chain the prisoners like so many pet bears inside a log cabin. I had many worse cases than Ladd's to deal with. Common sense and strategy had to be used, as well as pluck, when an outlaw was arrested, or someone would have been hurt.

After two terms as sheriff, the people again asked me to accept public office as their treasurer, and one of my deputies, Nathaniel Henderson, was elected sheriff. He had many bad criminals to deal with, as well as I had during my term. I shall tell of one among the many.

There was a man by the name of Ellis, who loved his dram and liked to fight if any other man meddled with his business, although he was considered truthful. When I was sheriff he was one of my stand-bys. He had a neighbor named Crow, who was in good circumstances, with plenty of stock and negroes. Crow had no children. He, too, loved his dram and they often drank together while going out to their farms, a distance of sixteen miles. On one of these occasions they had a fight. Crow indicted Ellis for whipping him and made him give a peace bond.

There was another man named Pearce who lived in town.

He belonged to the Baptist church, had a number of race horses, and kept people of a sporting character around him. He visited the saloons and gambling houses twice to where he went to church once. He was overbearing and was considered a dangerous man.

While Ellis and his neighbor, Crow, were at outs, Ellis called a consultation of his friends to advise him. He said to us, "This man Pearce is a dangerous man. He is the only man I am afraid of. I want you to advise me what to do. He thinks I am mad at Crow for swearing out a peace warrant, and he made me a proposition to kill or have Crow killed. He then wants to fix up a bill of sale for the stock, negroes, and deed to Crow's land, and says that we will then divide the property. I jerked out my pistol and gave him a good cussing. I know he will seek my life for fear I will expose him." It was, in a manner, a life and death case, and we told him that we would all go home and each give his case serious consideration, and that we would meet with him again the next morning.

The next morning we advised him to take the bull by the horns; that we would see Mr. Crow and advise him, as well as Ellis, to swear out a peace warrant for Mr. Pearce, because both had just grounds for such action. Knowing the situation, I could see trouble coming for Sheriff Henderson. When he arrested Pearce on the peace warrant from Justice Dixon's court, a crowd of about forty of his friends, all armed, from the saloons and gambling dens followed the sheriff into Dixon's courtroom.

Pearce told the justice that neither witness should give testimony against him, which intimidated the court and the sheriff from further proceedings. Dixon adjourned his court, and he and the sheriff gathered together all their friends who were in town and told them that if there were not enough law-abiding citizens to back them in their official duty that they would resign. We advised Sheriff Henderson to deputize a man from every neighborhood and summon every man in the county who had gray hair on his head (the young men to be held in reserve) to meet at Corsicana on the following morning with their guns.

By ten o'clock, there were over two hundred armed men on the grounds. When Pearce saw such a crowd, he and his friends fortified themselves in a saloon and gambling house. The saloon keeper talked pretty saucy, telling the old farmers that they had better go home if they did not want to get hurt, which only enraged them. In the meantime, the citizens prepared to dislodge Pearce and his followers by the use of explosives.

When the rowdies found there was an arrangement made to blow up their fortification, some of their forces began to sift out of the back doors. Then Pearce came to the front door and told three farmers that he would surrender if they would promise him that there would be no acts of violence by the crowd. They promised and he surrendered. These old gray-haired farmers told him that he had been a great annoyance to the county ever since he had come into it and that he must leave.

They put him and some of his friends on his race horses, tied ropes around the horses' necks, and led them across the county line. They were told never to come back, and they did not. We camped out one night with them and guarded them. They were very restless.

After this demonstration by these old farmers, Navarro County did not have, at least for a while, any but law-abiding citizens. Hal Ross, cousin to ex-Governor Sul Ross, later killed this man Joe Pearce on the race tracks at Waco.

At the May term of the county court in 1854, patrols were ordered against possible attacks by the Indians. I was appointed captain of the patrols. Meanwhile, the citizens of Navarro County had seen fit to elect me County Treasurer, in August, 1852. And in August, 1854, they again selected me as their sheriff.

In February, 1855, I heard that a man named Love had shot an acquaintance named Anderson. Anderson was apparently fatally hurt and there was unusual excitement about the affair, when, on the following day, the victim died. As sheriff, I arrested Love. After the preliminary hearing, the case was transferred to Squire Carroll's court at Dresden for the trial. Some twenty of the local citizens opposed my arrest of Love and carried guns with the probable idea of intimidating the law.

After the prisoner had been haled before the bar and the trial got under way, this opposition was less in evidence but still existed. On the day that the trial opened I had decided to spend the night with my brother Augustus. Some fifty armed men, of whom about thirty were from Freestone County, followed me nearly to my destination for some purpose. However, the case was tried and the defendant was bound over for his appearance in District Court in bond of eight thousand dollars.

Once, during my last term as sheriff, the courthouse was burned, supposedly by the murderer of one Wells, in order to destroy the indictment. Reinstating the cases that were destroyed by fire took quite some time.

I will relate one case that gave me more trouble than any other during my official terms, with all the technicalities which accompanied it.

There was a man by the name of Taylor who had come to Texas among the first three hundred families with Stephen F. Austin. The Mexican government had given each man a league and a *labor* of land. This man Taylor's league and *labor* of land was located on Richland Creek, covering some of the land on Pin Oak Creek, now in Navarro County. Taylor's wife died, and he took their children back to relatives in Tennessee. He returned to Texas and carried out all the duties of the colonists, as he had agreed to do. His land was a hundred miles from the settlements. He died at a man's house, whose name was Stout, in East Texas.

After annexation, there came many bad men to Texas. Among the worst were forgers, principally lawyers. In looking over and hunting up land titles they found this Taylor league, without a claimant. There were three different people who forged deeds to the Taylor league. One of these forgers was Jacob Elliot, a lawyer, a deacon in the Baptist church, and a Freemason of the highest order. He took possession of the Taylor land.

One day there came along a man, by the name of Wells, and his wife in a wagon. They stopped at Elliot's. He hired this man to boss a job of putting up a barn and stables. Elliot told Wells to take the negro boys and to cut cedar logs to build the barns and stables. He remarked at that time that he got a bargain when he bought the Taylor league. Wells remarked, "There was a man who died at my father-in-law's house by the name of Taylor, who owned a league of land somewhere in this section of the country." Elliot interrogated Wells, and found that he and his wife had evidence to convict him of forgery. The next thing, to his mind, was to get rid of them and he did. The Wells', however, secured more complete evidence against him.

He had two white-negro boys, said to be his children. He had them take two good mules, a watch apiece, and some money, and told them to go to Corpus Christi and stay until further ordered. Then he secretly went to the prominent men and high Masons of the county and declared Wells had robbed his house. He then had his other negroes testify before them that it was all as their master had told them; that after Wells had robbed the house, he had sent away the mulattoes and mules by a man who was missing from the neighborhood. (This "missing man" had merely gone to his home in Brazos County, as was later learned.) On these allegations he induced some of the most influential men in the county to conspire with him in killing Wells. They killed Wells, believing they were doing a good service to society in getting rid of such a man. Elliot's and the negroes' testimony to hide the knowledge of his forged deed and the conspiracy to get Wells out of the way caused no suspicion.

They took Wells twelve miles across the divide, killed him, took out his viscera, put a long pole on his breast, and sank him in eight feet of water in Chambers Creek. They put the other end of the pole in the fork of a tree that leaned over the hole of water to hold him to the bottom. Eleven days after he was missing, he was found by a cow hunter.

On the urgent plea of Mrs. Wells, who said she knew her husband was either killed or under duress, I sent a deputy and a posse to search for him. Many of the people, also, hunted several days. Mrs. Wells told them that she knew her husband had been killed because he knew too much about the Taylor league of land, and that she was afraid that she would be killed. She asked me to protect her until she could get word to her father to come after her.

I summoned a jury inquest, and Mrs. Wells recognized her husband by his clothes, plugged teeth, etc. The jury kept their verdict secret and returned it to Justice Dixon, who issued writs to me to arrest eleven men, nine of whom were men of influence and wealth for that country and time. Nine of them were Free Masons and appealed to me, as a brother Mason, to favor them by losing and destroying the papers, etc. I told them that I held my oath of office to be more sacred than everything on earth, except my wife and baby. Dixon would not allow them bail, although they waived the right of trial. They moved their trial before another justice, who was a Methodist preacher and a Mason. He permitted them to make bail. And, there I was, with these prominent men with their influence, angry with me. Most of the Free Masons were angry because I took the strange and heartbroken woman into my household until her father came after her.

Their trial came up in the district court and Wells was proved to be a man of worth and veracity. (There has been more than one man hung on more doubtful evidence than was presented against these men.) It was proved, by two witnesses, that the defendant and the deceased were going in the direction where Wells' body was found. It was also proved that two of the crowd were seen near where Wells' body was found on the first day he was missing. But the jury returned a verdict of "not guilty."

Here my tongue got ahead of my brains. I turned, and facing the jurors, I told them that they were the only men in the county who believed these men innocent. I have often wondered why the judge did not punish me for this act, but he only gave me a sharp lecture. He, as well as all in that crowded courthouse who had heard the evidence, knew they were guilty. But the jurors were such moral cowards that they had rather perjure themselves than to gain the ill will of those prominent men and their friends. (It is the moral cowardice of men today that destroys our free institutions, their own liberty, and makes them dangerous enemies to society. They hold policy above principle. They will uphold wrong and falsehood and condemn right and truth, rather than oppose popular sentiment.)

About the time I moved to Bosque County, there were two other forgers to the Taylor league. They brought suit against Elliot for possession. They were having an interesting three-cornered fight over this land when the Taylor heirs, who had grown to maturity, intervened and produced the old original patent to the land. They also had their father's will, witnessed by Stout, in whose house Taylor had died and who was Wells' father-in-law. Stout read the will which was recorded in the county in East Texas where Taylor had died. Here were three plain cases of forgery for possession of the same piece of land, and no grand jury had the moral courage to investigate these criminal acts.

When the patent and the will were read in court, the forgers ceased their three-cornered fight with a stain upon them, but they had the kind of lawyers criminals employ. The court gave the Taylor heirs all the league, except one section, held by limitation, which has prejudiced me against the limitation law.

CHAPTER VII

LIFE OF A TEXAS SETTLER
IN THE 'FIFTIES

FRONTIER life held a fascination for the early settler but that life soon made him into a realist who found many of his youthful concepts of western life mere myths. There was a less enjoyable side, a drab, monotonous side in the daily life of the frontiersman. All along the western line of the settlements men participated in events which were vital in the history of our nation, but their lives were not entirely made up of high adventure and noble deeds. I cannot here even try to picture the frontier nor frontier problems in the broader sense, but I would like to point out that most of the life of the frontiersman was spent in a daily routine of ordinary duties, although it is true that this routine was frequently broken by exciting events or occasional relaxation of a social nature. I shall indicate something of the daily work and also the diversions of myself as an average frontier settler in central Texas in the 'fifties.

One of the most prevalent means of contributing to one's livelihood was that of raising livestock. Stock raising was considered as profitable as any other business and more so than many, but it required much work. Raising of cattle was not my major interest although I had some, chiefly for beef and butter purposes. I was not at all a "cattleman," although I might have been a few years later when that day arrived had I been living in typical cattle country. But I kept a herd of a hundred and up. They were turned out to range, but a severe drouth meant fewer calves and poor beef, while an

72

unusually severe winter called for some feeding to tide them over the season. Although not really wild, they tended to become that way on the free range and would stray badly so that days of gruelling riding would be our lot in an effort to find them. Some of them had to be roped to round them up and would be "fighty." They were of some material value and a welcome addition to the diet despite the plentifulness of game. A norther and sleet was frequently the cause of their drifting. We broke some few of them for oxen. In this work of herding or looking up the cattle, my young son, Kossuth, although a mere boy, was soon of much help to me as he was a gifted rider. I remember that in the spring of 1860 I gave him ten cows and calves to encourage him to read the Bible. I branded them ƔB for him.

As i was raising horses, and sufficient mules for my own use, and occasionally buying and adding to their numbers, some time was devoted each week to looking after them. They were on the range but when we desired to brand or break them we generally drove them to the fields and thence to the pens. I did not have a large cavayard [caballado], but seldom, if ever, less than one hundred head. At times some of them strayed or got into some neighbors' crops and they would have to be found and shifted to other pasturage. They ranged the prairie, river bottoms, and the mountains, so we wanted to keep them somewhat in check. Then there were generally some mustangs or perhaps wild horses that might entice them away. Mares with young colts, if in poor condition, were driven to the pens and fed. In the winter season this was especially necessary, of course. We lost some of them from one cause or another—such as lockjaw, wolves in hard winters, and straying out of the country.

Both horses and cattle were branded. Horses were branded when colts and cattle when yearlings. In this work, I generally hired a man or two to assist me as my boys (negroes) were not skilled at this task. On one day in June of 1858, I remember, we branded thirty colts and a few days later two of us branded fifty-three calves. I found a few months later that one Smith of Meridian had the same mark as my own, so I bought his stock, including his hogs. Horses grazed mostly along the Brazos, Steel's Creek, Duffau Creek, etc., which lie north of the main Bosque River. And while we did not consider ourselves ranchmen, in the latter sense, we broke our stock to work and to saddle. Several years' experience in the saddle, almost daily, soon enabled a man to become somewhat accustomed to that seat even on a pitching horse. Horses on the range became wild and spirited and about one out of five horses gave real trouble in "breaking," but it was all a part of the horseman's work.

We tried to raise good saddle horses for the pleasure afforded by satisfactory transportation and because I always considered the best horses obtainable in a country subject to invasion by the Indians a part of the settler's fundamental equipment. Naturally we expected to market the surplus. A man's life frequently depended on the speed, stamina, and intelligence of his horse. I remember that one of my favorite saddlers was a high-spirited stallion named Blackleg, while another which I felt could carry me away from a party of redskins was named Blue Dog. One high-strung and fast animal that I liked to ride had some mustang blood in her and would buck frequently with me on cool mornings. Her sire was a well-bred saddler and gentle, but "White Gal," a one-man horse, was never entirely so.

Fencing during these earlier years was limited to pens and small pastures for both cattle and horses. Sometimes all hands would turn to and fencing would occupy our time for several days. These fences were made of rails although we sometimes simply used rocks and brush. The rail fences were of rails secured from cedar brakes and other timber along the creeks and even on the mountains. Ordinary rail fences were usually deemed sufficient for cow pens, a horse pasture, and the fields, but we had to supplement the rails with planks for our vegetable gardens to keep the rabbits out. There was much good cedar in the Paluxie River country to the north of me. Getting out these rails enabled some of my boys to become very proficient with the axe. Many of the axe handles we dressed out of the timber, also. At times neighbors traded labor in building cow lots or fencing a horse pasture.

In this connection, stock in pens had to be fed, of course. One big source of feed was the tall or prairie grass hay which was cut and hauled in the fall. Another was corn tops, while we raised some cane. Then there was straw from the grain which we threshed. When a corn crop had been made in our community, corn was to be had for a fair price if one had to buy to supplement his own crop. Corn was pulled and hauled in in order to have the cribs filled for winter. There was hauling of rocks for walling up of wells, bringing supplies by ox-team from Houston or Galveston over two hundred miles distant, and trips to mill for flour and corn meal. Some hauling was done from Waco, the county seat of McClellan County, the nearest town of consequence, which had a population of about one thousand souls. Timber for fences and lumber for houses of any type was generally hauled by oxen or teams of horses or mules.

My land was prairie, sodded in the forks of the Bosque and along the Brazos bottom. The plowing was chiefly done with oxen and I tried to keep from two to five plows breaking the land. When the ground was moist the effort was not so trying, but drouth sometimes delayed us or forced us to quit for the season.

In March corn was planted, oats sowed, and setting out of peach trees completed. Irish potatoes were planted in liberal quantities. September was a favorite time for sowing a turnip patch. Fall wheat was sowed in October, along with some rye for the chickens, and from two to four plows were used in plowing the seed under. Some wheat was sowed on fresh sod, just broken for the first time, and brushed in. Hard freezes often killed the fall wheat and we had to sow again in January; or perhaps, in the spring, rain would fail us and it would be necessary to try again. Grasshoppers proved trying in some years. If dry weather came in the summer, we generally cut and stacked the corn as fodder, in August. Yet, with some rain, even the sod lands yielded corn very well. I recall gathering four hundred bushels one September from new freshly sodded land. October saw us gathering potatoes if any had been made. Certainly we hoped to have something from the acres devoted to corn. No one neglected to cut and save the fodder if it became apparent that corn was not to be made.

Wheat was generally cut about the latter part of May or the first of June. Sometimes Indian raids delayed us in getting to this part of our farming and much of the grain was lost. But we worked desperately to save what we could, once we got to it, and neighbors frequently assisted each other. The scythe and cradle were in general use, although there was an occasional settler who cut with horse power. Then it was hauled in near the house and stacked in preparation for threshing. Potatoes, of course, were hauled to the houses and banked to preserve.

As for the threshing of wheat, it was done largely by hand power. It was placed in small cribs or timber containers that would not allow very much to be wasted, and trampled. After trampling it out of the stalks or straw, it was then fanned with a "fanner" or "fan" to separate it from the chaff. As this was done in July, when the weather was very warm, it was work.

"Hog killing" time came with the first apparently consistent cold weather. This occasion was thoroughly enjoyed by the children, but a job to be completed as quickly as possible by the grown-ups. The butchering, rendering of lard, the cutting up and salting down of the meat, making of sausage, and cleaning the premises of all evidences of disorder, refuse, and dirt, was the work of several days' duration in our family. Although the hogs were largely range fattened, they were ordinarily in good order when butchered because of the abundance of mast from the pecan and the oaks.

In preparation for this killing of meat, the smokehouses, built of logs and boards and generally without floors, were cleaned out. They were swept, boxes scoured in which the meat was to be salted, and hooks or strings for suspending portions of the meat and sausage from the rafters overhead placed in position. Sausage was placed in small, long sacks of simple cloth prepared by our women folk, or in vessels if it were to be soon consumed. After cutting up the meat it was spread out on boards before later being salted. Lard was rendered from the fats and the unedible portions of the hogs. Large pots and kettles over fires in the open were used in this process.

The weather was an important factor in butchering hogs, of course. We did not kill at one time all of the hogs selected for the meat supply. In January, I generally killed from ten to fifteen, depending upon the size, and would kill about the same number, say, in February. Nor did I always find it possible to have the fattest hogs driven into pens at the house for butchering. If I found others, on the range, miles from the house, and the weather suitable, I would kill them and send for wagons to haul them in. Then cleaning, cutting up, and salting in the smokehouse would follow. Of course we were on the range frequently to look after our hogs and had in mind the possibility of finding some fat ones among those we were looking for. When the mast failed us, as it did about once in every five years, the meat was poor accordingly. An abrupt change of weather from cold to warm soon after butchering meant spoiled meat despite efforts to save it. But usually some had already been preserved in a previous butchering or would be later. However, it was just part of the life and not an unusual experience to find the meat of eight or ten fine hogs spoiled in February, for instance, by a sudden warm spell. Spring or summer sometimes found the supply of bacon sorely depleted by losses through the activity of worms, although some of it could be saved by sunning before restoring to a freshly cleaned box.

Another type of labor performed by the early settler was erection of his buildings or houses. In addition to his own house of logs, or of logs and clapboards, there were the houses for the negroes, the smokehouse, the cribs, etc. Rafters and laths were obtained from the timber at hand as well as the logs for the walls. Doors were heavy but practicable in a country invaded by Indians and were constructed with the usual bars and notches. A small window or two was closed by a sound and heavy shutter as there were no window panes during the first number of years. So, the getting out of logs, rolling, and notching of them was an undertaking in which neighbors frequently came miles to assist. Smokehouses and cribs could be put up fairly quickly.

Mauls, axes, and wedges were tools to split the logs, while some men were quite proficient at notching the logs for corners and dressing them down on that side of the log intended for the inside. Equipment or tools, gauged by modern standards, were crude but we had grindstones on which to sharpen axes, hatchets and knives. Chimneys were of rock and mortar of selected clay and muds. They were large and afforded a fair fire although drafts caused them to smoke badly at times. I built a second chimney in a cabin for cooking purposes and this was known as the kitchen chimney, as it was really the kitchen and presided over by one of the negresses.

After some two years in log cabins on my Bosque farm, I had a more suitable house built by a very good carpenter, named Short. I was now the father of four children, three of them living, and needed more room. My wife and myself owned a few negroes and they had increased three or four, and another cabin was built for them. One of my wife's negroes, Soph, had five children. My new house was built of the same materials as the old—logs, but Short did a better job of it. There were two rooms sixteen feet square with a ten foot passage between and a piazza running the full length on one side. To this was added a lean-to room and others could be added as needed. Small windows were provided but there were no panes for two or three years. Nor was this additional house too much room as preachers, travelers, and neighbors sometimes stopped overnight with us. On one rainy Sunday night, some twelve persons stayed with us, five of them being ladies. I paid Short eighty dollars in trade for building the house.

Other duties with axe and hatchet were numerous but smaller operations, such as building ash hoppers, cutting bee trees, making clogs for horses, etc. I recall cutting a bee tree one November morning and hauling it in to add to my small collection of twenty hives, which were doing well, for seed. My son, Koss, was with me when I found it. I cut down the tree with an axe I had tied on the skirt of my saddle. The boy was riding a gentle gray mare and we cut a forked stick to use as traces for the mare to pull the tree with. We tied the prongs of the forked stick to the sides of the cantle of his saddle, on the order of buggy shafts, and the bee tree was tied to the apex of the forked stick. Koss then mounted and we rode slowly home without mishap.

As clogs, we generally used selected logs which we trimmed of branches. They were of sufficient weight to more than hobble an animal, practically staking it out, and yet not skin its legs nor endanger it from possible tangling as from staking with a rope. Ordinarily, I did not care for mustangs or wild horses nor want them around my stock, but in a few instances I captured wild horses which were especially attractive. Late one day I saw such a wild horse at a distance and creased him with a rifle bullet so that I was enabled to get close enough to him to rope him. He was left hobbled on the prairie overnight, when I returned and replaced the hobbles with a clog and again left him for further gentling. One of my friends in Navarro County, Lawson White, was seriously injured while engaged in capturing mustangs.

There were multitudinous small jobs about a stock farm. Attention to crippled or sick stock, looking after stock water, repair of the fences about the houses, going to mill ten miles below Meridian on the Bosque, or a distance of twenty miles, getting of wood for cooking and fuel, and building neighborhood roads. I remember wanting to see a road toward Duffau, but there were not enough settlers to petition the county court for such a road, so I marked and cut out the road myself. A log and my oxen were used to drag the new road. And on rainy days, when we were not forced to go outside to look after stock, some time was devoted to repair of saddles, molding of bullets, cleaning of guns, and plaiting of hair ropes, or perhaps dressing buckskin for clothing. Pecans could be gathered when fields were muddy and other duties were not pressing. There were many other tasks such as making cloth sacks for wheat, digging wells for drinking water, building sugar cane mills for our limited supply of cane, cutting wood to fit the fireplaces, milking and churning, feeding the stock that were always around the house, and mending clothing and shoes.

But life for the pioneer settler was not all work and no play. The two were mixed. Frontier life was lonely, especially for the women, but there was some opportunity for fun and social contact. Logrolling, house raising, harvesting, weddings and deaths attracted all the neighbors. But as the population was sparse, the crowds were small after all. There was an occasional candy stew in the private homes back in the older settlements, well regulated balls, and socials at the masonic lodge temples. I remember attending with my wife a few of these functions at Corsicana. An invitation to one of the balls read:

The pleasure of your company is respectfully solicited at a ball to be given at the Haynes Hotel in Corsicana on the 24th inst., at 5 o'clock P. M.

Corsicana, December 13, 1852

MANAGERS

P. M. Monnell   D. B. Hartzell
P. H. Carethers   W. B. McCabe
P. D. Hicks   A. F. Bartlett
D. R. Mickie   E. H. Root
J. H. Martin

Mr. B. Barry, *present*

A ticket to one of the celebrations of Washington's birthday stated:

Taos, February 9, 1853.

You are respectfully invited to attend the celebration of Washington's birthday on the 22nd inst., at the house of J. B. Hodge of Taos.

MANAGERS

E. H. Root   J. M. Riggs
R. C. Donaldson   Wm. Croft
G. M. Hogan   H. M. Allen
B. Handley   Jas. L. Lee

Wm. E. Hicks
Mrs. J. B. Barry, *present*

Of course one of our chief amusements was talking politics, particularly at the county seats where we gathered on court days or went to vote. Perhaps we were more interested than we had been before coming west as emigrants, as we felt keenly the need of strong government, particularly for the preservation of local order where it was frequently absent. Yet, no doubt, we all had a spirit of personal independence in the absence of the law. I remember voting for Sam Houston as governor, Baylor for judge, and Jack Evans for our representative, and attending the Democratic convention at Corsicana, although a new citizen. I voted for the same man as governor

at a later election and Alison Nelson for representative. And
one or two barbecues stand out in my memory as enjoyable
events. One given by our community for Walker's Rangers,
stationed in Bosque County for a while when the Indians had
begun their raids, was a great success. As game was everywhere
rather plentiful, we donated good beeves for the occasion.

Visiting or staying overnight was a welcome happening
in the frontier household. Afternoon on Sundays was a favorite time for visiting because everyone worked during the week
days. Preachers, newspaper editors, such as J. D. Shook of
The Prairie Blade of Corsicana, relatives, friends from east
of the Mississippi River, and neighbors were among these call-
ers. Then there was the peddler, the infrequent traveler, and
the surveyor or other officials. Sometimes one or two preachers,
say parsons Yell and Cooley, would stay with me and there
would be preaching at my house at eleven o'clock.   Again,
several couples from the nearest neighboring town would drive
to my house to have dinner with me. Perhaps Mrs. Barry and
myself would visit some of our neighbors and take dinner with
them; for instance, the Kimbroughs, Cogdells, Wileys, or
Hesters.

However, it was the church which provided a welcome
social opportunity and an outlet for pent-up emotionalism.
This was especially true for our women. Their life was hard,
nerve-racking at times, and despite their hopes for a better day,
something was needed to give them a chance to lift the restric-
tions of the daily existence. Not only was preaching held at private residences but in the absence of the preacher there was the
infrequent prayer meeting.

But it was the camp meeting which was the change most
thoroughly enjoyed. We attended Methodist, Presbyterian,
etc., at Meridian. One of the best attended camp meetings in
our section was held at Meridian in September, 1860, by a
Methodist preacher, and we carried bedding, food, etc., to
spend several days. Corsicana was an older town in a more

densely settled county where more and better church services were conducted than in Bosque, farther west. There was also more social recreation. About 1856 the white population of Navarro County was about 5,200 while that of Bosque was less than 900, with something over eight years difference in the time of their organization. While at Corsicana in the early 'fifties I heard some very good sermons by Robert King, Presbyterian, and the Reverend Cooley, a circuit rider of the Methodist church. We gave these men small gifts of money and provisions and were always glad to have them in our homes, but their work was hard and their remuneration must have been very inadequate in comparison to their good influence and work in the community. In the villages and towns, services were occasionally also held afternoon and were customary on Sunday nights. It was my good fortune to visit a session of the Baptist Association meeting at Waco, where I was visiting my brother. On another date at Waco, I attended a fair conducted by the ladies who were raising the means to buy a church bell. Weather was not allowed to handicap seriously our attendance on these welcomed services.

We had a few books, some of which I bought in Corsicana. I bought a two-volume history of Texas and some books on hunting in Africa. When any of the preachers happened to remark that they were going to Houston or Galveston, I sent by them for newspapers. I subscribed for the *Christian Advocate* at $3.50 per annum. Then we could secure copies of the *Texas Almanac.*

Such a means of relief (in the above mentioned church worship) from the daily struggle was not all that the church did for the settlers. The religion of the frontier settler gave him consolation at times when sorely needed. Injuries, deaths, and murders were to be expected by the frontiersman but, nevertheless, they always came as a shock. I had the experience of narrow escapes from death but received only serious injuries, and had my smaller son, Willie, seriously gored by a wild cow.

Medicine and surgery were crude. It was my lot to help hold some patients for the doctor when he was amputating limbs without anesthetic. Both men and women had falls from horses, accidents at the hands of stock, tame and wild, and other injuries too numerous to record.

But it was death in the frontier home from other than accidents or the hostile Indians that banished any youthful romantic ideas of the frontier that we once had. I helped husbands bury their wives and wives their husbands and saw the one that survived the other struggle to continue the plans that both had labored to complete. And I returned home one cold day in February, after an Indian hunt, in time to be present at the burial of our baby, Cora. Six months later we laid our little girl, Mary, by her. But the neighbors all came and were so kind, and next day the sun shone, and those of us who lived were well, and there was work that had to be done. So despite the loneliness we had to go ahead and no doubt it was better that we were so busy. Then my brother at Marlin passed away. But his going was not so sad as that of my nephew's little girl, Mary Bryant, who killed herself while at play by climbing to the top of the fence and pulling the top rail off on her when she slipped and fell. She and her mother were visiting us. We made her a coffin and buried her beside little Cora and Mary. And I was not through with sorrow, but I was more fortunate than so many people of my section that I could not complain.

It would be tiresome indeed to attempt to give a clear idea of the numerous business deals that I had over several years of life on the frontier. They involved from a few dollars to those few of several thousand. But perhaps it might be worth while to give some slight idea as to the prices of a few articles which were bought and sold in my section of the country by the frontier settler of the 'fifties.

In 1855, at Corsicana, I paid fifty-five cents for a saddle blanket, four dollars for a pair of firedogs, twenty dollars for two bedsteads, seventy-five cents for three bushels of potatoes, and thirty dollars for a five-shooter with flask molds. Six yards of domestic cost seventy-five cents, eight pounds of rice one dollar, while several of us bought *The Prairie Blade* from Editor Shook of Corsicana for $1,200. I paid twenty-five cents for a pound of powder, thirty cents for a quire of paper, ten cents a pound for nails, one dollar for a bushel of meal, and twenty-five dollars to a Mexican for a pony. An elementary spelling book for my little son, Kos, was twenty cents, and four boxes of matches were to be had for ten cents.

Labor, by later standards, was quite cheap. A blacksmith charged me only two and a half dollars for putting four felloes in one wheel, while I hired a white man to cut hay for one dollar per day. A white man was hired to do general farm work for me at twelve dollars per month and I hired out one of my negro boys during a prosperous spring season at $10.70 per month. In Bosque County, further west and near the frontier line, I was glad to let out a good negress at $2.50 and keep, during hard times, although I received five dollars per month with clothing and medical attention in ordinary years.

For experienced white women as midwives in attendance on my negroes, I paid ten dollars. At this time, while living in Navarro County and preparing to move out to Bosque County, I sold one negress and her child for $1,000.

When I moved to Bosque County from Corsicana, I bought wheat to keep from hauling it to my new home. I bought one hundred bushels in one lot for $1.50 per bushel. In Meridian in November, 1856, I sold 188 pounds of butter in a lot at fifteen cents per pound and some pork at eight cents. Cattle of the beef type averaged six dollars per head, although "the day of the cattleman" had not begun. A bottle of bitters cost a dollar and a quarter, while if wheat was scarce we paid two dollars per bushel, and a farm hand received fifteen dollars per month and board.

One of the most diverting forms of recreation open to the frontier settler was hunting. I enjoyed hunting and did a lot of it both for the sport and for the meat to be had. Game was plentiful and of numerous kinds. We had bear, panthers, deer, otter, wolves, cats, some buffalo, antelope, turkeys, prairie chickens, ducks, geese, and birds too numerous to mention. We seldom wanted for game to eat during several years when the population remained sparse. One had plenty of chances to practice marksmanship with both rifle and pistol while hunting, and there was enough hunting to obviate "buck fever." It was my privilege to hunt over much of the country of central, north, and northwest Texas as well as some in other portions of the State. Sometimes we hunted alone and at others in groups from a camp. I have already told of some bear, buffalo, panther, and alligator hunts, so I will here confine myself to the mention of other game and occasions.

On one of the first trips recorded in my diary, which I took in Ellis and Kaufman Counties, I listed as game killed: bear, deer, ducks, and turkeys. A few days later, while looking for some of my horses, I killed four prairie chickens, some ducks and geese, and four coons in one hollow log. But not always did we score a hit on game at which we shot. Some of the shots were fair and some were ridiculous misses. When we killed a deer running through the brush, or a moving turkey at about seventy-five yards we thought it fair shooting, everything considered. I also remember having killed flying turkeys on moonlight nights when out hunting varmints.

A hunting party I was with on a trip along Chambers Creek killed seven deer, a bear, and some smaller game. But deer and turkey were not difficult to kill although they soon learned to make themselves hard to find. There were pelt animals in plenty but we were not interested in trapping, although we poisoned wolves because they preyed on young stock. Game was so plentiful that we did not consider the question of sportsmanship, in the latter sense, in methods of killing, if we needed fresh meat for our families and our help. On the East Bosque, one day, I shot several ducks, one pot shot yielding several.

Another day I got five ducks at one shot and pot shot fifteen birds at a shot. Hunting turkey with a Mr. Davidson along the Palo Pinto, we bagged eight.

Once, when it seemed that we were consuming our pork too fast and no fresh meat had been encountered while doing the regular work outdoors, I secured seven deer in two days while on the prairie after stock. It was in a cold November. Deer, coons, and hogs frequently damaged our crops despite the fences. Of course the coons could climb through or over, the deer jump, but the hogs would find a weak spot in the fence and break in. When we went to the fields inspecting them for such intrusion, we took our dogs. One July day the wild hogs found in a field were not disposed to run from the dogs but bunched for a fight. The result was a wicked fight, some dead hogs, and some slashed dogs. It was an interesting contest for a few minutes, but the dogs were outnumbered and I did not want them seriously injured, so I took a hand with my pistol.

I had gone up the East Bosque one day to hunt horses. Passing alongside the creek, I saw and killed an otter, several coons, a couple of turkeys, and a deer. This was little sport, but I came to a flock of gobblers where there was some open ground and I enjoyed a chase on my pony after one of them. I ran him down and then shot him with my pistol. A few weeks later my small son Kossuth duplicated this act but chose to capture the gobbler instead of killing it. The others had scattered but I got two or three of them with my rifle.

Up in the Rockey community, between Iredell and Stephenville, several of us staged a turkey hunt one January, and killed twenty-seven. I brought four home. The weather was cold and in this same month hundreds of cattle on the range were frozen. So as bread had been scarce and now beef was apparently going to be, turkey would taste very well and was needed. Other game, including a couple of antelope I managed to get, supplemented the fare of much turkey during the weeks following. Fortunately, crops were very good the coming season.

The other outstanding sport we enjoyed, but which we also made yield some substance, was fishing. Our fishing was a real lark, although it was expected to yield something to take home with us or prepare on the grounds for the "fish fry." So our method of catching the fish was generally to use a sein. Seining was usually done in the summer and in the Bosques or the Brazos.

I went on one fishing spree in the North Bosque and caught over one hundred by seining with wagon sheets sewn together. We could not "round-up" in the water as with regular seins, but "drug out" on the banks. Most of the fish would thus escape us, but we caught plenty of good-sized ones. Fish frys were held at intervals during the summer, and we always had one on the fourth of July as a part of a holiday festival and celebration.

This hurried account of the activities of the settler does not do the subject justice in treatment nor in the enumeration of his duties. He was a busy man and his wife was more so, although no effort to discuss this last can be made here.

At home more, with certain types of domestic work, such as spinning, which might have been a blessing, at times, denied her because of a lack of materials such as raw cotton, and too much other work, with responsibility for the safety of the children in the absence of her man, and the worry over the absent and those present, there was some grounds for the old saying that early Texas was "hell on women and horses." Even where there was some help from a few negro women, the duties of the household were trying on the women's physical strength. But very few families in our section owned any negroes and during hard times these were frequently hired out. Keeping the home clean, food prepared, washing done, quilts made, rendering the lard when her husband killed hogs, and in the absence of the men, perhaps cutting wood and carrying water as well as looking after the stock about the house, was only a portion of the work of the women along the frontier of central Texas.

But behind this story of toil there was the background of much life in the open and some greater recompense. A realization was prevalent that the soil and the grazing, the fruits and the nuts, and the water and the climate, etc., would some day attract sufficient people to inaugurate a development which would yield returns surprising to the nation.

CHAPTER VIII

STOCK FARMING AND INDIAN ATTACKS

THROUGH my brother who lived at Waco, not many miles from the Bosque County line, I had become interested in Bosque County. Bosque was some distance from Corsicana, but only a few miles from the frontier line in its region, and was about to be organized as a county. Indians had not bothered it for quite an interval, although a scare was given the settlers of a portion of the county in 1854. In this raid several Norwegian settlers along Gary's Creek suffered much misfortune when their savage enemy decided to molest their household property and run off their horses and other live stock.

About the first of May, one of these Norwegians, Ole Canuteson, had to go to Dallas County with a prairie schooner, drawn by four yokes of oxen, to bring back new settlers who wanted to make their home in that community. His wife went to a neighbor's home until her husband could make the trip. They had no children. The first Sunday after Ole left, his father and another man went over on the Brazos to drive home five milch cows he had bought from Colonel Frazier, who lived where Kimball is now located. One Monday night, about eleven o'clock, old man Canuteson and the man with him, dashed up to the house where his son's wife was staying and began telling her, very excitedly, in their Norwegian language that his wife had been carried off by Indians, the bed ticks ripped open and feathers scattered all over the place, and $900 in silver, in a sack, was also gone. Their twelve-year-old son was gone, too.

They decided that the Wacoes and Comanches were the culprits, as they invariably did every devilish trick they could think of. None of the Norwegians had a gun, so they knew that if the Indians had decided to raid the entire settlement, they were at the Indians' mercy. So they took some blankets and quilts and went to a cedar grove about half a mile off. They spent the night there, expecting any minute to hear Mr. Red Man robbing the house. But when morning came and nothing had happened, they returned to the house, where the women cooked them a good breakfast.

After breakfast, they decided to go on a voyage of discovery, to find out what tricks the visitors were up to. They first went to Ole Canuteson's home, then to the man's house who was with old man Canuteson and found these two places undisturbed. But when they approached the elder Canuteson's home, they saw in the door what appeared to be Canuteson's wife. One of the men said, "There is your wife!" Then other figures appeared, and they saw that the persons in flowing robes were buck Indians in blankets.

When the Indians saw the settlers, they dashed into a near-by thicket. The white men also took to cover, and sent one of the men to notify several families living where Clifton is now located. The crowd then went to a Mr. McCurry's.

A number of men immediately started looking for the Indians. Some took their trail and went to the head of Gary's Creek, where they found old lady Canuteson and their son, who had taken refuge at Ole Pearson's. She said that when she saw the Indians coming, she grabbed the bag of silver and she and the boy ran down Neil's Creek until they struck the mouth of Gary's Creek, at Pearson's.

The other party followed the Indian trail some distance until they met a family in an ox wagon. They had been working on a cornfield of one of the men's. They said that the day before they had been away from the house to rob a bee tree and that when they returned they found they had been robbed of their supply of food and bedding, two guns, and several head of horses. They followed the trail to a noted crossing on the Paluxie, where beautiful and famous Glen Rose is now situated. They concluded not to follow the trail any farther and to return home. They thought the Indian raid was over, but such proved not to be the case.

About ten days later, when everyone thought the Indians had left the country, a man by the name of Chesser, who lived on the old Scrutchfield ranch, heard his dogs barking fiercely. He had staked his horse near the house, but when he went out with his gun to see about it, the horse was gone. As the rope was new and strong and had been untied from the stake, he knew that Indians had stolen him. He went into the house and took his wife and two children to a thicket.

After waiting awhile he decided to hitch a gentle yoke of oxen to a cart and go to where his mother and brother lived, eight miles across the brakes, to the North Bosque, which was the nearest settlement. He heard his oxbell and went toward the sound. When he reached the big prairie back of his farm he saw and heard hundreds of cattle in a stampede. He squatted in some tall weeds and directly saw six or seven Indians on foot and one on horseback come near him. He did not shoot, as he did not know how many were in the party and he was afraid that they would overwhelm him and then swoop down on his home and family. It was not a matter of personal fear, for Chesser was in the battle of Monterey in 1846, and his bravery made him an outstanding figure in that engagement. He heard them talking about their plans to kill several beeves.

So he slipped back to his house, and he and his family walked across the country to the Mabray place. After Chesser stated the situation there, they made haste to notify the other settlers in this community on the Bosque.

The next morning all the men met at Chesser's cabin. Nothing had been molested. But all the Bosqueites were on foot, as the Indians had stolen their horses several days before. So the party started toward the Middle Bosque. When they came to a certain ravine, or arroyo, about three miles from Chesser's cabin, they saw a cavayard [*caballado*] of horses with two Indians rounding them up. They began to run when they saw the white men and several of the settlers mounted horses and gave chase. They ran these Indians about twenty-five miles, when they finally decided that their wily red enemies were purposely leading them away from the arroyo. So they started back to where the rest of the party had stayed with the stock and were fighting the remaining Indians. The Indians then became their pursuers. When they neared the brink of this arroyo, which was about three miles long and a hundred and fifty to three hundred yards wide, they saw moccasin tracks leading down the banks. Several of the men knew the trail led to a cave, which was used as a cow house. Two of the men dismounted and disappeared over the side.

Directly, gunshots were heard, and the two men came tearing back over the side. They had killed a couple of Indians and reported that there were forty or more Indians in the arroyo. The Indians then began crawling out of the ravine, on the opposite side, about two hundred yards away. Every man took a shot at them.

By that time, it was sundown and men and horses were exhausted. They were thirsty and hungry, so they decided to go home to eat and rest and to go back the next morning.

Accordingly, the crowd met again at the Chesser place and went to the head of the ravine to hunt for the Indian trail. They went to the cave, which was astonishingly large, being fully thirty yards long and about forty feet wide and open at the south side. The roof was about ten feet high. There, they found several dead Indians. The other Indians had fled, leaving some bows and arrows, some dry and fresh beef and pork hanging on saplings. Some of the hog heads bore the marks of various men of the party. One rawhide lariat had "L. H." branded on it, which was made from the hide of one of Lowery Scrutchfield's cows.

An elm tree was peeled all around and some very good charcoal pictures were painted on it. One picture was of a mounted Indian with a lariat flourished over his head, like he was roping a horse. On the opposite side was pictured an Indian with a bow and arrow, with the cattle and hogs all around him. Old George Erath interpreted the pictures to mean that they were a notice to other raiding parties that this band which had left the arroyo had found plenty of horses, hogs, and cows in the neighborhood. He said that every stealing party of Comanches and Wacoes carried along their artist, who left a pictured story of their forays along the trail.

Several more dead Indians were found, and the settlers attempted to follow their bloody trail, but that was impossible, as the ground was so rocky. However, this vicinity suffered no more from Indian raids that year.

This raiding party of Indians was unusually large which was one reason they were readily detected and routed. They learned, as proved by later raids, to range in parties of from eight to fifteen. They skulked in ravines and along river beds, and took advantage of shelter in thickets, when they were few in number, and thus escaped conspicuous notice. The probable fate of these settlers is horrible to contemplate if just a few Indians had been in the raiding party; a mere handful, stalking their quarry with greater stealth, would have enabled them to have driven off the stock and then to have scalped these people, at their leisure.

Meanwhile, I had secured some land on the Brazos, near Waco, and was trying also to decide on a location in Bosque. When I desired to look over this land I would go to Waco, spend the night with my brother, Bryant, and then proceed to my place. Here, I drove a small herd of cattle and built a cow lot. In the spring of 1856, I had some new ground cleared and planted to corn. It came up the first of April, but when I visited it in mid-July it had had no rain. The Brazos was so nearly dry that seining parties were catching with ease a good many fish.

During 1855, some trips to my land in the forks of the Bosque, a large tributary of the Brazos, decided me on locating there. The land was in Bosque County, which had been organized in 1854. When, on December 16, my thirty-fourth birthday, I rode out to look at this land and the mountains nearby, there were few settlers in that section. On my way home I stopped overnight at Meridian, the county seat of Bosque County, and then rode to Waco where I spent the night with my brother, Bryant.

In August, 1856, rafters and laths had been cut for my house and the first days of September were devoted to its construction. An additional house was bought from a settler named Robertson, who agreed to move it in exchange for a horse and fifteen dollars. Then I sold my place on the Brazos to Ned Francks, rounded up my cattle there and drove them to the Bosque. Upon my return to Navarro, some of my cattle, chickens, etc., were gathered together and brought out in preparation for our departure toward the end of the year.

In my absence, one John Carr had driven out of my cavayard [caballado] a fine colt and suit was entered at Corsicana for its recovery. While the litigation was pending, I received word from our sheriff, Jessie Walton, to raise a company of men and meet him in Grimes County to prevent a probable attempt at rescue of a prisoner that he had gone after. The prisoner, Cooper, had been under sentence of death for a year for murder. We rode twenty-five miles that night and forty-five the next day before meeting Walton with his men. Cooper was jailed without an outbreak, and the posse celebrated by eating an enormous quantity of honey from one of my bee gums.

After rounding up my little cavayard [caballado] of one hundred and twenty horses, we packed up to start to Bosque. We got under way on the morning of November 25, 1856, after losing the greater part of it in bidding adieu to the neighbors. I had hired some of my neighbors to assist me in moving, and one of them, Robert Gregory, drove a four-mule team, John Gregory an ox team, and my wife, small son, William, and little daughter, Mary, rode in Dr. Dixon's carriage. Neighbor Newbolds, assisted by Mr. Hilliard, my son Kossuth, and Kit, one of my boys, drove the horses. We traveled by White Rock Creek, Hillsboro, and Meridian, and reached our place on East Bosque on December first. A cold norther was blowing but we found that the boys, who had been brought out with the things in September, had finished the cabin. Next month we brought out our hogs, one hundred head, and some corn, but waited until spring to bring out the remainder of the cattle, eighty-five head, eleven of which we lost in fording the Brazos.

The range was fresh and my stock did well. It was two years before the Indians gave me any trouble, although there were friendly Indians around me. Afterward they were my nearest neighbors and seemed to be bitter enemies to those that depredated on the settlements. They would go with us after our enemies, who were the Comanches. There were five tribes of the Comanches. Two of them claimed to be friends and were located on the Clear Fork of the Brazos River by the government.

In March, 1857, the Comanches came down in a large band which divided into squads of about a dozen on approaching the settlements. They raided in Brown, Comanche, and Erath Counties, killing in Erath, which adjoined Bosque on the west. The fall and winter saw them entering Bosque County in greater force, killing, scalping, kidnaping and plundering. In this, their first raid in our county, for about three years, they killed a man named Bean and his negro man, and Peter C. Johnson, carrying off his eight-year-old son, little Peter. Fifty miles away, they robbed the boy of his clothes and turned him loose to face the cold and the wild animals. They also raided my horses and drove off over seventy, together with some thirty of those of my neighbors. These horses were worth, on an average, fifty dollars each and two stallions of mine were worth more. Several squads of men from the neighboring counties of Erath, Hamilton, and Eastland followed the invaders but failed to overtake them.

It was on January 15, 1858, that I learned of the raid. After looking to my arms and securing extra cartridges for my pistol, I rode over my horse range and on to see some of my neighbors. I found them greatly alarmed. My horses ranging on Duffau Creek were not disturbed and a few days later Kossuth assisted me in driving fifty head from on the Bosque to the Brazos to hide them from the Indians. Neighbor Zach Medford and myself scouted the community on the lookout against any possible return of the Indians. We found no signs of their presence and I returned home to find my baby, Cora, dead.

Johnson's little son, Peter, later a citizen of Fleming, Comanche County, was released by the Indians after three days and nights as a captive. He told the story of his father's death and his captivity which, in parts, became familiar to his contemporaries and their descendants.

The father and son were returning from the mill ten miles below Meridian on the Bosque River to their home in what came to be Brown County. They had their corn meal and had purchased supplies at Meridian. They were traveling slowly in a wagon drawn by a yoke of oxen. As they passed a small round mountain peak, three miles southwest of Iredell and some eighteen miles west of Meridian, they were suddenly attacked by Indians. The savages had laid in ambush on the peak, at the base of which ran the virgin public road, and swarmed down on their victims. A desperate effort to make their escape was made by the father, who plied his long black-snake whip to the sluggish oxen. The oxen started on a lumbering gallop but a bullet from the rifle of one of the redskins toppled one in its tracks. The wagon crashed to a stop and the Indians killed and scalped the father.

In the meantime, little Peter had remained in the wagon crouching and apparently paralyzed with fear. But when he saw his father's murderer tear a bloody scalp from his victim and attach it to his girdle, he quickly came to himself. He seized the whip from the bottom of the wagon where it had fallen from his father's hands, and lashed out with a blow, into which he had put all his desperate childish strength, upon the back of the nearest warrior. For a moment it seemed that the boy would be slain, but the chief signaled a halt. While the Indians conferred, the boy stood gazing with horror at the body of his father on the ground.

Then the chief, who had scalped the father, urged his horse alongside the wagon, seized the boy and placed him in front on his horse. The other ox was killed and the wagon plundered. Holding the captive on his horse, the chief led the departure in a northwesterly direction.

Perhaps the Indians spared Peter because they admired his courage. Perhaps they intended to hold him for ransom. Or it may have been that they had some thought of adopting such a brave little fellow into their tribe. If this last was their intention, when they carried the boy away, they must have been disgusted at what followed. The captive would not eat raw meat as the Indian children did, he displayed no interest in his surroundings, and refused to talk. He became weak and pale. So at the end of three days and nights the redskins stripped him and turned him loose. An old squaw gave him a piece of ragged, dirty blanket as his only protection from the elements.

For several days, Peter wandered in the woods, cold and hungry, and with no sense of direction. Without food and yet continually walking, he became so weak that he could hardly stand. But one day he heard a cowbell and shuffled hopefully toward it. He came upon a small herd of milch cows, and either reason or a desire to be with something domesticated caused him to stay with them.

On the day that Peter wandered to the vicinity of the cows, two men in Erath County, named McKinney and Rough, were out rounding up some cattle and found the boy moving about with their stock. The men had heard of the tragic death of the elder Johnson and concluded that the waif they had found was little Peter Johnson. They carried the boy to Stephenville, about fifteen miles distant, where he was soon restored to health. His mother was notified and came for him.

On the same day of the Johnson's Peak tragedy, the boy saw the Indians driving in and herding together stolen horses. Years afterward (in 1889), Johnson offered the opinion that he was released by the redskins for the additional reason that some of the reservation Indians were along and, sharing in the murders and raids with some of their wild brothers, did not want to increase risk of exposure of their implication.

The news came in February that the friendly Wacoes had stolen some horses from the Northern Comanches and were bringing them in to the Lower Agency. So I concluded to go and see if any of them were mine which had been stolen the last of December. Messrs. Thornton and Hightower, two friends of mine, decided to accompany me. After riding over some very rough country, fording the Brazos five times, and passing through the Caddo village, we arrived at the Agency.

We found only one of my horses among the forty-five or fifty that the Wacoes had brought in. The Wacoes said that they had started with about eighty-five head and four Comanche captives, but they killed some of the horses which gave out on the way. Two of the Indian prisoners had escaped on the march. In fact, they actually had only one Comanche and a Mexican. These they executed in a few days in a rather brutal manner and proceeded to stage a scalp dance, which was continued so long that the onlookers grew tired of watching it.

After my return home, I wrote early in March to the Department of the Interior concerning my loss of horses. In the letter I requested that Indian Agents north of my section be informed of the loss of the stock and be on the alert for animals bearing my brand—the triangle-bar on the shoulder. Charles E. Mix, Commissioner in the Office of Indian affairs, replied that he was distributing copies of my letter.

After a few days, letters were received from M. Leeper, Special Indian Agent, and R. S. Neighbors, Agent, to the effect that some eight of my horses were on the Comanche Agency. The reservation Indians claimed that the horses had been taken from the Northern Comanches on the Big Wichita River. Perhaps the agents thought their wards innocent of all complicity in the Indian atrocities that were being renewed; perhaps they believed the troops of the general government sufficient protection against Indian raids.

The federal government had garrisoned the forts along the frontier with regular soldiers. But neither the dragoons on their big and awkward chargers nor the infantry understood how to fight the Comanches. This fact the Indians soon learned and they became so active that the people began to call for someone who could cope with them. The regulars generally did not know the country and the redskins would lead them over "hill and dale" until the troopers and their mounts were exhausted.

For three years the Indians annoyed the frontier settlers, paying them a bloody visit on every full moon, killing a number of people every raid they made and driving off hundreds of horses. And some of them lost their scalps on every raid they made on Texas. In a later foray they killed of my acquaintances and neighbors, the two young Munroes that were improving their land on Spring Creek, and a part of the families of Woods and Lemley. They took the wives of Lemley and Woods about a mile from their houses and murdered, scalped, and mutilated them. They also took captive two young ladies

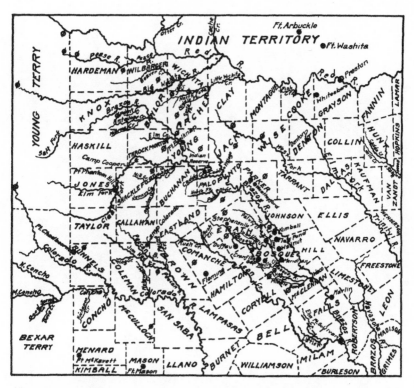

Map showing Counties in Barry's Section and indicating a portion of
the scenes of conflict between whites and reds in the '50s and '60s.
Explanation: "O" denotes scenes of conflict.

of the families. After two days travel they were going to murder the captives, when the girls appealed to an old warrior of the party who made some statement to his comrades which provoked a discussion. The young women were then stripped of all clothing and turned loose far from any house.

They killed in these raids of 1857, a school mistress, a brave and noble woman, who sacrificed her own life that her pupils might save theirs. She ordered them to flee to a dense thicket near-by, while she fastened and held the door in pretense that all were inside. On the following day, they killed one preacher and seriously wounded another. After he recovered, the preacher told me that the Indian who wounded him was riding my horse, named Blue Dog, a horse my oldest son Kossuth claimed, which was the only horse the Indians had that could outrun his mount. These same Indians came by my place and took several using horses. The horse Blue Dog and another, a nervy mare, they rode so completely down that we picked them up on the trail. The trail divided; one of them led to the reservation.

Other victims of these invasions into my section were Mr. Knight on Neil's Creek, Mr. Bryant on the Paluxie, and Mr. James Tankersly, one of the first men with whom I formed acquaintance when I first came to Texas. I bought my first horse from Tankersly's father, William Tankersly, who was in all the fighting under Jackson below New Orleans. Of course, the settlers would follow the Indians every time they came in but were seldom able to overtake them, as they rode the best horses that they had stolen from the white people.

We soon learned the route they went out from, in the section of the country they had raided. Whenever we could hear of their being in the settlement, we would try to beat them in getting to certain points where they would pass out at night and other points where they would pass out in the daytime.

One of my neighbors and friends, Zachariah Medford, had two about half-grown boys who went with every scout. I sent an expressman on one occasion to let him know the Indians had gone into the corners of McClellan and Bell Counties, so that he could strike them as they came out at the point of Bean's Mountain, on the Leon River. The expressman got together several men on his trip to Medford's. But he found Medford very busy at work, who said, "Boys, I am too busy, and I can't go. I've been and been on every trip and have never seen any Indians. I have lost so much time I'll never get my place improved."

"Well," said one of the men, "let Hill and John go. We'll get a fight this time and kill some of the yellow rascals."

Hill and John, Zach's boys, commenced begging their dad to let them go, saying, "Dad, we may have some luck and kill some Indians this time."

"If nothing else will do you, go! I'll eat all the Indians that are killed," their father answered.

One of the crowd said, "Uncle Zach, are you in earnest about eating all the Indians we kill?"

"Yes, and I'll chew the bones, also," he replied.

We had good luck and killed three Indians and recovered all the horses they had stolen, and only one man, Ross Cranfield, was slightly wounded. After the fight was over and the boys had all come back together, after chasing the Indians who had fled in all directions, they began talking over the promise Uncle Zach Medford had made. They agreed not to take all the dead Indians for him to eat. It was six miles to his house, so they took only a hind quarter of the fattest one. Uncle Zach went back on his promise, swearing that he would not let even his dogs eat a quarter of an Indian. He made his two boys take it off and bury it.

At another time, a crowd headed by George Layman and William Hitson waylaid a band of Indians, killed several and captured nearly a hundred head of horses which the Indians had stolen in the lower settlements. Some of these horses were mine.

Perhaps it may seem strange that the redskins could take such heavy toll of the stock of the settlers. But these Indians had had the experience of generations in the practice of carrying out raiding expeditions. They were well mounted and knew the country between the settlements and their camping grounds better than most of the whites knew it. They darted in, rounded up the stock to be stolen, and drove them away before the settlers were aware that the foe was in their midst. Before the citizens could organize to follow them they would be too far away to be overtaken. In later years, even the trained and especially mounted soldiers could not match the skill of the invaders at this game. Some of the more resolute and best mounted settlers could offer protection, if they were organized and already in a camp or group in the vicinity where the Indians were attacking.

In this connection, I received about this time letters that had some bearing on this subject of Indian raids and gave some information concerning horses I had lost in December. These letters read:

Buchanan County, August 2, 1858.

Dear Sir:

I wrote you some time ago by request of Mr. Harry Anderson, that he had one of your horses, which was given him by Mr. Leeper, the Indian Agent, to pay him for one of his the Indians had stolen from him and killed.

But as I have heard nothing from you, I suppose you may not have received my letter. I am collecting all the evidence I can against the Indians and agents, and want to know if you have any objection to my using a statement made by Mr. Leeper that "he would pay himself for all his trouble out of the stolen horses he had in his possession." I want everything that can be brought forward and this is important testimony. There has been, as you may know, Commissioners appointed to investigate the fuss between the citizens and agents. And we must not be careless or they will out prove us; remember they have the *money* and know how to use it. We have only justice and right on our side. But I am determined to do all in my power, and hope you can either appear before the Commissioners in person and testify to this matter, or send me a written statement. It is important testimony and I would like to have it. And if you can get the certificate of the man who told you that one of the hands at Ross' Agency was turned off for telling a man that he had seen his horse among the Indians I would like to have it. And any other thing that you think would be of use. It is important that the citizens should *hang together and unite.* I want Nelson in the place of Neighbors and will do all in my power to aid him. Hoping to hear from you soon, I remain,

Yours truly,

JOHN R. BAYLOR.

Camp Cooper, Texas, October 8, 1858.

Sir:

I beg leave to advise you that the Secretary of the Interior has appointed me special agent to inquire into the conduct of supervising Indian Agent Neighbors, and generally to investigate and report upon the difficulties that seem to exist betwen certain citizens of Texas and army officers on the one part and the friendly Indians and the government agents on the other part.

Being informed by Mr. Neighbors that your testimony would be of importance to the investigations, I would respectfully invite you to attend, at this place, at any time that may suit your convenience during the period that will intervene between the second Monday of this month and the second Monday of November following, for the purpose of giving in such evidence as you may be prepared to offer.

As this request is written at the instance and in behalf of the defendant, Mr. Neighbors, he assures me he will advise you of the precise time at which your presence here would be desirable.

I am, sir, very respectfully,

Your most obt. svt.,

THOS. G. HAWKINS.

J. B. Barry, Esquire,
Flag Ponds,
Bosque County, Texas.

Flag Ponds, Texas,
Bosque County, November 2, 1858.

Thomas G. Hawkins, Esqr.

Sir:

I have the honor to report this day the reception of your summons of the 8th of October, and am sorry that the time is too limited for me to make my appearance by the 8th inst., as it is full five days' ride. Being taken on surprise, it would require the other day to prepare for the trip, which leaves no time, &c. As for Mr. Neighbors assuring you that he would give me due and timely notice, I assure you, sir, that I have never heard a word from him nor do I expect to, although my testimony might not be worth much for or against him. Permit me to say in behalf of Major Neighbors, that he treated me very cleverly and gentlemanly in the informing me of some of my horses that were stolen. Notwithstanding, I am satisfied, from many circumstances, that the Indians on the upper reserve were aware of the stealing of my horses and that some of them were directly involved, although I was not thus convinced at the time that I made affidavit in presenting a claim to the Government for damage done. Therefore, those upper reserve Indians were not included in my affidavit, &c.

Yours with respect,
J. B. BARRY.

P. S. Sir, it has been feared, and even predicted, that the citizens would not have a fair and timely hearing on the subject now under investigation (I write this that you may manage the case so as to give general satisfaction to all concerned &c.). I would further take the liberty of saying (if it would meet your approbation) that it would save me a tedious ride and some two weeks' valuable time to answer interrogatories here at home.

You will please ponder the liberty I have taken,

Yours &c.,
J. B. BARRY.

On another occasion, a crowd of settlers headed off a raiding band of Indians in Hood County and killed five out of six. This brief account is of the raids made in my section of the country. Similar raids were made all along the frontier, from the Rio Grande to the Red River.

CHAPTER IX

"THE RESERVATION WAR"

IN THE late spring of '58, I started on a tramp with John Walker to the Indian reservations on the Brazos. When we came to Stephenville, in Erath County, we found the citizens organizing a ranging company as some protection against the forays of the Indians. We passed on and spent the night with Robert Martin. On the following day we made our way over mountain and prairie to the mouth of Caddo Creek where we stayed all night with a settler named Darnell. Here, several families were collected as protection against the Indians who raided and murdered two families in the community.

We rode through the Caddo village, where we stopped out of the rain, and took dinner with the Caddo chief. The rain continued and we rode on to the Agency, where we spent the night with Dike, the blacksmith. Next morning we visited the beef pen, as it was beef day for the Indians, and saw the slaughter of the government beeves. Their killing and butchering of the beeves was hurriedly and interestingly done. The beef was their weekly ration, but several hundred Indians were present and the meat was devoured in less than no time.

Our journey was resumed and we forded the Brazos below the fork, traveled up the Clear Fork to the home of my old friend Browning, where we visited all day. When our trip was resumed Browning joined us. We arrived at the Rangers' camp, at the mouth of Hubbard's Creek, where we ate dinner. Only about a dozen men were in camp as the others and some hundred friendly Indians were out hunting the Noconas or Comanches. We went on toward the Upper Reservation but became a little wary at Indian signs and camped at night in the woods east of the Clear Fork, keeping a sharp lookout for Indians.

We traveled through the woods to the upper Reserve where I found seven of my horses that were stolen in December. Walker found three of his. We visited with the agent, Colonel Leeper, whom we paid twenty-five dollars for taking care of our horses. We were told that the Indians at the Reserve had picked them up on the trail to which they had been driven when stolen.

On our way back we visited with Captain Baylor, of the Rangers, and camped at the head of Caddo Creek. In the Palo Pinto country we stopped to rest the horses. Here we wrote out a petition for the removal of the local Indian agent. Coming to Stephenville, we wrote out a similar petition for the citizens of Erath County to sign. Next day we drove home and found all well and right-side-up, with several of my neighbors cutting wheat and mine nearly sufficiently ripe to begin harvesting.

After several days devoted to cutting my wheat, branding my colts and calves, riding young horses, chasing the mustangs away from some of my horses that had gotten with them, and the many other duties of a frontier farmer-stockman, we celebrated the fourth of July with a community fish-fry. It was suggested by someone that the people of our section give a dinner to the above mentioned Rangers. So in the middle of the month we made preparations for a barbecue at the home of one of the neighbors, Captain Nelson. The Rangers had returned from an expedition after the Indians and had taken seventy-six scalps and recaptured three hundred horses with the loss of only one man. Most of the Rangers attended the feast in their honor and things went off splendidly.

The pleasures of the past several days were marred by the illness of our youngest, little Mary. She suffered with a swollen throat and congested lungs. We called in Doctor Robertson and some of the neighbors came to try to assist in our trouble. Though she was up and playing one day she was dead the next.

She died one morning at daylight. When the little creature was suffering from want of breath, she would look at me, as though I ought to help her to breathe, and say she was going. She was dying. She was aged three. We got Mr. Woods to make her a coffin. With all our neighbors in attendance, we buried little Mary beside her sister Cora, who died six months before.

. On September first, I started to the Indian Agent's on the upper Brazos. When I arrived, on the fifth day after my departure, I found much excitement in regard to Indians. The Kiowas, a few days before, had killed four men and driven off over a hundred head of horses and many cattle. The evening of my arrival they came in and stole some horses. Pursuit was made under the leadership of Lieutenant Fifer with thirty men accompanied by some twenty friendly Indians. A Mr. Goodlet and myself volunteered our services to the officer directing the pursuit and the later attack, but the invaders refused to pause and offer battle.

After spending the night with Mr. Shirley, the Indian trader at the agency, who presented me with a handsome Indian purse, I decided to return home by way of the lower agency. At Fort Belknap people were quite excited over the killing of a part of a family and abduction of the women and children. The ride home was without incident, although I heard much Indian news. But the constant threat of possible attacks seemed to demand scouting about the near-by rivers and mountains every few days. This, of course, proved irksome and several of us met at Doctor Toliver's to make arrangements for a ranging company. I then spent four days riding to see the citizens of the surrounding country to get them to help raise and equip a company. Meanwhile, our Governor had refused us aid.

We held a meeting at Meridian, passed some resolutions, and agreed to subject ourselves to a special tax to defray the expenses of the company provided we could not secure better assistance or get the defense without such a plan.

In the meantime, we continued to scout the Spring Creek, Duffau, and Paluxie country against surprise raids. Naturally, with the ever present expectation of the coming of the foe, there were some false alarms and "scares," some of which one could laugh at after the apparent danger was exploded. Sometimes mustangs were mistaken for Indians; at others, men thought each other the enemy. Such an occurrence as the latter was my experience one day when I went with my eight-year-old son, Kos, to "cedar rafter" mountain. We lost one of our hunting dogs and had just found him when seven horsemen were seen charging us. I hid Kos in the cedar brake and prepared to give them the best fight I could. When the men drew nearer, I was very glad to see that they were white men. They, likewise, thought we were Indians.

Only a few weeks had elapsed when another Indian raid was made in the Palo Pinto country. I started to the scene of action immediately. Upon arrival at Stephenville after night, I found a high state of excitement prevalent. The people were heavily armed. Some dozen of us started to Golconda, the scene of a skirmish fought between the invaders and the settlers. We met John Stephens who had been to bury his son who had been killed in the fight. One or two other men had been wounded. The night was spent on Barton's Creek, near the scene of the fight, and we returned to Stephenville the next day.

Two days later I returned with my little company to the battleground. The fight had been between about twenty citizens and some Caddo, Anadahko, and Choctaw Indians that were hunting. Believing that the hunting party had participated in the many recent acts of hostility on our frontier, the settlers had entered the conflict with the idea of discouraging Indians from coming into the country. Seven Indians were killed and four wounded. Both sides left their dead on the ground and returned home.

On the following morning, January 3, 1859, I started to

Stephenville to get reinforcements. I met a large group of citizens en route to the Reserve with the intention of demanding a change of Indian policy. They believed that the government plans of civilizing the Indians on these reservations had failed to secure good results. The Indians seemed to be given a better chance to do their horse-stealing and murdering, mixed, as they were, with the wild Indians, and, sometimes, with white renegades. This idea was in the minds of the settlers who had made the surprise attack at Barton's Creek.

The reinforcements were secured and we started on our return. Captain Erath accompanied us. Traveling on into Palo Pinto County, we found about one hundred men imbued with the idea of attacking the lower reservation of Indians on the Brazos. Next day, January 6, the men requested me to go on an express and spy to the agency. I took one man, David Jones of Meridian, with me. After a hard day's ride, facing a norther, we camped in a cedar brake near the Caddo village on the Brazos. On the following morning we arrived at the agency. The weather was sufficiently cold that the Brazos was frozen over completely.

Now that we had done what we could in ascertaining the attitude of the agents and soldiers and obtained general knowledge of the situation, we started back. We had ridden twelve miles on our way when we met sixteen men from the company who were going up to the reservation with instructions to either make war or peace, the condition being that the Indians were never to come among us on any pretentions whatever, under the threat of a war of extermination. Jones and myself rode on to the camp.

Next day, which was Sunday, we waited patiently in camp to hear from our commissioners. On the twelfth of January the Commissioners returned and reported that we would have no fight. The spokesmen of the commission were Norris, Captain Erath, and Dixon Walker. Our camp broke up and we

started to our homes. At Stephenville there were still a goodly
number of people assembled to learn the status of things.

An outbreak of hostilities from this dangerous condition
had been averted. But it was repeated Indian raids which
brought on what was known as "the reservation war." In fact,
about two weeks before the reservation war a noble young man
named Holden was killed and scalped about halfway between
the two Indian reservations. His slayers were trailed into the
Comanche reservation. It was either Peter Garland or Captain
Hamner who was in charge of a group of men doing the trailing, when they came to a camp of Indians. The pursuers were
all mad and asked no questions but commenced firing, killing
four warriors, two squaws, and one child. These Indians were
friendly Caddoes. This hastened the war with the reservation
Indians. This war, which was being waged by what the agents
chose to call a mob of frontier citizens, will perhaps never find
its way into Texas history. Yet it was a war of no little consequence to the people of Texas.

It should be kept in mind that there were two reservations,
the Comanche reservation on the Clear Fork of the Brazos and
what was known as the Caddo reservation on the main Brazos.
But there were other tribes on the Caddo reservation which included Anadahkoes, Keechies, Tonkawas, Wacoes, Tahwaccaroes, Delawares, and Shawnees. These latter tribes on the
Caddo reservation were a great protection to the frontier settlers against the "wild" tribes of Indians. But the Comanche
reservation was no protection. They had too many wild kins-
folk in the three tribes of Comanches that had made no treaty
with the government. When the settlers would follow the raiding parties beyond all settlements and return by the Comanche
reservation, they invariably found theirs or some of their neighbors' horses. At one time, I found thirty-two of my own and
my neighbors'. After every raid that was made in this section,
a number of horses would be later found on this reservation.

Even the conservative historians of the State have said that there were some Indians who could not resist the opportunity to plunder and steal, an old habit. Occasionally, these joined the "wild" Indians, and perhaps, certain white criminals, in forays against the settlers. I asked Colonel Leeper, the Indian agent, permission to talk to the chief, Long Tree. Then I questioned him as to how and why our horses were found on his reservation. Jim Shaw, a Delaware Indian, acted as my interpreter. The chief told me his wild brothers would come to see his people and that they would have a war dance and persuade his young men to depredate against their white brothers; and the horses that I had found there were those of his stepson, which he received when they apportioned after the raid. When I reported these facts, they coincided with the statement of Fred Gentry and others.

The citizens asked the government, through their congressman, to move all the Indians out of Texas so that we might know that when we saw an Indian he was our enemy. As it was, they would pass themselves for friends and often take advantage of men under pretext of friendship. It sometimes happened that they would take a woman and kill her and her children after she had fed them, thinking them friendly Indians. We went to the trouble and expense of getting up a petition to Congress to have the friendly Indians moved across the Red River, and we paid Colonel Nelson to take it to Congress with sworn evidence of the situation as above stated.

When Colonel Nelson returned, he told those who had sent him with the petition that we would have to fight it out the best we could, as Congress thought more of an Indian, a foreigner, and a free negro than it did of American citizens. They had told our Texas Congressman on the floor of the Representative Hall that they would never vote one dollar for appropriations to move the reservation Indians across Red River or to furnish any more protection to Texas until Texans freed her negroes; that the Indian and the negro were more preferable as citizens than the slaveholder. Such insults made me a secessionist.

We held meetings all along our frontier and determined that we would move the reservation Indians across the Red River ourselves, whether the government (Congress) wanted us to or not. It was agreed to drive only the Comanche Indians out of Texas, as we knew the Caddoes, Tonkawas, and other small tribes were our friends.

The threatened reservation war of January, 1859 had been averted, but in May there came an alarming report about the reservation Indians. It was to the effect that many citizens were collecting to break up the reservations, some one hundred fifty miles up the Brazos from me. I made plans to start to that place. Several of a Minute Company, which had been organized a few weeks before in Meridian, with Hanna as captain and myself as lieutenant, had gone. I got others to agree to be ready to go with me. The harvest season was on and leaving meant sacrificing it and neglecting other affairs.

We started and rode beyond Stephenville where we stopped with Chandler Roberts. Next day we fell in with some men from Coryell County who were also on their way to the same destination. Another day's ride brought us to the camp of some four hundred men. Some of them had had a skirmish with the Indians on the Reserve in which three citizens and seven or eight Indians were killed.

Finally we decided to advance to the Comanche reservation and they fled to the Caddo reservation, forty miles distant. We pursued them. When we arrived, we sent a message, or rather started it, to the captain commanding the United States troops; Captain Palmer, I believe, his name was. They were shot at and one of them was wounded. This act opened the fight, which was bloody for a while. We lost several good citizens, and we soon saw that two hundred and fifty men could not hold out against a thousand or twelve hundred Indians, backed by United States troops. Colonel Baylor, who was

elected to command, ordered his command to fall back from
the reservation lands in order to avoid fighting United States
troops.

Baylor fell back into Palo Pinto valley, where he received
recruits every day until his little enthusiastic band of citizens
had grown to an army that felt itself invincible against the combined forces on the reservation, the United States troops included. We knew that if we should fail in the next fight that
there were at least ten thousand as brave men as ever looked
through the sights of a gun barrel, anxious and waiting to be
notified that their services were needed. Some scattering recruits who had had their relatives and friends murdered by Indians, came two hundred miles to join us.

After recruiting had doubled our forces, it was thought
best to reorganize. We reëlected J. R. Baylor, Colonel, Alli-
son Nelson, Lieutenant Colonel, and Hood, Major. We knew
that if we went on the reservation we would have to fight the
United States troops, also. We kept a reconnoitering force
around the reservation, cutting off their supplies and not even
allowing the Indians to get out and kill buffaloes. At this time
it was thought advisable to demand the surrender, or rather
that the agents, Colonel Leeper, agent for the Comanches,
and Captain Ross, father of ex-governor Sul Ross, who was
agent for all the other tribes and the commanding officer of
the United States troops, move all the Indians across Red River
at once.

Baylor and Nelson put the hazardous duty on me to go
into the reservation and make this demand. I was acquainted
with both agents and many of the Indians. I call this a hazardous trip, for the agents and the Indians were angry to the
point of desperation as were also our little army of frontier
citizens, or "mob," as the agents called us. I took one man
with me.

We bore no flag of introduction but our rifles and six-shoot-
ers. I carried no written communication to anyone, I was only

instructed to demand of those who were in authority that all the Indians be moved across the Red River.

The agents and their employees were mad and sullen and would not talk with me, although one did inform me that the Indians were frenzied and that I was in danger. They did permit my companion and myself to sleep on our blankets spread on the floor of the council house, which was a log cabin. When the agents refused to talk business, I turned all my conversation to Captain Palmer (I believe that was his name). I told him we were now strong enough to cut off all supplies, which he knew to be a fact, as our scouts had already captured their meat, bread, beef, salt, etc., and that every man in Palo Pinto valley had friends and acquaintances who were swelling our ranks every day. As soon as the cold spell was over, our friends from the Rio Grande to Red River would make haste to join us. I also told him that Governor Houston could not check the excitement and determination of the people of Texas to move these Indians across her border. His reply was, "I am here under orders to protect these Indians as well as the frontier settlers. I can't afford to disobey orders. There is nothing I would hate more than to get into a deadly conflict with American citizens, but you tell your officials and the people that if they come on this reservation for the purpose of molesting these Indians that I am ordered to protect, I will have to fight them."

Everything looked dark and gloomy. Every person—agents, soldiers, and Indians—was all mad, and it seemed that blood had to be spilled. When I was ready to leave, the captain commanding met me out a distance from the agent's office and told me to tell Colonels Nelson and Baylor to hold their people off and keep them quiet for three days, and he would take the responsibility of seeing that the Indians were moved out of Texas, if it cost him a trial by court-martial and his position in the army, which he'd rather lose than shed the blood of American citizens. He said, "It may cost me my position in the army, but I am not going to shed the blood of American citizens while I am here to protect them. I've no means of counseling or communicating with my superiors, but I'll risk the consequences rather than shed the blood of American citizens. The agents and all who're employed by them, as well as the Indians, are mad at me for the conclusion I've determined on."

When I returned to the headquarters of the citizen soldiers and related (no one wrote a word) what the captain commanding had said, there was a mixed feeling in camps. The majority seemed to be vexed because they were swindled out of a fight, while others were well pleased that every Indian would soon be moved out of Texas.

After a day's rest in camp, I started with eleven men on a scout up the Clear Fork of the Brazos toward the upper agency and to look after the safety of several families living there. All night we rode through the woods and mountains and got to the settlements just at daybreak. Two days were used in getting the families together and preparing them for a march toward the more peopled settlements. Several families and nine wagons were escorted to the Brazos.

Upon our return to camp, we found the citizen soldiers dispersed. They had gone home rather than have a conflict with the federal troops who were at the agency protecting the Indians while they depredated at the expense of the frontier settlers. The federal government was no doubt blind to the fraudulent conduct of some of its agents.

Three days were spent in getting home; forty miles was ridden on a tired pony the last day. My crops and stock were in poor condition due to neglect. Some of my wheat crop was lost, of course. But after a few days occupied with rounding up horses and branding calves, I was called to Meridian. A commission of five men from Governor Runnels wanted an interview to inquire into the difficulty of the frontier citizens and reserve Indians on the Brazos.

The Indians were assembled by the general government several weeks later, and escorted across the Red River to the vicinity of Fort Cobb in Indian Territory. Then they became bitter enemies to Texans, but when we saw an Indian we knew how to treat him. They depredated on our frontier so heavily that Governor Houston commissioned several of us to raise companies and patrol at intervals between the posts where the United States troops were stationed. We patrolled from the Rio Grande to the Red River and protected our frontier better than the United States soldiers had, with all the friendly Indians to help them.

CHAPTER X

TRAILING HORSE THIEVES

THE INDIANS had been moved across Red River into the Territory, but their invasions increased in frequency and they were even more troublesome. In February, 1860, I had gone to Mr. McCarty's on the Duffau and stayed overnight. On going on to see Mr. Duncan, who lived on the Bosque, I heard that the country was infested with Indians. They had killed two women, Mrs. Woods and Mrs. Lemley, and had taken the two Misses Lemley captive. Many horses were driven off in the same attack.

I at once set out for Camp Cooper to get out the regular soldiers. As I passed the homes of the settlers, inquiry generally brought the information that the heads of families were out after the Indians. Two night rides and a portion of a day found me at Camp Cooper. Out with the soldiers looking for Indian signs, we found where they had crossed the stage route. We marched on to Fort Phantom Hill, on the clear fork of the Brazos, where we learned that there was a general Indian disturbance on the whole frontier.

As we rode back we found a fresh Indian trail some six miles from Phantom Hill. Fourteen men from Leon County were trailing these Indians. We joined forces and followed the trail until late in the day when we quit it to kill some buffaloes. The Leon group went on next morning and we headed for Camp Cooper. Several buffaloes were killed, and the choice parts were taken for our meat as we had no other. That night carelessness gave the Indians a chance to steal some of our horses, which were recovered only by pushing the stealers in a hard race. An all night's ride brought us near Camp Cooper.

After an interview at the camp concerning Indian depredations, I rode down to my old friend Browning's on Clear Fork. All the news he had was Indian news. Apparently, horses were being stolen in all the section. At Lemon's, on Iron Creek, after leaving Browning, I was told that he had just had a fight with the Indians. Some Indians had been killed and over fifty horses recovered. My next call was at Captain Peter Garland's, who stated that all the horses grazing on Rush Creek and some on Barton's Creek had been stolen. I spent the night with Chandler Roberts, near Stephenville, and then rode home on February 21, 1860.

During my absence the Indians had taken a good many of my horses and the saddle horses of my wife and son, Kos. Eight people in the community had been killed; two girls taken prisoners who, after being treated very brutally, were turned loose. I hurried to Meridian where I found twenty men assembled waiting for me to lead them in search of Indians. But the trails were cold and as a company of local rangers organized under Lieutenant Walker were to range above the county, we did not make a hunt. Conditions were so intolerable now that practically every man physically able was equipping himself for vigorous pursuit of future raiders. The country seemed to be dotted with bands making forays for robbery and murder.

I decided to go with Walker's men to Duffau but we encountered nothing on the way. After my return, I heard rumors of a band of the horse-stealers and watched with five men on the mountains at Bean's gap. A twenty-four hour wait was rewarded by the appearance of a band of Indians driving some horses. We charged them when they were abreast of us and secured twenty-nine horses. The thieves escaped by fleeing on our appearance. We had remained under cover in hopes of a chance at them, but the scarcity of timber prevented us from getting close enough for fatal shots. Mounted as they were on the pick of white men's horses and given a start, pursuit of them would have yielded nothing.

The horses were herded and our watch resumed. A company of men from Leon County came by and reported killing and plundering in their region. No Indians had appeared, and I decided to leave the boys and drive the horses home by way of Cranfill's gap. The drive was made without incident and I arrived home to learn that more of my horses were missing. Meanwhile, the boys at Bean's gap had another chance in which they secured another drove of horses and three Indian scalps. None of them were injured in the fight.

News came of the killing of six families on Hog Creek, and I rode to Meridian to attend a public meeting called on account of such occurrences. Resolutions were passed in regard to the frontier and the increasing depredations. It was the general opinion that some white men around the agencies were encouraging these more numerous attacks. Other mass meetings were held, which at least had the effect of causing the citizens to become more vigilant.

Scouting parties during April, May, and June of 'sixty seemed to clear the local atmosphere, at least. A party I was leading in April killed one Indian and another secured three scalps. Vigilance was not relaxed and horses were now guarded some at night, but more time was given to crops and stock, although drouth and Indian troubles had blighted prospects for the year's crop. I took an occasional distant ride for Indian signs, going toward the west as far as Comanche. This precaution seemed warranted since the Rangers under Walker in Bosque County had been discharged, and it had been in moments of relaxation that the larger crimes had been committed.

Some surcease from worry over the number of our horses diminishing at the hands of the Indians, was interrupted by the work of white horse thieves. Captain Clark, Mr. Ferris, Kos, myself, and Clark's negro, Simon, started on the trail of thieves who had taken some of Clark's horses. We were led by way of Sulphur Springs on the Lampasas, where we were joined by Colonel John Burleson, and on to the south of Fort Gabriel. We were camping when night overtook us. The trail led near Austin to Rogers where the thieves had traded a horse to the deputy marshal and received a dollar to boot.

We passed through Austin where Kos, nine years of age, had a rather interesting conversation with General Sam Houston. Below Austin we had our horses shod and continued along the San Antonio road to the Yeguas. Here we picked up a straight clue but got off the trail and went through Caldwell and four miles along the Brenham road. We crossed the main Yegua, reached Brenham and parted. Some went to Washington and some to Hempstead, where several men joined that portion of the posse.

We met at Navasota, those who had gone to Hempstead bringing their horses up on the train. Here we decided to separate again to follow what appeared to be two trails. My crowd went to Milligan's depot and toward Port Sullivan. We again divided, Mr. Stark of Brenham, Kos, and myself started to Marlin but discovered that the thieves had gone the Port Sullivan road. I dispatched Kos to Marlin, where all were to again meet, with the news. Six miles west of Port Sullivan the trail turned back across the Brazos and Mr. Stark and I rode into Marlin that night.

At Navasota we had learned the identity of one of the thieves. We now lost little time. On to Waco in one evening's ride and northwest to Meridian before breakfast next morning was made possible by steady riding. Our crowd was increased to fifteen and John Hanna was elected captain. Before night we rode to the vicinity of the thieves and camped.

Just before day we charged the camp of the thieves and captured one. He made an effort to escape and was shot badly. His pal, Tucker, got away and was off to Arkansas, we learned from the captured one. By the next day a good many citizens had heard of the capture and came to where the thief was being guarded in camp. No information was divulged by the prisoner that was not already known, and he was hung after having been given the opportunity for confessions and a last speech. His name was Covington. Three men were appointed to go after the other thief, Tucker.

We reached home on the twentieth of June, after more than three weeks of hot and dusty travel and an expenditure of more than one hundred and thirty dollars and had captured only one horse thief. When I rode up, neighbors were gathering in attendance to hear the Reverend Fleming preach. Attending to the stock and seining in the Bosque during the next few days was a treat by way of a change.

At the end of the week I attended a public meeting at Meridian concerning the horse thieves. Two days later a similar meeting, held at Mr. Lott's on the Brazos, was attended by citizens of Bosque, Erath, and Johnson Counties. A resolution was adopted to rid our country of thieves and cutthroats. A second resolution provided for the public execution of Bob Tucker on August tenth, near the county line of Erath and Bosque Counties. Tucker had been brought back after a several days' chase by Messrs. Hanna, Jacobs and Brown, and three men appointed to do just that.

The prisoner was taken to the home of Captain Clark where he was given a hearing which occupied about three days. Over one hundred men were gathered there, but Tucker's and other suspicious characters' hearing was conducted by a vigilance committee. It was decided to turn Tucker over to the civil authorities and he was jailed. But about ten days later, I was asked to attend a meeting at Sulphur Springs on the Paluxie, where I found a general committee from adjoining counties reopening the case of Tucker. After a thorough discussion of the crime, circumstances and conditions, it was decided that the horse thief should be publicly executed by two o'clock the next day.

The deliberations and arrangements of the general committee were completed, and Tucker was led out and hung to a post oak tree on August 10, 1860. Over one hundred men were present and there was no voice of dissent raised at the quiet execution which justice and conditions demanded. In fact, the end of the same week saw many of these men at my house on Sunday to hear the Reverend Montgomery preach. But while at Meridian a few days later, qualifying as justice of the peace, I was told that six men, heavily armed, were hunting me to kill me for having actively participated in the hanging of the two horse thieves.

Only two other meetings of the vigilance committee during the next few weeks were of serious consequence. One of these had to do with the case of John Garner who was implicated with some Indians in the killing of two families in Jack County. Captain McCarty came by my place and I accompanied him to Waco after Garner. On our way we overtook a negro who was driving some horses for a white man who had stolen them.

Three days early in September were spent in consultation with a committee of Waco men in a room secured for the meeting of the Vigilance Committee. The cases of Garner and others were discussed. Finally, the Waco men decided to turn Garner over to us and, accompanied by several others, we left with him. After traveling about a mile, he asked of us the privilege of praying, which was granted. He then requested that his body should be left above the ground, whereupon he was left hanging to a live oak limb.

Map showing Counties and Principal Towns of Texas in 1860. Explanation: The heavy, irregular line indicates the border line of settlements.

CHAPTER XI

WAR: THE NORTHWESTERN FRONTIER

NEXT month, October, 1860, rumors of Indian forays were again echoed in our county. County court was in session at Meridian with Judge Battle presiding. Here, two public meetings were held by citizens to discuss the protection of the frontier and consider ways and means to secure remuneration for losses already sustained. It was the conclusion of the meeting that no confidence could be placed in officers that had been sent to our relief and that an independent company should be sent out. They asked me to take charge of the company.

Three days sufficed to get our equipment, consisting of wagons, guns, etc., in fair condition for a trip to the Indian country. Twelve men accompanied me. We met Captain John Lowe of Stephenville with ten minute-men and Captain Hamner, on the fourth of November, at Hubbard's Creek, making a total of twenty-five men. Our united group started on what we intended to be a several weeks' tramp, and we soon ran afoul of several Indians, from whom we recovered the stolen horses they were driving. However, the thieves got away.

Marching by way of Camp Cooper we came to the Givins ranch where we traded our wagons for pack mules and saddles for our scout. This was the last settlement on the Clear Fork of the Brazos. We camped for one day in order to allow the men to kill some buffaloes, which were fairly plentiful at this place. Forty were killed in the day's sport.

Two men quit me and two others had their horses frightened by the buffaloes, thus leaving them afoot. The two men walked back to the nearest settlement and another man decided to go with them which left us twenty strong. We decided to catch the two runaway horses. While hunting them we had some good chances at buffaloes and I killed several with my pistol. In sight of the Double Mountains, I became separated from my company and had five lonesome days by myself in an Indian country but fortunately encountered no Indians.

We traveled down the Colorado by Fort Chadbourne and learned that the marauders had killed several teamsters on an overland mail route to California, while we were some miles above. Traveling back to Camp Cooper we went on to Mountain Pass where I had to leave Captain Lowe, who was very sick. With four men, I went home by way of Jacksboro to see about the Indian excitement in that region. The weather was cold and the horses of the other men already needed rest, hence only five made this ride. Several families around Jacksboro had been killed and over one hundred horses driven away.

When I arrived home on Christmas day I found a commission from Governor Houston to raise a Lieutenant's company of twenty-five men for defense of the frontier. The order specified that the company was to be mustered in at Fort Belknap for three months' service. All general orders issued to Rangers were to be regarded and Indians committing depredations were to be pursued and punished. We were to cooperate with Captain Sul Ross. The instructions were carried out and I reported the company at Captain Ross' camp, near Belknap, on January 14, 1861.

While in the frontier service under call and commission from Governor Houston, with my headquarters at Flag Mountain, on Hubbard's Creek, there was issued a call from some of the leading men of the Democratic party, for the people to send delegates to Austin to consider the propriety of seceding from the United States, forming what was to be called the Southern Confederacy. All of this was done in conformity with the call. The convention deposed Governor Sam Houston in March. He was a man possessed of more intellect, patriotism, and statesmanship, and was the safest counselor for the mass of the people, than anyone who ever sat in the executive chair of Texas, and I might say, in the executive chair of the United States since the Confederate War. He had refused to take an oath of office by which he was to swear allegiance to the Confederate States. So the convention declared the office of governor vacant and directed that Lieutenant-Governor Clark fill the unexpired term.

The president, O. M. Roberts, of the convention, had been authorized to appoint a "Committee of Public Safety." This committee organized the defense of Texas by appointing Colonel Ben McCulloch to take charge of the post at San Antonio, Colonel Henry E. McCulloch to command the forces on the northwestern frontier, and Colonel John S. Ford to command those on the Rio Grande.

The order from Governor Houston's Secretary of State, Cave, had resulted in my being near Fort Belknap hunting Indians. I ordered camp made some distance up on Hubbard's Creek. From this base, half the company at a time were used as scouts. Living without tents in the heavy sleets and with buffalo meat as the principal item on the bill of fare this was not so glorious, but we continued our work. No Indians were encountered and I dismissed my company for five days and went home at the last of January. Here I found my order for scouting countermanded by Governor Houston and received another order from the convention of the people of Texas to raise one hundred men and assist in taking the forts and posts of the United States along the frontier of Texas.

Thus I found myself with two commissions, from two governments, without a precedent to be governed by. But the only conclusion I could arrive at was to stand by the voice of the people of Texas, who had voted by a large majority to secede. So I paraded my old company and explained the whole proceedings of the convention to them and told them that they were discharged. But I told them that if they wanted to they could help make up the company the convention had commissioned me to raise. About half my old company went home as they said they did not care to fight their own government, and the other half stayed with me.

The convention had commissioned Henry E. McCulloch to raise a regiment to aid in capturing the military posts on our frontier occupied by United States troops. This was in February, 1861. Colonel McCulloch ordered me to raise all the men I could to form a company, up to one hundred, rank and file, and meet him on the Jim Ned River. Six miles below Camp Colorado, there was one regiment of federal cavalry and one of infantry who saw themselves cut off from all means of escape and, after two days' parley, they surrendered. McCulloch permitted them to carry off their side arms. By this time there were about three regiments of Texans under his command. But as only one was organized under orders from the convention, he called the other two his heelfly force.

We now moved on to Fort Chadbourne where there was a similar force with company artillery added. Here a few days were devoted to making inventory of ordnance, commissary, and quartermaster stores, for all of which we receipted. A captain was left in charge of these posts and we marched to Camp Cooper. Here the heelfly forces were discharged.

We arrived on March 7th. The camp had already been surrendered to troops in the old State service which had been under Governor Houston. Now, however, it was promptly turned over to Colonel McCulloch, who left me in command of the place and of that portion of the frontier. Captains Frost and Halley had been placed in command at Colorado and Chadbourne, respectively. We held our positions until the fourth of May, keeping scouting parties in the field in a manner we thought best for the defense of the frontier. We were not able to keep the Indians from doing any mischief but broke up their camps and prevented them from doing serious injury at this time. Our companies were stationed an average distance of about one day's ride apart and we were required to patrol this distance twice each day, meeting each other's company patrols and returning. For over a year we continued this patrol.

In the meantime, L. P. Walker, Secretary of War of the Confederate States, ordered Major Ben McCulloch to recruit a volunteer regiment for protection of the Texas frontier. The Major transferred the order to Colonel H. E. McCulloch, his brother, who at once undertook to get the men into the field as early as possible. Colonel McCulloch was already in the field, under the authority of the State, with five companies of men distributed from the Colorado to the Red River. He now asked that he be assigned to this area alone, as it was as much territory as his command could very well undertake to protect.

A letter from Colonel McCulloch to me at this time throws much light on our volunteer companies serving on the frontier under the Confederate flag, during the next twelve months:

                                        Austin, March 27th, 1861.
To Capt. James B. Barry.
  Sir:
      You are hereby authorized to proceed at once to enroll a company of Mounted Volunteers to consist of one Captain, one First Lieutenant, two Second Lieutenants, four Sergeants, four Corporals, two buglers, one farrier, one blacksmith and from forty-four to sixty-four privates. The men will elect the commissioned officers, and the captains are to appoint the non-commissioned officers, bugler, farriers, and blacksmith. The men must be over 18 and under 45 years of age, sound and healthy and as far as possible good riders and good marksmen, and of good moral character and steady sober habits. And in no instance, will you enroll a professional gambler or habitual drunkard, as such men are unworthy of and unfit for place in our service. The horses must be of good size, not less than 5 nor more than 10 years old, and in good condition; saddles must be on the Texas style, good and strongly rigged with a good blanket and a good strong, single reined Curt bridle. Each man will provide himself with a Colts six shooting pistol if possible, and, when it can be conveniently done, have a good double-barreled shot gun or short rifle with him

also. Each man should enter the service with a tin canteen, covered with cloth, that will hold half a gallon of water, and each mess of six men will have two other canteens that would hold one gallon. Each man should possess a good heavy blanket. The officers and men will be entitled to the same pay and allowances allowed volunteers in the army of the "Confederate States" and subject to the same rules and government. You will rendezvous at such places as you desire and organize the company in time to report at Camp Cooper on the fourth day of May, next, where your company will be mustered into the service of the "Confederate States" for twelve months unless sooner discharged. The Lieutenant Colonel and Major will be elected by the Regiment after they are received into service. The utmost good order and good conduct is expected of your company in passing through the country, and no unnecessary interference with the persons or property of the citizens of the country or others will be justified or excused by me under any circumstances. The pay and subsistence of your men will commence on the day of your company rendezvous and your rations and forage commuted (I presume) from that time until you are supplied by the Government. I confidently expect you to bring into the service a company of which Texas will be proud, and that will nobly sustain her reputation in the service of the "Confederate States."

Very respectfully, your obd't servant,

H. E. McCulloch,

Col. by Appointment, Vol. Army Confederate States.

At about the same time, the Colonel wrote L. P. Walker, Secretary of War of the Confederate States, concerning the protection of the Texas frontier, and requested permission to use some of the friendly Indians of the Territory in his scouting trips and drives against the hostile Indians. He stated that he believed they could be of great service to the Confederacy and that the expense of maintaining them would be proportionately small. Forts Arbuckle and Cobb across Red River were to be seized after getting control of the frontier posts held by the United States. In fact, they were taken over by Confederate forces in June, but the raids of the Indians into Texas continued.

CHAPTER XII

SCOUTING WITH THE
TEXAS MOUNTED RIFLES

Now that the Provisional Congress of the Confederacy had passed an act providing for a provisional army, two regiments of mounted troops which had been authorized by the Committee of Public Safety of Texas in March, 1861, were mustered, under this act, into the service of the Confederate States. We were mustered in by Captain Sayre of Montgomery, Alabama, on May 7, 1861. Our regiment was Colonel McCulloch's First Regiment Texas Mounted Rifles, who garrisoned the frontier posts, formerly held by the United States troops. A month later, McCulloch ordered us to fill up our companies to eighty men. The highest officers of the command, in the future, were to be elected by the men of the regiment; elections for Lieutenant Colonel, Major, etc., being held in each company on order of the commander of the regiment at a specified time.

Our section of the frontier, which extended from the Red River to the Rio Grande, was considered the most difficult to defend. The other two portions were from Brownsville to New Mexico and from the southwestern corner of Arkansas to the northernmost boundary of ours at Preston on Red River. Our frontier line was thus several hundred miles in length. The settlements, at intervals along this line, had been moving westward a few miles each year but were subjected to constant depredations from the wild Indians of the plains.

The Comanches and the Kiowas, particularly the former, struggled against the encroachments of the whites in this region of the Southwest which was the most desirable portion of the unsettled country. Settlers realized the possibilities for grazing, and perhaps for farming, while the wild Comanches who inhabited the country of the headwaters of the Colorado, Brazos, and the Canadian Rivers naturally wanted to preserve the game, fish, wild fruits and nuts for themselves. The Kiowas were largely in the Panhandle.

From the Canadian River and Antelope Hills country in the Panhandle through the "Plains" and on southward to below the Staked Plains, the Comanche horsemen had long roamed and hunted. The country east of the Staked Plains was so well known to them that they could enter by small canyons and ravines and raid the settlements along the upper Colorado and the Brazos and be on their way toward New Mexico in comparative safety. Farther north, the region of the headwaters of the Little Wichita, Wichita, and Pease Rivers was even more desolate and rugged, being broken with hills, small canyons, and brakes, which offered a convenient means of escaping pursuers or made a desirable rendezvous and means of entrance if attacks on the settlements below were contemplated. The country was so irregular that a war party might scatter and the warriors hide themselves until the pursuit had passed, overlooked them, or been abandoned.

Particularly during the last decade these Indians had entered stealthily in small parties, stolen horses and plundered, and killed families which were least protected. McCulloch found insufficient horses to mount the men in such sections as Camp Colorado. He saw deserted homes, devastation, and recommended ample protection or else he believed the frontier would be practically broken up. Because of the very nature of the incursions of the Indians, their superb horsemanship, and rapid movements they could only be overtaken if immediately pursued. Even then when a pursuit was about to overtake them, they would often scatter and hide themselves.

In his volunteer rangers, Colonel McCulloch looked for men who possessed the qualities which were demanded by this

peculiar service. He wanted only men of courage, good horsemanship, and of good physical condition; men who knew the
traits of the redskin, who knew the country, and who would be
ready to take the trail at a moment's warning. Such troops were
to be kept constantly moving instead of being confined to the
vicinity of permanent military posts. Not only were we to
range along the line of defense, but were to be often sent high
above it into the very lands of the Indian to hunt them out.
The federal government had quartered gallant officers and
men in this country but proper means had not been provided
for by the general government and the defense had been
inadequate. Neglect was one cause for the loss of affection toward the government by the people of this frontier.

When letters of the companies were drawn in April, I
drew "C." How quiet everything had seemed in March. But
we began to drill our men and send out scouting parties, not
only for drill but also because depredations had been reported
as beginning in some portions of the frontier. I led the first
scouting party on a two weeks' trip and sent out four other
scouting expeditions in the same month, but we encountered
no Indians. Hardee's *Light Infantry Tactics* and the *Cavalry
Tactics* of the U. S. Army were used in instruction and drill.
Ammunition was scarce and we were ordered to use it sparing-
ly, which was not such a hardship in drill, as the men were
largely frontiersmen.

In addition to the weekly scouts which made contact with
the other companies in picket fashion, we often sent out larger
scouts. Also passing wagons or trains were furnished with escorts so that proper guard against the Indians was employed
most of the time. But the conduct of the men was rigidly regulated by enforcement of orders forbidding card playing, even
for amusement, horse racing, gambling, and drinking of in-
toxicating liquors unless with consent of the post commander.
Guard duty, care of stock to prevent stampeding, and vigilance
kept the soldiers occupied.

All the conflicts we participated in during the next few years total a sufficient number to be impracticable to set down nor do I recall all the details, although my old "Post Returns," made each month, make a fine supplement to my memory. But two engagements had by detachments of "C" company at the end of the spring of 'sixty-one, were interesting introductions to what was to come in the months following. They were both fought approximately fifty miles north of Camp Cooper (our Post), on the Little Wichita, in the month of July.

The first fight was between Corporal Ercanbrack's little group of ten men and some forty-seven Indians. Colonel Mc-Culloch ordered me to send ten men as a guard for some supply wagons going to the station on Red River. I selected Corporal Ercanbrack to take charge of the guard. On their way back they encountered the Indians. The Indians were better armed, several of them using Minnie and Sharp's rifles. Seven of the men of the corporal were wounded and five of their horses killed, while the known losses of the Indians were two killed. One of the men's wounds (James McKee's) proved fatal next day, while four were seriously wounded.

For six or seven hours the battle was on. Tied on their horses, in order to prevent themselves from falling into the hands of their enemies if killed, the Indians charged the corporal's party on the open prairie. They were repulsed but immediately surrounded the soldiers for a finish fight, apparently confident of victory. But victory was not to be theirs as is shown in a rather accurate reminiscence of the battle many years later by one of the participants, Frank Wristen, which I read in the Dallas *News*, clipped, and deem worthy of reproduction here:

> This company was composed of young men, Capt. Barry himself being at that time a comparatively young man. With us life was then in the romantic stage and at first our occupation was a sweet taste of the mind's desires. We were kept sufficiently busy

with scouting and drilling to avoid the monotony that makes
the soldier's life a dread around the post and we had encountered
no dangers and only pleasant experiences. Game was plentiful and
our commissary had only to provide sufficient breadstuff for our
supplies to be abundant. We were stationed at Camp Cooper early
in the spring and the country was simply one magnificent picture. Rains having been abundant, the lakes on the prairies were
full of water, the grass was green and the trees were in full leaf.

We had been at Camp Cooper perhaps two months, nothing of
interest or importance had transpired and the rollicksome spirit
that had first entered into our lives as frontier guards was now occasionally interspersed with a desire to go back home and see the
folks. We had made several scouting expeditions into the surrounding country and yet we had never seen Indians nor the sign of
Indians and the prospects of our doing any real active service was
not encouraging, and if there was anything we craved about that
time it was military glory. "But all things come to him who waits."

One morning it began to rain. It was a chilly, gloomy, late
spring rain. Of course the rain had not caused the Captain to
relax his military vigilance and sentinels had kept watch during
the entire day, one of these sentinels being kept on a mountain
about one mile north of the post. Soon after the storm closed the
sentinel on the mountain turned in an Indian signal and then
proceeded to turn himself in as fast as a Spanish pony could tumble
down a mountain side, and he had scarcely reached the post when
another picture came into view where the sentinel had formerly
stood, for there silhouetted against the receding clouds appeared
about two hundred Comanche Indians. How many, if any, Indians
were in reserve we could not, of course conjecture, but there were
enough in sight to afford more military glory than we had bar-
gained for. From the top of the mountain the Indians commanded
a full view of the post and the surrounding country. The chief
and some of his sub-chiefs rode a short distance in front of the
main column and there seemed to hold a consultation and by their
actions and gestures indicated that they had viewed the situation
to their entire satisfaction, whereupon they rode back and the
whole band disappeared.

The corral in which the horses and mules were kept every
night was inclosed with cord wood, the wood being piled to a height
of eight or ten feet and two cords deep. Into this corral the horses
and mules were quickly gathered and thrown and every possible
preparation was made to resist an attack, which the Captain was confident would be made during the night, but for some reason no
attack was made and the Indian trail showed that the redskins had
approached no nearer the post than the top of the mountain.

Perhaps they were surprised to find the post there and had over-estimated its strength.

This incident impressed upon our minds, however, that there were plenty of Indians in the country and that we had something to do besides killing time and buffaloes. From this time on experiences came thick and fast. A scouting party seldom went out and returned without having anywhere from an incidental skirmish to a hard-fought battle with Indians. Frequently a scouting party would return leading a few riderless horses or bringing into camp one or more severely wounded companions.

Early in the fall the tribe of Tonkawa Indians appeared at Camp Cooper and appealed to Captain Barry to escort them to Red River. The Tonks were terrorized and could not be dissuaded from the belief that if they attempted the trip unescorted they would be attacked and annihilated by the Comanches, their implacable and relentless foes. About forty miles north of Camp Cooper, at a post which was known as Willow Springs, a company of soldiers was stationed, and on the Red River, about forty miles north of Willow Springs, there was another company and the three posts were kept in constant communication with each other by pony express and by this route the Captain sent an escort of ten men with the Tonks. The Tonks were safely landed on the banks of the Red River and the returning escort encountered no noteworthy incident until about eight miles south of Willow Springs. At that point they were crossing a long stretch of open country and were suddenly attacked by a band of fully fifty Comanches.

The Indians divided into two squads, their evident purpose being to prevent the soldiers returning to Willow Springs or going forward to Camp Cooper. The men knew that a small scouting squad was then stationed on Fish Creek, about fifteen miles further south, and realized that owing to the character of the country they would have a better fighting chance to reach Fish Creek than they would have to retreat to Willow Springs, so they decided upon this gloomy alternative. Then began a running fight in which ten men on tired horses were pitted against five times their number of well-mounted Indians. As the men would charge upon the line in front of them the Indians would disperse, form a new line and confront the men at another point. Within a distance of ten miles the men broke through the Indian lines not less than a dozen times, three of the men had been severely wounded and the Indians were gradually drawing the cordon of death nearer about them. From behind them and in front of them and on each side of them the bloodthirsty devils yelled in triumph and rained arrows about their intended victims more in a spirit of tantalization than with a desire to kill. For the men there was apparently no hope of escape and to fill their souls with terror was the height of the Indians' joy.

Once more the men dashed through the line before them, but at the cost of one brave fellow's life, for Private James Mc-Kee received a fatal arrow wound. As he fell from his horse Corporal Urkenback [Ercanbrack?] who had the mail and express in his saddle bags, jumped from his horse and picked up the wounded man, but in doing so his horse jerked away and started in the direction of Fish Creek camp. How the horse got through the line of Indians is a mystery, but he did and when he dashed into the camp on Fish Creek the saddle pockets had been ripped almost into shreds and only contained an unimportant letter or two. The men in camp knew by this that a fight was then in progress or had taken place between that point and Willow Springs, but just what to do was the question.

There were only seven men in the Fish Creek camp and it was getting late in the evening. If the escort had been killed they had certainly been attacked by superior numbers and if they had not been killed a messenger instead of a riderless horse should have dashed into their camp. The Sergeant in charge of the camp finally decided to send a runner to Camp Cooper and with the other six men make an effort to reach his comrades, dead or alive.

Then in the distance appeared a horseman, a messenger from the little bunch of men he had left in the very jaws of death. His story was quickly told. Three miles back on the road to Willow Springs were his companions, three of them dangerously wounded, one of them dying, surrounded by Indians, and five of them able to fight, battling for their lives, a hopeless task without immediate assistance. All of them might have dashed through the lines and reached Fish Creek except the wounded men. To protect them only one man could make the break. No messenger was sent to Camp Cooper, but the seven men and the messenger rushed to the assistance of the besieged men and as the relief came in sight the Indians fled. Where the men had made their last stand was a ghastly sight. Within a radius of a few feet were four dead horses, three badly wounded men and one in a dying condition.

It was then dark and two men were dispatched to Camp Cooper for a surgeon. Early the next morning the surgeon arrived, accompanied by twenty-five soldiers. The fatally wounded soldier was dead when the surgeon reached camp, but the wounds of the other three were dressed and all of them recovered and were soon again in active service.

The wounded men were sent into Camp Cooper and Captain Barry decided to make a scouting expedition covering a large portion of country, this expedition starting from the point where the ten men had made their last stand against the Indians. Three days later this scouting party was attacked by a large band of Comanches and a desperate fight ensued. The pack drivers were a short distance behind the other men and the Indians dashed upon them. There were three of the drivers and all of them were killed. Several Indians were killed and after the fight we dug a big grave with our butcher knives and buried our three comrades, piling rocks over their graves to prevent their being dug up by the wolves. This was undoubtedly the same body of Indians that had attacked the escort between Willow Springs and Fish Creek.

About a month later Captain Barry decided to make another scouting expedition as far west as the foot of the plains, covering the Pease River country and the head of the Clear Fork of the Brazos. We reached the head of the Clear Fork without discovering Indians, but at this point we collided with quite a band. There were about twenty-five of us and perhaps sixty or sixty-five Indians. They succeeded in stampeding the pack mules, cutting the packs all to pieces and leaving us entirely without supplies. After scattering the pack mules the Indians made a running fight, traveling northward. We followed them a short distance and then resumed our course and soon ran into what had been doubtless intended as a kind of permanent camp, for it was now late in the fall. The Indians had evidently abandoned this camp in a very great hurry. There was a big scaffold of buffalo meat, freshly and finely barbecued, and near by were three Indian ponies and several blankets and there were quite a number of women's and children's tracks about the place. It was only a short distance from this to the place where the Indians had attacked us and doubtless their object in trying to lead us north was for the purpose of allowing the women and children time to make good their escape and our unexpected return had made it necessary for them to abandon their camp in the manner they had. It was now very late in the evening, so we preëmpted the camp and being without provisions gladly availed ourselves of the barbecued buffalo meat.

Notwithstanding the loss of his supplies the Captain decided to continue the scouting expedition, so the next morning we continued our way around the foot of the plains, nor had we to go very far until we encountered a band of about fifty Indians. A running fight ensued and the Indians divided into two bands, after each of which the Captain sent a band of men in pursuit. A small bunch of us pursued one band of the Indians for several miles, killing several of their horses and wounding, perhaps killing some of their own number. Being closely pressed the Indians dashed up the mountain or cap rock and going some distance on the plains awaited us. We dashed into them and then engaged in what might be termed a hand-to-hand engagement.

The Indians were armed with bows and arrows and lances and we were for the most part armed with pistols, consequently effective fighting must necessarily have been at very close range. The Indians would dash at us, hurl their spears and then dash away, only to repeat their tactics, and how we escaped annihilation is little less than miraculous, especially considering the superior number of the Indians. I was the only man seriously wounded, being shot in the neck with an arrow. In this fight there were twenty-two Indians and owing to a mistake in understanding orders only six of us were engaged in the hottest of the fight. Reinforcements reaching us the Indians fled, leaving six of their dead on the battleground and taking four other dead ones away with them. After this fight Captain Barry returned to Camp Cooper, scouting the country as he returned, but encountering no more Indians. . . .

The second engagement was fought within a few miles of the scene of Corporal Ercanbrack's fight. It was on July 29, only three days later. In the main, it was a running fight between thirty-two men led by myself and about seventy Indians. About fifteen miles were covered and the Indians were routed with a loss of not less than a dozen. Among the killed was one of the head men of the hostiles, dressed in a United States soldier's coat. The loss of this man seemed to discourage the Indians. Three men, Wetherby, Connelly, and Lynn were killed by the redskins and seven others were wounded. This fight is mentioned by Wristen, in the above story. On a scout a few days later to join with Major Ed Burleson on an expedition to the Canadian, I found the trail again. This trail was followed beyond the Wichita Mountain, where numerous herds of buffaloes had put it out entirely. These last traces indicated that the redskins were fleeing beyond the Texas line.

One of the boys who was with us in this fight, wrote me many years later in regard to it and some few other experiences. The letter read:

Colonel James Buckner Barry,
Walnut Springs, Texas.

Dear Colonel:

I will write you again, for I want to hear from you once more while on earth. I hope my brave Captain, as I used to call you at old Camp Cooper where I first made your acquaintance, is well and yet alive, and will take pleasure in answering a few questions about the Ranger days. If you remember, one July we were attacked by about one hundred and twenty-five Kiowa and Comanche Indians about twelve o'clock.

There, during battle, an old chief was shot through the head by some of the rangers. Thomas Erkenbrack [Ercanbrack] halted me and made me hold his horse until he could take off the old chief's scalp. I watched him take off his topknot. If you remember, he had a bone whistle platted in his hair. He also had a beautiful necklace, or beaded sash around his neck, a bow and a quiver full of arrows, and an old Mexican scopet. It seems to me like you fell heir to them. Did you get them and if so have you got them now? I remember very well just how that old rascal looked. We buried Tips Conley, Thomas Weatherby, and "Bud" Lynn in ditches; you know they were killed the first dash the Indians made at us. I remember Bushong's horse gave out.

The next day, I was a way off on the lookout guard about one-half mile from camp, and I found a white horse staked out a way up on the little Wichita River, two miles above camp. You came up and brought that great long spy glass and looked at the horse. You said it was a horse with a red blanket and an Indian saddle and for me to go to camp and take two men with me and get the horse. You said if none of the boys would go willingly for me to tell Bill Johnson to detail two of them, but Wils Biffle and some other one said before they would be detailed they would go. So we went and got the Indian horse and saddle. You gave the horse and all his rig to me.

If you remember, at another time some of us boys ran some gobblers down and caught three of them. A little while after we caught the turkeys, we saw a smoke coming up out of some mesquite timber about a mile away. You told us to lay our blankets and turkeys off and fasten our saddles and fix for another charge on Indians. We went a little way and saw ten Indians coming from the smoke. We took our six shooters in our hands and started after them. We ran them four or five miles and overtook them. When the row commenced, six shooters rang out on the air like a hot skillet full of popcorn. The result for the Indians was Eli Franks' horse lanced through the hams, Frank Wristen shot in the neck, and John Hardigree shot in the arm.

We went back and found an Indian camp with buffalo meat plentiful on a scaffold; there had been women and children there from the sign. So we camped on the spot or not far away. If you remember, on that trip John Billner, and Andy Truit got lost from us one evening and were several days getting back to Camp Cooper. Now on that same trip, one night we had no meat to eat. So you took off your shoes and waded in the water and picked up some mussel shells and brought them out, cooked them in a fry pan and you and I ate them; none of the other boys would eat them. If you recall, you caught a turtle that the buffalo had stepped on and had mashed his shell on his back. You and I ate him after broiling him on some fire coals. We ate him without bread or salt.

On the trip the time we had that big Indian fight on the Little Wichita, we got out of meat and rode all night. The next morning we came upon old mammy bear and two large cubs and some turkeys. We killed one bear and two turkeys. We also ate this game without salt or bread, but we had plenty help that time.

Well, I will digress a little from this subject as it might become monotonous. I hope you are well and are in good health. I want you to send me one of your photographs. If I had one I would prize it very highly so please send me one if possible. I had two or three ribs broken 27 days ago. If I had one of your photos to look at it would cheer me up; so please send me one.

I am going to relate a circumstance that happened on one of our trips which I suspect you do not remember. After we had left the Wichita Mountains, we went to the head of the false Washita and camped on the head or near the head of the stream. That night we bunched our horses close, and placed a heavy guard around them. A long time after dark the alarm was given that Indians were lurking around camp. So you took a half dozen men, (I was in the number) and scouted the surrounding country for some distance. Finally we came to the creek; it was dry as usual. We stopped on the bank and you told Burr Brown to go down into the bed of the creek and see if he could see any Indian sign. Burr looked at you and said, "Captain, suppose you go first; you are sure getting the most pay." You looked at him and a smile came over your face and then you took the lead and told us to follow. We went back and reported at camp that no Indians had been found.

But I will say one thing, I never did hear such a howling of Lobo and prairie coyotes in all my life before or since. Can you remember all these things?

If you still have that bow and other things I have mentioned, I would like some time to come and see them again.

Well, I will close for the present and ask my dear comrade to answer as soon as possible, for I want to hear from you anyway once more on earth.

I am your comrade, with much love for you,

C. K. Hackworth.

(White House, Texas, is my address.)

Regular scouting was continued during September. A party of Indians, numbering about thirty, was seen on Fish Creek, between Camp Cooper and Fort Belknap, and two groups of men were sent after them. The mountains and woods in Buchanan and Palo Pinto Counties and the brush along the Leon were scoured to no avail. During the full moon, two other squads of men were kept out on Elm and Paint Creeks, and until near the close of the month, Lieutenant Combs and twenty men were stationed on Camp Creek beyond the Brazos. But no redskins were encountered nor sign seen.

At the last of the month, Captain Boggess and his company were moved from Phantom Hill to my post and I was ordered by the Adjutant General to prepare to winter the additional company. There came an order, also, for a ten-day scout, with fifty picked men under myself, in a northwesterly direction across the Big Wichita and up Beaver Creek for a distance of a hundred and twenty-five miles from camp. A large war party of Comanches was reported approaching in this direction and we were to investigate the "positive" information for the Regimental Head Quarters. Captain Boggess of Company "H" was asked to take thirty men and I took thirty-one and the expedition was off against the hostiles, leaving Lieutenant Combs in charge of the post.

On the first of November, of the same year, 1861, we discovered a party of Indians on the Pease River, a tributary of the Red River, and, after some precaution in an effort to get within striking distance, had a warm encounter with them in a running fight which extended over several miles. Ten "good Indians" were found after the battle was over and several, seemingly seriously injured, were given assistance by their comrades in fleeing from the scene. Some of these last were no doubt mortally wounded. Two of my men were wounded and two horses. We captured about six hundred dollars worth of ponies and peltries. Colonel McCulloch saw fit to cite the victory in a circular to the Regiment as the "first decided victory" gained over the marauders.

Drilling and disciplining of troops continued, under strict orders, although not a "single round" of ammunition was to be used unless actual necessity demanded. Ammunition in private hands was not considered private property when it was so scarce and citizens wasteful with it faced having it impressed for their carelessness. It became my duty to take some ammunition as contraband from a disloyal citizen named Knox, near the post. As a supporter and sympathizer of the enemy, his effects were clearly ours and my act was approved by the Adjutant General in a letter. Perhaps much of the drill was of little value because when men were once in the midst of a running fight with Indians, each man was generally his own commander. But officers were strict, in hopes, perhaps, that promotion and transfer would take them to a more glorious field than that of the redskins.

In the meantime, it had been our duty to act as escorts for a party of Seminole Indians en route to the Red River and to become the guard of fifty prisoners of war brought to us from San Antonio. Care was taken that they did not escape but there was little "glory" in it and some of the men only smiled wryly at the message of Adjutant General Yager: "Good luck to Co. 'C' in its next engagement with the Indians. Already she wears the palm."

The opening of the new year, 1862, saw new expeditions being made from the various posts of the First Texas Mounted Rifles. On the fifteenth of January my company was ordered to make a scout to the plains on the head of the Big Wichita River, thence by way of the North Fork of the Brazos to our post. Fifty men as a minimum were to be taken.

Meanwhile, T. C. Frost, the acting commander of the Regiment had resigned ánd Major Burleson was placed in command by Colonel McCulloch, who was regretful that he could not be with us. He was in charge of the Military Department of Texas and maintained headquarters at San Antonio. It was obvious that no hope for any other service than the protection of the frontier should be nursed until the year's enlistments had expired, and then we would probably be retained if depredations of the Indians continued. So we tried to perform our duty faithfully as men and soldiers. Protection of even portions of the frontier could be possible only by labor, patience, and perseverance.

On February 1, the men of the Regiment elected me Major to succeed Major Burleson, resigned, and I was given command of the north end of our line—from Camp Cooper to Red River—with permission to choose my headquarters. I celebrated the promotion the same month by leading an expedition of fifty-eight men and two commissioned officers to the head of the Pease and the Brazos Rivers for possible Indian sign. But no redskins were met. All the while rumors continued that the Regiment would soon meet at Fredericksburg or Fort Mason for reorganization. But the assembling of the parts of the Regiment were delayed and an order came from Richmond to reënlist men whose first enlistment periods were expiring.

In obedience to an order from Colonel Frost I ordered some companies whose time of enlistment was up and who were to be mustered out, to report to Fort Mason, the Regimental Headquarters, on April 12th. I started there with my old company and encountered Indians on April 9th, 1862.

This conflict, on the headwaters of the San Saba, was a bloody little affair and came near proving to be the finish of my career as a fighter of Indians. We charged the redskins and were soon in their midst. They probably realized it was too late to run as it would prove even more fatal and so they fought desperately. I found myself in conflict with two big Indians who launched six arrows into my horse which brought him down and as he fell I was unable to jump clear and was pinned by a leg. They were rushing me as I lay prostrate, when one of my men, M. L. Webster, later of Whitesboro, Texas, ran up and took the fight off my hands. I believe my bones would now be decaying on the scene of the battle had not Webster come to my rescue and given me a chance to get on my feet to continue the fight. A few minutes later, the boys had so acquitted themselves that the Indians changed their minds and plunged away in flight.

This fight was our fourth major contest during the "quiet" first twelve months. We knew of three Indians killed and one wounded. Four of my men and four horses were wounded. Corporal Ercanbrack was seriously wounded.

At Fort Mason, my time of enlistment having expired and wanting to go home for a few weeks, I was relieved from duty. In fact, the enlistment time of six companies of the First Regiment of Mounted Rifles had expired and the Regiment was disbanded. I did not immediately join its successor, the Frontier Regiment Texas Cavalry, under Colonel James M. Norris, but within a few months I was tendered the position of Major McCord, who had been promoted to Lieutenant-Colonel after the death of Obenchain. There were things at home which needed my attention, but I was fortunate in getting away from the service for even a short period.

CHAPTER XIII

THE TEXAS FRONTIER REGIMENT
VERSUS INDIANS

In February, 1862, the Frontier Regiment, Texas Cavalry, was organized to succeed my old organization, McCulloch's First Regiment Mounted Riflemen, as our terms were soon to expire. Governor Lubbock appointed James M. Norris, colonel; Alfred T. Obenchain, lieutenant-colonel; James E. McCord, major; and ten captains of as many companies. In passing the act creating the regiment the legislature intended that it should see service with the Confederate armies when organized. But when Governor Lubbock, months later, tendered the regiment to the Confederate War Department he specified that it should not be removed from the frontier. This condition the authorities of the Confederate government rejected, and the unit was destined to remain in the service of the State for some two additional years.

---

[1]The reminiscences, which extended nearly to 1865, become thin after the Civil War had been in progress for a few months, while the diary ended with June 1, 1862. There were additional entries, but these pages, approximately sixty in number, have been cut out of the large ledger in which the diary was kept. These missing pages probably contained information, statements, and allusions to individuals or bore on local events occurring during the war and, possibly, the bitter years of reconstruction. Colonel Barry was wont to express his opinion freely and fearlessly, but some member of his family probably deemed it expedient, some years later, to cut away these last pages lest they fall into the hands of someone outside the family. Mr. Koss Barry, mentioned in the introduction, only knows that a member of the family deliberately mutilated the diary.

In five of the six remaining chapters (Chapter XV practically amounting to an exception), Barry is allowed to tell his story in the first person, although the narrative as he left it has been filled out by the editor from other papers. The base of the narrative henceforth, becomes the military papers which throw much light on the history of the Frontier Regiment, although no effort has been made to give a full account of that famous cavalry organization. Nearly five hundred pieces were used by the editor, exclusive of the "Order Book," in the treatment of these five chapters, and woven into what would have been at least the core of Barry's reminiscences, had they been completed.

Only a few weeks had passed since I had been mustered out and had gone home, when I received notification from both Adjutant General Dashiell and Colonel Norris that I was appointed major of the new regiment. The letter of the colonel was cordial and sufficiently complimentary that it gave me pleasure, although, of course one would hardly have expected such a message to be the opposite. I had already learned that Obenchain had been killed, where Breckenridge, Texas, now is located, in a difficulty with two soldiers of the regiment. McCord had been promoted to the vacancy and the position of major was open.

When I accepted the commission I learned that the strength of the unit was over twelve hundred men. Horses were well selected, perhaps because they were the property of the troops, and the men were furnished arms. Frequently, however the guns were of inferior make and, at times, some of the ammunition was worthless. Occasionally powder in one hundred pound lots proved to be unfit for use.

As there were ten companies to patrol from the mouth of the Big Washita at Red River south to Fort McKavett, Colonel Norris ordered that patrols should travel south to their camps and thence back to their posts each day. Thus there were twenty camps and the country between each two camps was scouted over twice daily. From his headquarters, at Camp Colorado, on January 25, 1863, the colonel ordered the start of these patrols, which were to prove so effective.

The well-known posts which had been established a few years previously and which we garrisoned upon occasion as a part of our chain of defense in this northwestern section thus began with Preston in Grayson County, which is bounded by the Red River. Going south from Preston one came to Fort Belknap in Young County; Camp Cooper in Throckmorton County; Fort Phantom Hill in Jones County; Fort Chadbourne in Runnels County; and Fort McKavett in Menard County. Then there was Fort Croghan in Burnet County, and

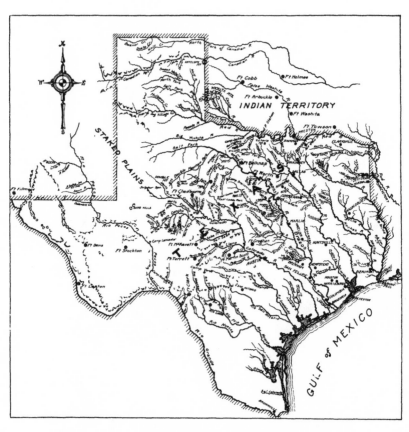

Map showing location of Camps and Forts along the
Texas Frontier in 1863.

Fort Mason in Mason County. Such counties as Wichita, Young, Stephens, Brown, and McCulloch had been on the outermost edge of a movable frontier line when the war between the States opened. Most of the important operations along the northern part of the Frontier Regiment's line of defense centered around Fort Belknap, which faced the hostile tribes across Red River.

Colonel Norris tendered his resignation hardly a year after accepting the command, and Lieutenant-Colonel McCord was promoted to the command, and I to succeed McCord, on February 11, 1863. There was no lapse in the defense of the frontier, but not all of an officer's time could be devoted to this hazardous duty. There were some tasks even more unpleasant than those which involved exposure to the elements and the risks of hunting wild Indians. In truth, they were not nearly so distasteful as the occasional court-martial conducted for indifference to duty or impudence of some surly soldier. The very individualism of our men which made them good Indian fighters occasionally made one of them restless under the discipline of some company officer.

Then there were instances where our lieutenants who were acting adjutants complained of the disloyalty of citizens who refused to sell wheat or flour for Confederate money. One such report came in from Lieutenant Roberts of Camp Breckenridge, Texas, who stated that a citizen of Parker County would not sell flour for twenty dollars per hundred pounds in Confederate money but had asked five dollars per hundred pounds in gold. The same owner offered a large lot of wheat and flour for sale at five dollars in gold but flatly refused certified accounts against the State and declared that he possessed more Confederate bills than he wanted. This was in early February, 1863.

Also, some of the horses of the men had died and they could not afford to buy mounts again for themselves. Furthermore, there were calls for financial aid from the widows of men in our regiment who had been killed by the Indians. Such problems must be expected by the military frontiersman; but as there was frequently no solution, it was a relief to act as a military escort to a commissioner of the Military Board of the State making a survey, or to some other party which had secured the service of a guard. Forage, pack saddles, and camp equipage were often lacking when sorely needed and had to be brought from Austin and San Antonio before a big scout could be made.

In fact, the problem of securing adequate ammunition, forage for the horses, and meat for the men, was ever present. Poor ammunition tended to cause the men to have less confidence in themselves while on expedition, although an onlooker would not have been aware of it when watching the men going into action against the Indians. Extracts from a letter from Colonel McCord, which I have among my papers, is pertinent here:

Unofficial

Head Quarters Texas Frontier Regiment

Camp Colorado, May 20th, 1863

Lt. Col. J. B. Barry,

Commanding N. Div. Fr. Regt.,

Camp Belknap, Texas.

Colonel:

Not a pound of powder or a single cap has been received at these Headquarters since you left here; why such is the case, I am at a loss to know. My requisition for ten thousand pounds of lead, five thousand pounds of "*good*" powder, and three hundred and seventy-five thousand water-proof percussion caps is on file with the adjutant general, and I had every assurance from that department that these articles would be forwarded promptly to this Camp and for fear that it wouldn't get here in due time I sent an express to Austin but as yet nothing has been received nor have I the most distant idea when any will be sent. I was very anxious to have your division supplied with ammunition by the time you returned from the present expedition, but from the prospects now there is but little hope of accomplishing such results.

I have ordered the Quarter-master to procure ammunition for the Regiment by purchase or otherwise, and I suppose we will get some now soon, if it is not countermanded by my superiors. I send you a copy of an order to Lt. Peveler to inspect the arms of those companies of your division. If anything should occur that he can't proceed immediately to the inspection of the arms, you will order some competent officer to do so without delay in his place— as I want these reports at the very earliest moment possible as a data by which to make my requisition for *arms* for the *Regiment*.

If consistent with the interest of the service—I would be glad to see you on your return from the expedition, but if you can't conveniently come to see me, give me your views of the propriety of making a three-month's expedition into the Indian Country the coming fall. Say start the first of September and return the first of December. Each company could start from their respective camps with a month's supply and then have two months' supplies for the number of men on the expedition, concentrated at Belknap, with transportation to take it to any point we might suggest. And I would like to have an expression from you—as to the most suitable place to concentrate the provisions after leaving the line. Do you think the horses can stand the trip for that length of time without forage that season of the year? What time will the buffalo come down and how will the range be? And everything of interest pertaining to the same. Wouldn't it have a tendency to prevent them from going into Winter Quarters in Texas during the winter? . . .

Yours truly,
J. E. McCord.

The proposed expedition into the Indian Country was postponed, for one reason or another, until it was no longer feasible. In the first place, Governor Lubbock would not issue an order for the expedition, although he professed to be pleased with the plan, because he thought following the fall of Vicksburg, that the Regiment might be needed to repel the federals. Second, the citizens around the Red River Station solicited captains of the Command not to make the scout because they believed the Indians would immediately invade in vast numbers, and they contemplated leaving their homes if the troops departed. Third, the appropriation for the support of the Regiment was practically exhausted. Fourth, strong rumors were conveyed to State Headquarters, in part through the

Osage Indians, of an invasion from above the Canadian by the Northern Indians, who were said to be concentrating for a raid, supposedly on Texas, and an order followed not to try to operate above the line of defense. By the end of November, reports that the Regiment was to be shortly taken over by the Confederacy were verified, and any lingering hope that the planned excursion might be carried out was terminated.

Colonel McCord's letter reached me on June 15th. I had gone on a big spring scout in May with Captains Ward and Rowland with portions of their companies and half of the force of my headquarters company at Belknap to above the Washita and Red River country. The force was divided before starting back. At the head of the Washita, Captain Rowland's company was ordered to begin the return march. He traveled by way of the Washita, Otter Creek, Cash Creek, Beaver Creek, and Carter's ranch. This was rather a direct course but the captain and some of his men were not well and struck for camp. There they were confined to quarters with fever for several days. The captain's report, however, on the grass and water along his line of march was important.

On May 26, two days later, Captain Ward's company parted from my group at Red River and reached Camp Brunson, their post, on June third. The first four days of their march were through great herds of buffaloes. Grass was rather short and the water found was not drinkable, with the exception of a spring and that of Otter Creek. No fresh Indian sign was observed but, upon arrival at camp, it was learned that Indians had been below and stolen some horses.

The troops left in camp had seen only one Indian, however, and they tried to capture him. It was the opinion of the men that the lone Indian was a spy from some reservation above the River. This spy was the only Indian the captain's company saw on the return march, some one hundred and eighty miles from where we had separated forces. Good water had been found at springs on Red River below the mouth of the Pease, but it was scarce from there home. Fever attacked some of the men after they got into camp.

Still the year 1863 was not to pass without several encounters with the redskins. To attempt to record all of them would be tiresome even if one could recall the various details. I shall mention a few in which men of my division of the Frontier Regiment engaged and tell a few of the details in some of the cases.

On the nineteenth of July, Captain Loyd of Company "E" at Camp Colorado, took seven of his men and started on a twenty-day scout. They traveled from Camp Salmon, later named Camp McCord, up the Clear Fork of the Brazos for about five days and thence in a northeasterly direction for a day and camped on Paint Creek. Descending this stream a few miles they found a hobbled Indian pony and other signs of the presence of Indians. Apparently the Indians were about a day ahead of them and also going down the stream. Captain Loyd decided to go down the Clear Fork to Camp Cooper and replenish their supplies and ammunition and then resume the trail. It was not probable that the Indians would return at once.

At Camp Cooper, Sergeant Collins and seven men of Company "H" joined them and they returned to the place on Paint Creek where they had seen the signs. New Indian signs were discovered. They found a shield fastened in a tree which appeared to have been placed there as a guide. An Indian saddle and a lance were also found. These articles decided them on secreting their horses and putting a spy upon a high point sufficiently close that he could communicate with them without being seen.

The spy was sent to his position and the captain and sergeant discussed plans whereby they might come in contact with the Indians. It was the opinion of Captain Loyd that it would be best to try to ambush the marauders, but it was thought that they might not come near enough before discovering that they were being waylaid and would escape. The decision was then reached that a charge on horseback should be attempted. Two hours later the look-out announced that the Indians were approaching and the men were ordered to prepare for the attack. The Indians were about a mile distant and advancing.

After the distance had decreased to only a quarter of a mile, the men dashed from their cover. The Indians gave a yell and turned to flee, with the soldiers in pursuit. Blankets and other loose articles were discarded by the redskins. Only a short distance had been covered when the captain's stirrup leather broke and his horse became unmanageable. But he could see that the Indians were being rapidly overtaken and that they were running in two lines about forty yards apart. Whereupon, the captain shouted to his men to check their pace and not break through the rear line of the Indians and find themselves between two fires.

Some two or three men heard the order and slowed their pace but the others continued the charge. The captain managed to check his horse, intending to mend the stirrup leather in order not to lose the stirrup; but it was already lost and he darted forward again to overtake the contestants. He overtook his men just as they came up to the Indians and the fight opened. As his horse was difficult to handle, the captain could only use his pistol.

As the captain had expected, after the men plunged through the rear line of the fleeing redskins, the front line wheeled about and the soldiers were between the lines. Brandishing their shields and uttering warwhoops the front line of Indians frightened those horses which were leading the charge, and they, turning about, terrorized those animals just behind them. The Indians were quick to see their advantage and began firing. Sergeant Collins was killed and privates Tankersly, Howard, Hester, and Powers were wounded. Three horses and one pack mule, which had come up to the fight, were struck by stray bullets.

Checking their horses, the men charged in better formation only to find the Indians again in flight. Two horses dropped dead and two others were crippled, so the pursuit was halted. The wounded and dead were taken to the nearest shade and men were dispatched to Camp Cooper for assistance, which came early the next morning. The dead and wounded were turned over to the Camp Cooper men and the captain with enough new men to bring his force to fifteen, started on the trail of the Indians.

The trail led in a northwesterly direction, but it gave out after twenty-five miles as the Indians divided and scattered in different directions. All efforts to pick up their trail again during the next few days were of no avail. With good arms and splendid mounts, perhaps furnished them by or through the influence of the federals, these skilled horsemen of the plains, had acquitted themselves well in the running fight. The forces were equal in number and Loyd's men might have secured a real victory, but for their eagerness, untrained mounts, and carelessness. But it is fair to give credit to the opponent when he is not despicable.

Men furnished their own mounts, as has been previously stated, and frequently were unable to replace with good ones those that had been killed or lamed. Indian ponies were frequently captured and the stolen horses of settlers recovered, but the former were generally in poor condition because of short grass or limited forage in camps, while the latter were not to be used but advertised as recovered animals and held for claimants. Most of these were generally claimed before the end of ninety days, but, if unclaimed, they could then be purchased at auction.

Nevertheless, just before the first of December, 1863, special orders came from the commanding officer that only effectually armed men, mounted on strong, active horses should be permitted to enroll as members of companies, and that improperly mounted and armed men should be discharged. At this time, unshelled corn was quoted to some company commander at two and a half dollars per bushel, or about five dollars per bushel if shelled. Convenient water was scarce and the range poor, at the same time. Some of us were fortunate in possessing good horses and guns. It was my own good fortune to have replacements from my small and somewhat depleted herd of saddle horses. These, together with good guns, I considered fundamental in trying to cope with the Indians who often had similar equipment, which, now the war was on, the federals either gave them or encouraged them to steal.

Still, on the whole, the two-year record of achievements on the part of our regiment was scarcely tarnished. Victories by small squads and by companies which had been able to involve the Indians in a fight came often enough to encourage us. At times, the express of our companies, chiefly moving to carry the mail, had a brush with the invaders. Such was the experience of Private A. B. Smith, of Captain Ward's company, who started the express of some five men to Camp Belknap about the last of October.

In Jack County, about four miles northeast of Murphy's Station, they met five Indians coming from the settlements with four horses they had stolen. The boys of the express attacked and the redskins fought desperately. For some thirty minutes the conflict was undecided and then the Indians were driven to retreat to a ravine. Here they managed to get one of their number, who was crippled, on a horse and mounted another, who was only slightly hurt, behind him. By this time the boys drove them from their position and they made a desperate effort to reach a mountain. In the efforts of the redskins to climb the mountain, the men saw how well the Indian knew the physical geography of the country he was in, and took advantage of it when he was being bested in a fight. While the Indians were trying to ascend the mountain, the two on the horse managed to ride away, one holding the other, who appeared to be fatally injured, on their mount. The three Indians still in the fight covered the retreat of their comrades but were themselves soon killed. One of our men, F. M. Holden, was injured. Three horses, bows, shields, knives, guns, blankets, buffalo robes, and some money were taken from the victims.

Perhaps it was only to be expected that hard service in the field would be accompanied by other troubles over which the man on the frontier line of defense had no control. A letter of Lieutenant Chapman, written in August, from Red River Station, our northermost company, reached me in September and brought a report of his recent trip to Austin for caps and commissary sacks. While at the capitol, he had learned of the nearly exhausted condition of the last legislative appropriation for the expense of our regiment. He could only secure some four thousand dollars of quartermaster funds to pay for forage, which meant that it would have to be bought on time if it could be purchased by that method at all. He stated that he found farmers unwilling to sell on time unless they received enormous prices and a great many would not sell on time at any price. Some stated that they preferred their grain to a claim on the State or even the current cash. He wished to know therefore, what to do in case he could not obtain forage. Flour and beef could be contracted for and forage was to be found plentifully within fifty to seventy-five miles if it could be bought.

Thus the quartermasters had funds, despite the small remaining balance of the appropriation, and the frontier counties were teeming with abundance, but it seemed possible that our men might suffer from want of supplies. The appropriation had been used more rapidly than had been anticipated because of the rapid depreciation of the currency, and the accompanying rise in prices. We were ordered to purchase supplies and forage at the lowest specie rates if we could not secure these articles at fair prices in currency. The parties purchased from were to be furnished with certified accounts to be paid in specie. Such was the remedy tendered for an ailment which seemed not so easily cured.

In the meantime, some of our men, able fellows, were applying for furloughs, and renegades and deserters began to attract notice to themselves by their growing numbers. Rigorous discipline on the part of the officers did not, of course, prevent some few desertions from our own regiment. Courts-martial took the time of needed officers and it was decided that the good order and discipline of the regiment might be best maintained by discharging parties deemed unfit. These would be transferred to the armies of the Confederacy, and those not in the conscript age would be subject to the draft of their home counties. This was the suggestion of Adjutant General Dashiell.

CHAPTER XIV

THOSE TONKAWAS

FAILURE to encounter Indians on the spring scout of 1863, by my division of the Frontier Regiment, did not alter the plans I had suggested to Colonel McCord, at his request, concerning a big expedition to the Indian country which he had contemplated making in the fall. We proceeded with the preparations during the summer, although the governor had delayed in issuing the order for the march, because he felt that the expected fall of Vicksburg would require our services against a probable invasion by the federals. The governor was reported to be pleased with our plan and desirous of seeing it executed. Guns, lead, caps, buck shot, and powder were promised me through McCord. The powder, however, would have to be tested to determine whether it was good.

Adjutant-General Dashiell wrote from Austin, in August, instructing the colonel to be in readiness for the scout in the fall, but to continue the other scouting movements, keeping scouts out above and below the line of defense. Meanwhile I helped bring in some of the Tonkawas from their reservation at Fort Cobb in the Indian Territory to assist us. They had been taken there from the lower reservation on the Brazos in 1859.

There had been two of these reservations for Indians in Texas, covering something over 55,000 acres of land, provided in 1854. The Tonkawas, numbering only 171 in their entire tribe, were located on the first reservation near Fort Belknap on the Brazos, with the more numerous Tahwaccaroes, Anadahkoes, Caddoes, and Wacoes. All of these tribes together numbered only about eight hundred. The second reservation was given over to about 280 Comanches in 1855, but, within two years, this number had increased to over 425. Obviously, the first band had been joined by other Comanches from one or more of the numerous groups of these Indians who roamed the Platte, Arkansas, Canadian, Red, Colorado, and the Brazos Rivers and the great plains between.

The Comanches were great horsemen, well mounted, well armed, quick on the march, and they offered battle bravely. They were as quick to retreat, however, when the tide of conflict began to turn against them. Many interesting individual conflicts in battle between the Tonkawas and the Comanches could be mentioned during the days of the Tonkawa chief, Placidio. For instance, such duels were fought between these two ancient foes in the campaign of the spring of 1858, when the Tonkawas led by Placidio assisted the Rangers under Captains Ford and Ross.

It was the work of Tonkawa scouts that enabled the forces of Ford to surprise the Comanches at the Canadian under their chief, Iron Jacket. Iron Jacket rallied his men and offered battle. It is said that he wore a coat of mail, probably having secured it indirectly from Mexico. Anyhow, the chief thought he bore a charmed life but one of the Tonkawas got in a well-placed shot and killed him. Later in a continuation of the same fight, Comanche warriors offered mounted duels to the Tonkawas.

While the lines of conflict faced each other, the opposing Indian champions fought several duels on horseback. The Comanches were armed with lances, shields, and bows and, as cavalrymen, the Comanches were undoubtedly superior and generally were able to so demonstrate in a horseback duel. But this fact did not detract from the courage of the Tonkawas in accepting a challenge. This tenacity and courage, from such a small tribe as the Tonkawa, the Comanche deeply resented, especially since the Tonks were allies of the whites.

Old enemies of the Comanche, and always friendly with Texans, the Tonkawas had been located at Fort Belknap. For years Chief Placidio had assisted the whites in their fights with hostile Indians, particularly the Comanches. Now taking advantage of the Civil War, the Comanches attacked the Tonkawas on their reservation in the Territory and killed Placidio and most of the tribe. So they were now indeed a small tribe, but they made good trailers and scouts, were known as efficient buffalo hunters, and had generally shown themselves to be thoroughly dependable. It was now our intention to use this remnant of the tribe as they had been used for years past— for the defense of the whites against the dangerous Comanches.

They arrived at Camp Brunson in August, 1863, and Captain Ward wrote me about the middle of the month that they were hungry, needed better horses, guns, and that some of them were sick. He gave them beef and bread and attempted to persuade four or five of them to remain as scouts with him. But they wanted to see me and have a talk before they separated, if I desired that. These reports were true. The Tonks were very poor and their horses were inferior; their opposition to the wild Indians contributed to this condition. I was authorized by Colonel McCord to subsist them at Fort Belknap, their old home during reservation days, with as little cost as possible to the State until the matter could be laid before the governor for orders.

Colonel McCord suggested to the authorities at Austin that the remaining portion of the tribe, now at Belknap, be used as spies and scouts during the war. Frontier citizens never objected to the residence of the Tonkawas within the State; in fact they welcomed them back during the war. Moreover, Colonel McCord was apparently so confident that the Tonks would be given a home, at least during the war, because of their value on the frontier, that he was to be considerably taken aback at the vacillating policy of the legislature.

The colonel wrote me for four of the young Tonks to serve as guides and trailers at his post, Camp Colorado. At the same time he suggested distributing the other warriors along the line as far south as San Saba, at least. He felt that their service to the regiment would be equal to that of two or three companies.

While the governor was absent in the late summer at Marshall, Texas, conferring with the governors of other states in regard to a policy of state defense for their military district, the contemplated scout was in abeyance. A good many Indians were reported below the line and Captain Rowland at Red River Station had reported Indian signs in his section.

Now came word from Colonel McCord that the governor declined, in the absence of legislative sanction, to take the responsibility for authorizing the subsistence of the Tonkawas at State expense. The cost of transportation of the Tonkawas from Fort Arbuckle to Fort Belknap was a little over one hundred and fifty dollars. Not only did the governor disallow this amount but also the estimates of Quartermaster Strong for subsistence for the first two quarters. Yet the governor would give no orders to turn the Indians adrift. It was suggested that the matter be laid before Brigadier-General Bankhead, commander of the Sub-military District which included that portion of the frontier. So for some weeks, actual defense of the frontier was handicapped and plans for its future protection could not be carried out, because neither the legislative nor administrative departments of the State government would assume responsibility for the subsistence of the Tonkawas, although the State had profited in the past from the aid of these Indian allies; and these departments apparently desired to see it profit in the future—if no demands on the State treasury were to follow. As early as March, 1861, Colonel Henry E. McCulloch had written the Secretary of War of the Confederacy requesting permission to use these friendly Indians of the Territory as scouts and on expeditions against Indian foes.

He had given as his opinion that the service rendered would be much and the cost little. So the movement to use these Indians was not a new one. Some legislators apparently wanted the protection for the frontier of the State but wanted the Confederate government to pay for it. But meanwhile these Indians were needed, just as they would be needed later.

So in obedience to orders to drive out any invaders below the line, we continued to feed the Tonks and at the same time send out companies which would have benefited by the assistance of these allies. We worked our men hard, sometimes having as low as twenty-five present at roll call in the company camps. Calls came in from Captain Loyd and others for Indian trailers for scouting trips as they were better than all the dogs. We had to await the action of the legislature to decide the status of the Tonks but had them take buffalo hunts to assist in providing their food.

Even Colonel John R. Baylor who had been so bitter against the retention of a single Indian within the boundaries of the State in the late 'fifties, wrote to me from Weatherford in November, 1863, asking for the services of the new Tonk chief and some of his men as spies on a proposed scout. He asked that I use my influence with the Tonkawas to get them to assist him. Aware that these Indians had not forgotten his former attitude, he requested that they be informed that all was forgotten. As a clincher in his plea, he stated that they should be told that he wanted to kill the Comanches who murdered the Chief Placidio who was his friend. He added that, "I know I may rely upon your aid and assistance as we have been working together in this thing [defense of the frontier] for years."

Cold weather was at hand and we had to select a place to settle the Tonkawas. Captain Loyd thought Deep Creek in Callahan County would afford water, grazing, and was near the range of the buffalo, while flour mills were reasonably convenient. While considering this question, we learned that Governor Murrah disapproved of our actions concerning the Tonks and Colonel McCord decided to lay the affair before General E. Kirby Smith. Beef and salt were the only rations we were allowed to issue them in the meantime.

But the problem of a winter camp and feeding the Indians, while using them in defense of the State, was not to be ours longer, because an order came from Colonel McCord that we must transfer them to the nearest Confederate authorities at once. The Military Department of the State would not allow the estimates for the subsistence of the Indians to enter the proposed expenditures. This was at the close of 1863. Still McCord wrote me at the end of the year that the legislature had voted an appropriation for the good of the Tonks and that we would probably be eventually remunerated for our personal expenditures in their behalf. This letter of Colonel McCord's, which came from Austin, also charged me with seeing that the Indians were provided with beef for food.

With the transfer of McCord and six companies of our regiment to detached service, for a while I commanded only four companies in the Northern District and was ranked by Colonel Bourland, of the Border Regiment. In January, 1864, Bourland ordered me to call upon the quartermaster or agents who collected the county tithes to furnish subsistence for the tribe—warriors, women, and children. This he wanted done and he would cover with orders the necessary expenses later. We had about decided to move them to or near his quarters on Red River where he could "protect" and feed them. He added that he thought they would be of much service as trailers.

But the State decided to retain the Indians on their old Reserve, near Belknap, and Y. H. Isbell, from Company "D" of my Command, was selected to take charge of them. This was in June, 1864. We were now in the Confederate service, through an act of the legislature and the recommendation of Governor Murrah, and Isbell had to be recruited from the Confederate service by discharge or transferred to the State service. I so recommended to the Division Commander. Isbell gave bond to the State for ten thousand dollars for the faithful performance of his duties as agent of the Indians. Meantime, I had left that region for service near the coast.

While I was in south Texas, Isbell had charge of the Indians. I had hardly returned to Belknap before I learned, through Major Sparks of the Confederate Headquarters at Waco, that they were no longer a unit at Belknap. One group of the warriors under their chief, Castile, was doing most of the scouting, while another chief, Campo, was at Waco with another group of the Tonks. Sparks wanted me to come or send for them as he was unable to induce them to leave and go back to the agency. Evidently the Indians felt that they had some excuse for getting out of hand; or perhaps they were not handled properly.

Brigadier-General Throckmorton, commanding the First Frontier District, ordered our new State Agent of the Tonkawas on January 9th, 1865, to be transferred and turned the Indians over to me to be subsisted by the Confederate authorities. Isbell transferred the Indians to me on the twentieth and wrote me concerning it. He thought that they were well pleased to be placed again under me. It was his opinion that the Tonks at Waco whom Major Sparks was complaining about should be brought back and forced to assist the others in the frontier service, as they were only a nuisance at Waco. He was to continue to subsist the Indians, although they were no longer his responsibility.

In February, Isbell was on the job securing shirts and guns for the Tonks. The shirts he had made for them and the guns were rifles which used ounce balls. He hoped to secure more guns for them by means of donations through the assistance of Throckmorton. Meanwhile the Indians had to eat and it was hard to get a State man to check the brands of the cattle that they were butchering, because no one wanted to become involved in a lot of red tape and personal expense. I appointed

a Mr. Slaughter to look after this matter until the plan of the
Confederate authorities for furnishing them could be arranged.

This same month I ordered Private A. B. Smith, of Captain Thomson's Company "C", to proceed to Waco or wherever
it should become necessary to go to find the missing part of the
Tonkawa tribe. He was to bring them back to Belknap. If
Campo refused to come and bring the others with him, then he
was to be arrested by the nearest military authority Smith could
find and thrown into jail. Any necessary food and assistance
were to be furnished by quartermasters between Belknap and
Waco.

When Smith arrived at Waco he found the Tonks had
gone. Major Sparks of Waco informed him that the Indians
had been issued five days rations and that they had gone to
Captain Totten's in Bosque County. Totten was to pay them
for recovery of some horses. Sparks thought that they were
now on their way back to the agency having, no doubt, learned
that they were being sought. He advised Smith not to follow
them for that reason. The ponies of the Indians were in bad
condition and some of the Indians were afoot, so they could
only make about eight miles per day. Sparks' advice was supplemented by that of Captain Conner, the inspector general,
and Smith decided to accept it, as the Bosque and Brazos were
swollen and could not be forded in an attempt to follow the
Tonks.

As the war came to a close, I received information that the
governor had suggested to the comptroller that my claim for
subsisting the Tonkawas, while en route from Fort Arbuckle
to Fort Belknap in 1863, should be paid as a debt against the
State. But I was never paid, although the amount was small.

Captain W. T. Moseley was the white officer in command
of the Tonkawa Indians' company and I ordered him to feed
two rations of fresh beef per day until meal or flour could be
procured for them when the regular ration was to be again
issued them.

For some years following the end of the war the Tonkawas were cared for at Fort Griffin on the Clear Fork of the
Brazos by the United States government. Although they were
now only a remnant, some of them acted as scouts for the
United States troops and in the 'seventies some served as guides
for the Rangers. For example, they did effective work with
the Fourth Cavalry and the Sixth Cavalry in 1870. Ten Tonkawas were scouts for the Fourth and five of them scouted for
the Sixth. Again, in 1872, nine Tonkawa scouts were doing the
trailing and spying for General R. S. Mackenzie in a vigorous
campaign against the Comanches in Wheeler County, Texas.
It is said that the Indian scouts did not want to go west of the
Guadalupe with the Rangers against the Lipans because of past
alliances. Some have said that they were afraid, but perhaps
this idea should be taken with the proverbial grain of salt, as
history supports the statements of the Tonkawas. Certainly
there were alliances between the Lipans and Tonkawas against
the Comanches who reviled both tribes. Then, too, raids of
the Tonkawas against their too powerful enemy had decimated
their ranks.

This waning tribe of Indians was moved to the Indian Territory and placed on Oakland Reserve in 1884. There were
about eighty of them. By the time this story was begun they
were said to be almost extinct. The deeds of Placidio are not
forgotten by the students and recorders of Texas History. I
well recall the contact with Castile, my friend and clever scout
of the Tonkawas.

CHAPTER XV

A TRANSFER AND AN INDIAN INVASION

WHILE Colonel McCord and myself were still hoping that the big scout might be made in the fall of 1863, news came of Indian atrocities in Wise and Parker Counties. Some of these were reported in writing to Governor Lubbock in August. The drouthy season and poor mounts made it practically impossible for Captain Rowland's Company at Red River Station to intercept the Indians who came from that direction. It was the opinion of McCord, of the Commanding General and others, as well as of the Tonkawa scouts working with me, that there would be an invasion by the Indians in the fall. If the invasion materialized, it was the desire of the Governor that the companies of the Frontier Regiment under my command be concentrated at Belknap to oppose the expected raid.

Meanwhile, failure to see its plans materialize for raids against the redskins and the lessening of activities of our command above the line, as has been mentioned, did not mean a total cessation of the Regiment's activities. In fact, as the year 1863 faded, and before we were mustered into the Frontier Regiment of Texas Cavalry, Confederate States Provisional Army on March 1, 1864, our regular frontier duties were carried on. One of my companies, C, at Camp Brunson, was to be as embarrassed while on a scout as some of Bourland's men had been when the marauders raided and slipped away before they were discovered. Lieutenant Campbell was commanding a portion of the company on a scout trip up Beaver Creek and along the Big Wichita River. When they found the

Indians, or the Indians found them, it was about the middle of November.

Just before dawn, when the light of the moon was fading, the Indians made a furious surprise attack. Some of them were on horseback and some on foot. They were armed with guns and six shooters. Those on foot engaged the guards while the mounted ones rushed through the horses, stampeded them, and ran them off. Five minutes was the approximate time of the whole engagement. Twenty-four horses and six pack mules were driven away, while one man was seriously wounded in the arm and shoulder. If the Indians were injured by the fire of the troops, it could not be ascertained in the darkness.

The loss of the horses was indeed unfortunate, but the company was further handicapped by sickness of some thirty men with typhoid and winter fevers. No doctor or medicines were available. The nature of the food and the water that had to be consumed while on some scouts was almost sure to cause some sickness among the men. I was to be so fortunate in March, 1864, as to secure a contract with Dr. W. H. Robinson of Tarrant County to perform the duties of medical officer at Belknap. He was to be paid eighty dollars and a soldier's ration. Forage was furnished for his horse. The men who lost their horses were in better luck, in a sense, in that they were given twelve days leave of absence to remount themselves and resume the scouting.

Captain Rowland of Red River Station had thirty men scouting on Cash Creek. These were relieved by another thirty at intervals, so that a fair sized scout might be kept in the field. These men had to be subsisted by supplies sent up from the Station, which, in turn, were secured by details of men and wagons protected by an armed escort. It was doubtful whether this thirty-man scout should be maintained when the question of forage was a problem. The buffaloes were in that section by the thousands and had eaten the grass as they went along, and it was burned on one side of the river.

Encounters with Indians came in series and by 1864 the Indians were clothed, better armed, and equally sagacious and active. When a fight opened, they were for the moment, apparently, cooler headed than some of their opponents, who, in many instances, would have a large per cent of raw recruits present. So engagements between small parties of Indians and whites were usually desperate, with losses nearly equal.

Despite this unromantic and plentifully "risky" type of warfare, there were moments of relaxation in the various companies. There were occasions when we were in camp and had an opportunity to exchange a few books, write letters, and enjoy our mail. I recall that February, 1864, brought a letter from Austin to the effect that I was to receive the money on my muster roll for services under Colonel McCulloch long before. The legislature had made a special appropriation to pay claims of this nature. Now an opportunity would come whereby I could send money to the destitute widows of some of my men who had fallen in conflict with Indians. Powers of attorney had to be forwarded and the money sent to me as I could not leave my district.

Word now came from Fort Arbuckle, through Captain White in command, to the effect that the Northern Indians were concentrating in the Canadian River country. Colonel James Bourland, in command of the Border Regiment with headquarters at Camp Wichita, Texas, wrote me that he thought hostile Indians of different tribes were being concentrated by chiefs Jim Ned, Jim Pockmark, and others, along the Canadian. So he transferred the Chickasaw Battalion to Fort Arbuckle and brought Captain White's company south and placed it on his line of defense.

The companies of Captain Patton and Captain Baylor, which were volunteer forces, had lately joined Bourland. Bourland wrote that with the assistance of the friendly Indians and the aid of my companies, which I was glad to proffer, he felt sufficiently strong to make a move against the hostile tribes. In the same letter he asked for a consultation with me.

Only a few days before, Colonel McCord sent me a copy of a letter from Colonel Bourland to General McCulloch, dated November 10, which had been placed in his hands. The letter contained accusations against the company of Captain Rowland at Red River Station, with regard to their efficiency and loyalty. McCord wrote me that the document was being used in the legislature by enemies of the Regiment. Bourland stated that he had discussed these suspicions with the citizens. Of course the officers of Rowland's company deeply resented the charges, although there may at least have been some lack of industry in their movements. Such talk to the citizens by an officer was dangerous, since there were always those who objected, wisely or unwisely, to the presence of soldiers in their community, although they might be present for their defense.

Regardless of the record of the Frontier Regiment in 1862 and 1863, it was decided by the governor to transfer it or most of its companies to the Confederate service. To take its place, there would be organized state militia companies and these would be assisted by Bourland's Border Regiment. Unfortunately, it was contended by some of the settlers, and no doubt suggested to members of the legislature from the frontier, that this defense would be sufficient. From eastern Texas, since early years, there came an element in the legislature which opposed the appropriation for any force of men that were referred to as Rangers. At this time, Colonel McCord was in Austin and learned that the legislators, in general, were tired of the expense of the Frontier Regiment being on the State. One or two officers, of what later became known as the Border Regiment, another unit near Red River, who were jealous of the accomplishments of the Regiment, and some of the frontier legislators, who had been influenced by adverse criticisms and arguments that the substitution of the state militia for the Regiment would be of less expense, were lobbying, with some effect, against the maintenance of the Regiment, the colonel thought.

Despite these developments, I felt somewhat cheered by a letter from my old commander, Brigadier-General Henry E. McCulloch who wrote:

> Headquarters, Northern Sub. Dist.,
> Bonham, Texas, Dec. 2, '63.
>
> Colonel:
>
> Yours of the 15th of the last month is at hand. I was gratified to hear from you, and proud to see you promoted and still in a position where you can and will be useful to our country by protecting our helpless women and children against the savage Indians; and knowing your faithfulness and energy I need not say a word to you about your own duties but urge you to make others do as you have done. Be vigilant and watchful and whip the Indians when they approach the settlements. Yours is a responsible position; you have not only the great interest of the Service to look to, but to you is entrusted the sacred duty of defending the helpless and to protect those who cannot protect themselves.
>
> I approve the views you express in the letter but do not know that it is practicable to carry them into effect as it may be impossible to furnish supplies to forces as far out as you propose to send them.
>
> I would be gratified to hear from you at any time and let me assure you that I cherish the recollection of our service together on the frontier with great pleasure and satisfaction and most heartily reciprocate every feeling of friendship you entertain for me.
>
> Most respectfully and truly,
>
> Your obt. Svt. & friend,
>
> HENRY E. McCULLOCH,
>
> *Brig. Gen. Cmg. N. S. D.*
>
> Lt. Col. J. B. Barry,
> Texas Frontier Regiment,
> Belknap.

The dawn of the new year saw the Frontier Regiment virtually disrupted. Colonel McCord was transferred with six companies and attached to Bankhead's Brigade. I was stationed at Fort Belknap with the other four and ordered to operate in conjunction with Bourland's Border Regiment. Now with only four companies, I felt the absence of those I had formerly had at my command. Occasionally I was ordered to be on a coöperative march to the south or southeast and, in our absence, in came the Indians and the renegades to regain, in a measure, some of their lost territory. Deserters were increasing and congregating and the burden was increased for those remaining who tried to uphold, in so far as possible, the standards of the years past. In the meantime, as had been expected, the fall brought a heavy Indian raid on Colonel Bourland's portion of the frontier. He pursued but the raiders escaped to their camps which were either on the Pease or the Prairie Dog Rivers. Now it was too late to do anything but try to prevent future raids which were to be looked for when the "light moon" came.

Colonel McCord, who had regretted seeing the Regiment removed from the frontier at the season when danger threatened, through the influence of those who didn't realize or understand the needs of the frontier, was of the opinion that all the forces available would not have been too many to prevent the recent inroads. Adjutant A. H. Lee, who held similar views, wanted me to write to General E. Kirby Smith about the matter and thought that writing would do no harm. In early January, 1864, following the Indian raids in Colonel Bourland's section, in the course of a letter to Adjutant Lee, Colonel McCord couldn't resist writing, "I wonder what the immortal Colonel Bourland thinks now of keeping the Indians out?" But it is more pleasant to recall that Captain Rowland wrote from Red River Station, May 28, 1864, that, "Bourland has done a great deal against our Regiment, especially against this company, and in fact enough to make us have very hard feelings toward him. But he now seems anxious to act jointly and gives us any information of which he comes in possession. And I believe he is doing very good service toward capturing deserters." These deserters were from our old organization as well as Bourland's.

Early in 1864, the organization of the Frontier Militia, as provided for in an act of the legislature, was completed and Major-General J. B. Magruder received the Frontier Regiment commanded by Colonel J. E. McCord. The Governor had tendered the regiment to the Confederate authorities in accordance with the act of the legislature and Magruder had accepted it. Six companies were ordered concentrated at Camp Verde, Fort Inge, and at Fort Duncan, two companies to the camp, while the battalion of two companies was divided; one company being stationed at Camp Colorado and one on the San Saba. The other four companies, "D," "C," "G," and "H," under Captains Rowland, Thompson, White and Whiteside, respectively, were assigned me at Fort Belknap. An order from the State Adjutant and Inspector General's office, by command of Governor Murrah, on February 12th, directed us to muster the regiment into the military service of the Confederate States on the first of March for three years of the war, dating retroactively from the eleventh of February, 1863. Section three of the order praised our services against the Indians and lawless whites infesting the frontier.

In the spring of 1864, we began to take steps to hunt out deserters who were collecting above our line. There was little doubt that there were many in the southwest in the Concho country. Colonel McCord declared that he was going to make them leave there or bring them back as prisoners. He wanted one of my companies for the trip. This was merely the beginning of a drive which was to make, at least, renegades, deserters and over-stayers-of-leave decidedly uneasy during the year.

Many of the deserters congregated in Colonel Bourland's territory in Wise and Denton Counties where Union sentiment was strong. A man named Fox, reputed to be a renegade and leader of a gang of robbers, was a source of terror, for a time, to the people who were for the Confederacy. Colonel Bourland was appealed to and he sent an officer and detachment of men to harass the deserters and bandits.

Another man that the colonel had to drive from the country was named Parnell, formerly of Denton County, who had joined the Union forces at the opening of the war. Parnell returned and became an organizer of the anti-Confederate men. An attack planned by Bourland on Parnell and over a hundred of his followers was heard of and the "Unionists" fled to the southwest to the Concho country and thence made their way toward New Mexico. Even a leader of the state militia in Parker County, J. M. Luckey, turned Unionist and was arrested and taken to Houston when he tried to incite his men to desertion.

I set to work to harass those on the Wichita. Such characters ought, of course, to have been in the ranks. Possibly the service was better without them since no dependability could be placed in them anyway. They should have been made to leave the country. Robbery, plundering and murder could be expected of them later in the spring, with the arrival of warm weather. In some instances men with their families had moved above the line with the idea of emigrating to California with their stock and belongings. Deserters were flocking to them. To see men apparently planning to remove to the country of the enemy or remain outside the settlements among the Indians and threaten to become criminals, was a queer sight when the times and conditions should have called up more than the best in them.

Captain Henry Fossett, of Camp Colorado, moved up the Concho on a scout in late May and found that the deserters had left a week before. There were about five hundred deserters, some families, and forty loaded wagons in the train which had left the head of the Concho. These reports were from settlers who saw them near the mouth of the river. A few of the deserters were men from the companies of Loyd and Whiteside. Later, some fifteen of this type of deserter from Loyd's company were on their way to serve stiff sentences down at the Confederate headquarters at Houston. Some extra stock and beeves were herded along with the caravan. Courts-martial held as frequently as necessary sentenced men absent without leave or those who had overstayed their furloughs to forfeiture of a month's pay and a few weeks at hard labor, in an effort to discourage further desertion from any of our command. To portray these courts-martial would prove tiresome, even if interesting to any possible reader.

During the month of July, 1864, Company "C" sent out four separate scouting expeditions looking particularly for deserters. These scouts, composed of from eight to twenty men, lasted, on an average, for three days and were under the command of Captain Rowland and Lieutenant Giddens. As deserters were not encountered, we began to feel that they were either making themselves scarce or no longer dared to fluant the authority of the State.

In April I was ordered to report with my four companies to Anderson, Grimes County, but the order was revoked early in May by Brigadier-General P. O. Hébert, with headquarters at Houston, and I was ordered to remain at Belknap but to report to General McCulloch by letter. With rumors that we might or might not be ordered away to assist in intercepting a federal invasion, I decided to instill some better discipline than we had deemed necessary for frontier service. Such duties as camp and horse guard, having men sleep at their quarters only, reports of companies daily by eight o'clock, officers of the day duties, and careful posting and relieving of guards, as well as Sunday morning inspection and parade ground monthly inspection, with the men mounted, etc., were rigidly demanded. General McCulloch sent a lieutenant to give special drills, and to coach the men in various unaccustomed regulations of the regular army.

But about the first of August I was directed to take my companies and report to Columbus, Texas. While making this march, we were ordered to change our destination to Harrisburg on Buffalo Bayou, six miles below Houston. A month later brought an order to join Colonel McCord and his companies of our old regiment at Hempstead. Here forage and subsistence were to be had in abundance, quite a delightful experience for men who were accustomed to the limited pack saddle rations of frontier duty. Enfield rifles were furnished us, and we felt ready for action. It happened, however, that our duty was to guard five hundred prisoners sent there from Tyler.

Out on the frontier from which we had been transferred things now became more lively than they had been in some time. Marauding parties of Indians invariably came into the settlements on the full of the moon and there was hardly a moon that settlers did not have more or less conflicts with them. In fact, there were many, but I shall mention only one. These Indians were known as the "Pin Indians;" that is, all the Indians who were on the side of the Union, mostly Comanches.

On one occasion, these "Pin Indians" came in on the Brazos, near old Fort Belknap, in the fall of 1864. According to their own report they were one thousand strong. They killed and carried away into captivity over twenty persons and drove off hundreds of cattle. They would have done much more damage but for the opposition of the company of forty Rangers who met them in a desperate fight. At the same time some two hundred of them attacked George Bragg's little one-room picket house, in which seventeen women and children had sought protection, with only four men to defend them. The little house had but one door and there was no shutter for it. However, the four men had plenty of arms and were expert shots. Twice the Indians tried to charge through the door, but the four men, with six shooters and bowie knives, soon had the doorstep, a large flat rock, slippery with blood. When one of the charging Indians had been fatally wounded and could not get off the rock, the others would drag him off.

Then they attempted to prize down the house, but when they would prize apart the pickets, they were met with a volley of bullets through the crack, which their levers, or prize poles, had made. Meanwhile, the Indians maintained a crossfire through the door which ranged into every portion of the little house except the corners, on each side of the door, where the women and children had taken shelter and were loading the men's guns for them. One of the men, "Doc" Wilson, was killed, another, Joe Bragg, was shot through the lungs, while the third, old man Hamby, was wounded. But they had those women and children to protect and they never ceased shooting so long as the women would hand them a loaded gun. The fourth man, young Hamby, who was home on furlough, was also slightly wounded.

The Indians would have killed and captured them all soon, but at this critical moment, the company of Rangers, mentioned above, and some citizens entered the fray. Messrs. Bragg and Hamby once told me that they could hear the firing of the Rangers, although they were two miles away. The Indians attacking Bragg's house also heard the shooting and ran off toward the scene of the battle being waged by the Rangers. Several of the Rangers who had come to the rescue were killed while the others were now driven by the Indians to seek refuge in Fort Murray, where there were some forty odd men. In the fort there were also over a hundred women and children, and my wife's parents and five of her brothers were with them.

In this fight between the Rangers of Colonel Bourland and citizens against the Indians, two men were killed at or near their own home, which was the scene of the fight. (I believe their name was Prophets.) Two of the Rangers took the wives of these men up behind them on their horses, during the thickest of the fight, and resumed the retreat to Fort Murray, across the Brazos River, which they safely reached. It was in covering their retreat that many of the Rangers and citizens sacrificed their lives.

One of the citizens who was in this engagement, a Mr. John Wooten, with whom I was well acquainted, afterward told me of an interesting experience he had at the time. Just as the Rangers were retreating across the river to Fort Murray, his horse was shot from under him. When the horse fell, his gun was propelled into the mud so that the muzzle was filled. The gun was empty at the moment of the fall and now that the mud had clogged the barrel, he could not have reloaded it if he had had the time. As he was on foot with the Indians now between him and the retreating Rangers, he saw no chance of escape.

But he started in a run across the three miles of prairie in an effort to save his life. Two young warriors ran up to him, and although his gun was not loaded and dirt was in the barrel he presented it as though he would shoot. One of the Indians hurriedly spoke to him in English, calling him by name. The Indian exclaimed, "Don't shoot me, Wooten! Don't shoot! You run!" Every time Wooten would point his gun the Indian would tell him not to shoot but to run. They presented their arrows at him and told him that if he did not run they would shoot him. "Run, Wooten, run! You know me, Wooten. I know you long time 'go. You fed me on beef, Camp Cooper. Me know you, Wooten. You run!"

So Wooten ran. He ran for three miles across this open space. Then the two warriors wanted to talk but he had no talk for them. So they left him and started back toward the conflict, with the parting admonition, "Run, Wooten!" Wooten told me that he was convinced that these two young warriors had formed an attachment for him while he was butchering beef and issuing rations to them when they were reservation Indians in Texas several years before. Now they had joined the "Pin Indians," after their removal to the Territory. He thought they had done all this running to get him out of sight of the other Indians and thus save his life. The long run caused him to spit up blood and, it was thought, shortened his life.

The Indians hovered around Fort Murray until dark, apparently counseling whether or not to storm it. The surrounding country was open prairie and the redskins were in plain view all the evening. My wife's father, David Peveler, and Judge Harmonson, with the use of their spy glasses, counted over seven hundred. But as the Indians had large number reconnoitering, no doubt there were the full thousand they claimed. They paid a heavy price for every cowboy or ranchman they killed.

The family of Joseph Myers, a ranchman, and also a neighboring family, fled when they saw the Indians coming. They hid in a thicket, under a large rock. Myers had been cut off from the house and was killed after a bloody, desperate, and single-handed fight with over a hundred of the Indians. It was believed from the signs of the fight, and what was afterwards learned, that he killed at least half a dozen or more before they had the opportunity to scalp him. They cut off his arms and legs and otherwise mutilated his body in a savage manner. His body was found in this horrible condition the next day.

The dogs followed Myers' family into the thicket and betrayed their hiding place under the rock. The Indians were on the rock and tried to persuade them to come out, saying that they were friendly Indians and would do them no harm. But the women had heard too much shooting, knew who had been doing it, and so they remained silent. These Indians now heard the shooting at the little house of George Bragg and they left to go there.

In Fort Murray, the people had been praying for darkness in order that a messenger might be dispatched for aid. As soon as it was dark a volunteer was called for who would go to Weatherford, in Parker County, for reinforcements and to carry the news of the invasion of the redskins to the people of the settlements between Fort Murray and Weatherford. One of my wife's brothers, Francis Peveler, (later of Granbury, Texas) about grown, said, "I'll take that job! Not because I'm brave, but because I believe the Indians will storm Fort Murray tonight or at daybreak and I've the best horse in the fort; he will carry me quicker to Weatherford than any other." So he mounted and rode the distance, seventy-five miles, without dismounting. By sunrise he had organized a relief crowd and was on his way back.

The Indians had had, on the whole, rather poor luck in killing and capturing families. They had driven the company of Rangers into Fort Murray but they did not know how many men there were in the fort. So they decided to start on their homeward journey toward Red River. They drove off several thousand head of cattle belonging to the men they had been fighting in and around Fort Murray. The reinforcements from Weatherford arrived and followed the raiders almost to Red River. But the Indians had a two-days' start and the chase was given up near the river as futile.

Among the few prisoners they did take with them was the family of Brit Johnson, a well thought of colored man and daring frontiersman. He was away from home at the time. The same raid saw Johnson's late master lose two daughters. Master and former slave were frantic in their desire to attempt a rescue. So it was decided, several months later, that Brit should be equipped by the white man and go among the Comanches in an effort to effect a rescue. After living with the Indians for a time, winning their confidence, and being adopted into one of their families, he found a chance to try for a rescue. He secured one of his old master's daughters and his own family and stole away with them when the redskins were away on a hunting trip.

But the noble fellow lost his life to some of these same Comanches about five years later. He was out hunting with two negro friends in Parker County, when a band of Comanches rushed them. Brit's comrades were quickly killed but he fought in frontier style against some two dozen Comanches. It was later learned that the opponents recognized each other. Poor Brit was finally killed and his body was horribly mutilated. He must have taken some toll as his body was found by a heap of cartridge shells.

Before these events occurred, I had been ordered by General Walker to Houston. My companies were to take the place of troops who had been sent to Louisiana to check the advance of the federals under Banks by way of Red River. When General Walker became convinced that a thousand hostile Indians had invaded the settlements on the Brazos River, he forthwith ordered me back. On my way to my old headquarters, I felt sick and thought that I was taking the yellow fever. (General Walker had trouble with sickness among his men and moved out to Grimes Prairie.) So I lay over at Marlin two days and never took over my command until they arrived at Fort Belknap. Their families and all that they had was on the frontier and they wasted no time in getting back.

It was during my absence that this raid of October, 1864, in Young County, was made. Five of the Rangers were reported killed and several were wounded while eleven citizens were killed and seven women and children were taken captives. During my absence, Colonel James Bourland, commanding the Border Regiment, took charge of the frontier from the Brazos to the Red River, and it was a company of his regiment that the Indians drove into Fort Murray. When I had had command of that portion of our frontier from the Colorado to the Brazos, the first advice I gave to the frontier settlers was to fort up the best they could. They could attend to their stock and have their children safer at school in a fort than they could if they were scattered, each family to itself.

I will here give a brief description of the plan of the construction of these hurriedly built settlers' forts. The houses were built in line on four sides, leaving a hollow square of one hundred yards or more. They filled the spaces between the houses with logs set up end wise, two or more feet in the ground, and on a direct line with the outside or back of the houses. There were packet or picket bastions at two corners

large enough to hold ten or a dozen men whose firing would
range down all four sides of the picket fort. It was on the
blockhouse plan although they did not have the blockhouses.
This means of defense, no doubt, saved many women and
children from the scalping knife.

CHAPTER XVI

THE DOVE CREEK FIGHT

ON OCTOBER 1, 1864, an order arrived from Major-General J. G. Walker at Headquarters of the Military District, directing me to proceed with my four companies of McCord's Regiment to Fort Belknap. There, I was to make such disposition of my troops as would best protect the inhabitants of the frontier. A second special order on the heels of this one ordering my return to Indian warfare, authorized me to take a tax in kind in the counties in my vicinity. If necessary, I was to impress forage and provisions essential for my men's subsistence, under the provisions of the Impressment Laws. Of course, needs of families for bread, forage for their horses, seed, and gifts purchased by counties for needy families were not to be impressed. Prices were to be fixed by the commissioners.

I reported to Colonel Bourland of the Border Regiment, as I was to coöperate with him. The colonel saw fit to attach Captain Henry Fossett's Frontier Battalion to my command. Our work largely consisted of scouts to prevent the Indians from coming in and driving off the cattle of the settlers. Furloughs and details of men on other business was forbidden, and care was taken on marches to discourage any possible quitter from attempting to leave.

The regular work of scouring the country for Indian signs and any men absent without leave from their commands was resumed. I made it a point when ordering out troops on scouts to caution the officers about keeping their commands in regular and good order, taking care of any public property, and posting a strong guard when camped, especially during the night. Flankers or spies were frequently cautioned when traversing certain sections of the country. Rigid requirements concerning Sunday inspection by the company commanders and monthly inspections by the commanding officer were made.

Still the hours of service were not unreasonably exacting. Roll call and mounting of the horse guard, at sunrise, which was then on duty until seven P. M., and roll call at six o'clock in the evening saw the companies assembled. Regular guards were posted immediately after the morning roll call and the night guards were on duty at eight. The sound of the bugle assembled the men at the parade ground at the above morning and evening hours. Blasts of the bugle at other than the regular hours of assembling required all officers and men to repair to the parade ground immediately.

Monthly returns were sent in to my headquarters at Fort Belknap by the fifth of the month. Failure to do so meant disobedience of orders and arrest, unless a reasonable excuse in writing was rendered by this date. In turn, I forwarded my reports by the tenth. These company statements were generally sent by the regular courier, but if he did not bring them a special courier was to be sent. If corrections were essential they were returned to the officer commanding the company and twenty-four hours allowed for the correction.

The captains generally drew up rules to be observed by scouting parties from their companies. Captain Fossett, in command of Fossett's Battalion, sent me a copy of the rules he had issued on December 14th, for use during the winter of 1864-1865. They were as follows:

Camp Colorado, Dec. 14, 1864.

I.   There will be a roll call every morning and evening at which every man will attend who is not on duty or reported sick. One non-commissioned officer will invariably attend.

II. There will be a guard every night of eight men who will act as relief officers.. When not enough non-commissioned officers are in Camp, lance corporals will be appointed. A commissioned officer will visit the guard at least four times a week.

III. Six men will accompany the horses on herd during the day. The men on horse guard will carry their usual arms— always a gun and ammunition—they will keep their horses saddled and staked. No sleeping or card playing allowed on horse herd. If horses are lost the men losing them will hunt them up.

IV. Men will not leave camp to be absent from roll call without permission of commanding officer of Company.

V. Horses or mules will not be brought upon the parade ground except with loaded wagons—and no trees will be injured.

VI. Men will not suffer their company horses to run loose day or night.

VII. There will be an inspection of post every Saturday morning, and the men will be required to keep their rooms orderly and to remove all brush and filth from the barracks and parade ground.

VIII. No public animals will be used for any other purpose than that for which the regiment intended them and they will not be used by the men either in or out of camp.

IX. It is the duty of all officers commissioned and non-commissioned to see that the foregoing are carried out.

Col. Barry:

The above have generally been the rules usual for the government of the battalion when in camps—always when there has been a guard or more in camps—of each company.

HENRY FOSSETT,
Capt. Cmg. Fos. Batn.

Shortly after I received this note from Captain Fossett concerning camp rules for his command, he participated in one of the most widely heralded Indian fights in the history of Texas. It occurred early in January, 1865, and was, perhaps, the big fight of the times in that so many were engaged on both sides. It was not a victory for the whites but was courageously enough fought by the contestants. This interesting engagement is known in the histories of Texas as the "Battle of Dove Creek", but it has been very briefly mentioned. The details of the conflict came to me through letters, special reports, company returns, and personal interviews, so that I had both oral and written accounts of what occurred. Perhaps it is sufficiently interesting to record here.

A letter from N. W. Gillentine, captain of a company of militia of Erath County in the Second Frontier District, on December 9, 1864, reached me a few days later and introduced the story. He was out on a scout with twenty men and had come to the Clear Fork of the Brazos at Phantom Hill. Ascending this river about thirty miles he found considerable horse sign. A brief examination revealed that a large party of Indians had camped. Apparently, there were nearly one hundred wigwams and some ten tents. The party was judged to total five hundred (it was learned later that there were over three times this number) and to have broken camp some forty-eight hours before. They had moved off slowly up the Clear Fork, leaving a trail some one hundred yards wide.

Following the trail they found a grave, which they opened in an attempt to identify the tribe of Indians. The grave contained the body of a female, just buried, and very richly adorned. Some articles in the grave and some of the decorative articles of dress were taken and the captain stated that he intended to send me one of the moccasins. He thought that the Indians were not aware that they were being followed and wanted me to join him with a sufficient force of men to make an attack. He wrote that he would wait for me on Paint Creek. Meanwhile, he gave the alarm throughout the settlements in the counties of Bosque, Brown, Comanche, Coryell, Erath, Hamilton, and one or two others, and the militia began to assemble to take the trail. But I could spare only a portion of my force, and the uncertainty of the strength or the identity of the Indians, together with other duties, did not seem to me to warrant my joining him. But I dispatched what force I had available to act as scouts and assist the militia in any possible engagement.

Out of the opening of the grave incident there came a story which came to be a tradition related around camp fires and firesides for many years afterwards. It was to the effect that some of Gillentine's men opposed the opening of the grave in which was found the body of the squaw. Finding their opposition to be of no avail, they protested against the taking of various trinkets, beads, and portions of clothing as souvenirs. But they were laughed down by some of their comrades who took the relics with which the body was so richly dressed. Those who were jibed for their protests asserted, with wry grins, that their trinkets might prove to be "bad medicine" for them. But the men encountered no visible results of their ghoulish act until the battle, a few days later, with these Indians they were trailing, when every possessor of a trinket met death in the fight.

This discovery of Indians in numbers I mentioned in a dispatch to General J. W. Throckmorton. In his reply, written from Decatur, he gave the opinion that these Indians were the same band of Kickapoos that had been reported to have left the Kansas border to depredate below the Red River. They probably intended to remain along the fringe of the border settlements during the winter and plunder, thought Throckmorton. It was his opinion that the forces we had to spare in attacking these invaders of the State would prove too small and that more men mounted on good horses might capture "the whole body."

The general was commanding the state forces of the First Frontier District with headquarters at Decatur, Wise County. He wrote two or three days later that everything was quiet in his section, but that he was anxiously waiting to hear of our success against the "band of Indians reported moving toward the Colorado." He was not to have to wait long to hear of the battle which occurred.

On December 23, I issued "Special Order, No. 31" to Lieutenant Giddens to take some men from the four companies, C-D-E-G, of my battalion, and others from the two companies of Fossett's Battalion and proceed hurriedly to Fort Chadbourne. At Chadbourne he was to meet with other forces of the two battalions and turn over his men to the senior officer of either Fossett's or my battalion. This order carried by Lieutenant Giddens also required the senior officer who assumed command to coöperate with any state troops that might be there, for the purpose of capturing or routing any Indians on our frontier. The senior officer in command was to return to my headquarters a correct roll of the officers and men who participated in the scout, with remarks of interest and information. In the meantime, I had ordered Fossett to Chadbourne.

Fossett arrived at Chadbourne the last day of the year with fifty from his battalion. He was joined by Lieutenants Brooks, Carpenter, and Giddens with sixty men from the Frontier Regiment. Captain Cureton from Bosque County had seventeen militiamen and Lieutenant Morton of Brown County had thirty. Two days were devoted to waiting for the arrival of Captain Totten, commander of Company "A" of the Second Frontier District, who brought up several times more militia than those already assembled. Approximately four hundred men of the militia were present when all had arrived. Among the leaders of this last group of militia who arrived under command of Captain Totten, were Captains Rice of Hamilton County, James Cunningham of Comanche County and Culver of Coryell County. The two forces were not to march together, however, as Fossett with his small command of Confederate troops was to scout ahead. The march of Totten's men from the settlements to this point was briefly portrayed by my friend Judge Scrutchfield of Bosque County, in his diary, which he kept of the entire expedition. His entries read:

Friday, December 16, 1864: Order came for the militia to meet at Meridian on the 18th. Captain Gillintine had discovered a camp and trail of Indians on the Clear Fork of the Brazos, thirty-five miles above Fort Phantom Hill. Capt. Totten and I started to Waco in the evening and I rode until late in the night.

December 17: We got to Waco, bought 6,000 caps, got four Tonks (for trailers). Captain left that night for home. I stayed.

December 18: Came home with Indians.

December 19: Reached Meridian at 9 o'clock in the night in rain.

December 20: Reached Wiley's store in the snow.

December 21: Reached Stephenville. Snow deep.

December 22: Camped six miles above Stephenville.

December 23: Marched to Jamison's Peak and camped; horses stampeded in the night.

December 24: Stayed in camp all day. Hunted horses.

December 25: Marched all day, camped above Flanigan's ranch.

December 26: Reached Camp Salmon. Company organized. Whole strength 500 men.

Fossett led out up the Colorado to find the Indian trail. Next day they found where the Indians had camped on the banks of the river. Two camps had been made; one with one hundred and fifteen wigwams and another large one a short distance up the river. Some two weeks had elapsed since the Indians had left these camps. As there was no grass along the river, the men decided to follow the trail to grass and water.

Some ten miles farther was found the site of another camp and at night, twenty miles distant, they came to where the redskins had had a camping place on the North Concho. Here were signs of some one hundred and sixty wigwams which were many more than had been supposed. The Indians had left this camp only a week before. Captain Fossett and his men waited here two days, sending spies ahead and waiting for the other division of the men, led by Captain Totten, to come up.

On the morning of the 7th, the spies returned to report that they had discovered the Indians encamped at Dove Creek. This stream emptied into the South Concho on the south side. It was about thirty miles distant. Captain Totten's men had not yet appeared.

Fossett and his officers concluded that perhaps Totten had followed another Indian trail which was reported as being situated above theirs. So it was decided to advance and attack the camps at daylight the next morning with the forces in hand. A halt was made at two o'clock P. M., some twelve miles from the camp of the Indians, to eat dinner and put their arms in readiness. Lieutenant Mulkey and some men were sent forward to look over the plan of the camps and report back by night.

Just before night, as they were about to move forward, Captains Gillentine and Barnes came up. They reported that Captain Totten and his men were only fifteen miles behind. It was believed that he could arrive in time to assist in the planned attack. Men were sent back to guide him forward to those waiting, but he was farther back than supposed, and did not arrive until next morning, January 8th. The progress of Totten's men may be visualized quickly by again referring to the brief recordings in Scrutchfield's diary:

December 27: Marched all day and camped at night in mesquite flat on Hubbard's Creek.

December 28: Left camp in the evening and marched five miles and camped.

December 29: Marched three miles and camped.

December 30: March all day. Camp on the Clear Fork. No grass. Very cold.

December 31: March half day to grass. Kill several buffaloes.

January 1: Marched to Elm Creek, close to Indian Trail. Camped and killed several buffaloes in the evening.

January 2: Marched to Little Elm Creek on the trail. Went out in the evening and killed a buffalo. Saw the Double Mountains, high-topped hills on the head of the Brazos.

January 3: March on trail to head of Elm Creek and camp in a flat.

January 4: March on trail to Oak Creek.

January 5: Reached the Colorado.

January 6: [Manuscript too dim to decipher.]

January 7: Camped on the Concho. At 9 o'clock express came from Captain Fossett that the Indians' camp was discovered thirty-five miles distant. In saddle in ten minutes. March until two o'clock. Halt, form a line and issue caps. March on until day the

8th, dismount, load guns, mount and ride on across Spring Creek.
Join Fossett. . . .

Totten's men reached Fossett's camp about nine o'clock.
The officers held a council of war. As the camp of the Indians,
which was some three-fourths of a mile in length, was in a
large thicket, accessible only by a few narrow paths, and along
the creek, it was well fortified by nature. The horses of Totten's men were rather spent, and it was decided to have him
attack the camps with his men dismounted. Fossett would lead
the troops to cut off the Indians, in which he was to be assisted
by the Tonk scouts, and try to intercept any Indians rushing
from them or attempting to scatter from the camp. Fossett was
to attack the upper and Totten the lower division of the camp.

When all was apparently in readiness and every eighth man
was detailed to hold horses, because an effort was to be made to
drive the Indians from the thicket, the attack was launched. To
get at the Indians, it was necessary to wade Dove Creek which
was from knee to waist deep, and afforded the Indians a fine
opportunity to inflict severe losses. But Captain Totten and his
force rushed bravely in and took possession, it seemed, of a
greater part of the camp. For an hour the fight was fierce and
bloody. However, as the militia held a portion of the camp, it
seemed that they were winning. But now the Indians began to
scatter through the brush, keeping up a rapid discharge of
their arms, which were long ranged and of good make, and
there was little chance of returning their shots with fatal results to many. Among those who fell before the fire of the
redskins was Captain Culver of Coryell County. More of the
men fell, and the others were becoming discouraged by seeing
their comrades shot down by a foe it was impossible to reach.

Captain Totten saw the critical situation and shouted an
order to his men to load their guns and prepare to retreat. The
war chief of the Indians heard and understood the order and
ordered his braves to charge through the thicket and they came

pouring back and sifting through the irregular line of whites. There was a moment of hand to hand fighting and then the men began to give back under the force of superior numbers. But among those men who were anxious to get in a fair shot at the foe which had paused to pour in a heavier fire and now remained hidden behind embankments as much as possible, was Captain Gillentine. Together with Captain Cunningham and John Anderson of Cunningham's men, he was firing from behind an embankment but realized that he was overshooting as he could see little to fire at. So he declared his intention of climbing on top of the bank and trying for just one shot. His companions attempted, without success, to restrain him from what meant certain death. He climbed to the top of the bank, took a step forward, and fired his gun. Then he turned to Anderson, who had asked him if he was hit, and handed him his gun, with the reply, "John, I am a dead man." Anderson helped him down and started to the rear with him but met some of the captain's men and was relieved of his burden. Captain Barnes and more of the men fell and the others were about to become panicky at the realization that when they started to retreat the fire of the wily foe had increased in effectiveness. Fossett's men were completely cut off from those of Totten. So when the retreat was begun, it was hard to keep the men in any kind of order, although Captain James Cunningham's men were attempting to act as a sort of rear guard of the retreat. The losses of the whites were kept down by the poor marksmanship of the Indians who overshot most of the time. The Indians flanked the retreating men on both sides and also attacked in the rear with their long range rifles. But Totten's men were determined not to be forced to endure this sort of retreat and they halted, rallied, and drove the Indians back into their camp. This last aggressive movement was then followed by a resumption of the retreat. After falling back to another creek some three miles distant, camp was made about

the end of the day. Just as the sun went down, the wounded
Captain Gillentine died.

At the beginning of the fight, the Confederate troops of
Fossett, aided by the militiamen of Cureton and Morton, and
the Tonk scouts, made a mounted charge and captured most of
the horses, nearly a thousand in number, which were near the
camp. Skirmishes with the Indians were continuous as they
wanted to recover their horses. As parties of them attacked,
the men resisted bravely, killing them and driving them back
into the thicket. But later, when the fighting at the camp had
ceased, the Indians pressed forward in numbers, fighting
furiously. For five hours the struggle raged, sometimes the
troops giving ground and again driving the Indians back into
the thicket. It was easily seen that these Indians had come into
Texas with better guns and ammunition than the troops had.
With their longer ranged and superior guns they tried to fight
at long distances. The men would charge them bravely and
when the Indians would sally after them, they would frequently manage to cut one of the braves off and kill him.

A large portion of the Indians now carried on the fight
with Fossett's men, who were on the defensive, and the others
were enabled to concentrate on stealing back their horses. This
they were able to do. It was not realized by the troops at the
time, but the Indians were no doubt preparing to begin a retreat and rear guard defense if driven to it. This they were not
forced to do. Some two hours before night the Indians with-
drew into the thicket, and the whites did not follow them. The
fight had closed.

Fossett reported that his officers had acquitted themselves
honorably, and many of the soldiers fought with marked courage. Armed chiefly with shot guns and common rifles, they
were at a disadvantage. One officer of the troops, Lieutenant
Giddens, a good officer and a splendid man, was mortally
wounded and seven men were killed. (The lieutenant died
later at Chisum's Ranch on the Concho, and his effects at Bel-

knap were turned over to the quartermaster for safe keeping.)
Ten men were seriously wounded. Twenty-three Indians were
known to be killed and it was believed they lost seven others.

Fossett had had no chance to unite his force with that of
Totten, but he now came into Totten's camp at the close of
the day. The combined losses were checked and showed twenty-
three killed in the battle and some sixty seriously wounded, a
few of whom died later. Sixty or seventy horses were killed
or disabled in the fight. Plans were suggested concerning a re-
newal of the fight, if the Indians could be found. But, pack
horses and provisions had been left behind when the last few
hurried miles of marching to the battle had begun, so now
there was no food. And about ten o'clock it began snowing.
Next morning there was a nine- or ten-inch snow on the ground
and there was no forage for the horses. So the only alternative
seemed to be to seek the settlements at the mouth of the Concho. Captain Gillentine and the other dead would be buried
there. Totten was to go back with twenty-five men and see if
the Indians had left. He was to bury the dead left on the field
of battle. With no food and deep snow to impede their return
march, the men were becoming very hungry. So, for supper,
they butchered some of the few Indian ponies which had not
been recaptured by the Indians because the Tonks saw what
was coming and pushed away toward the pack mules some
seventy-five head of them.

After the snow had melted somewhat, next day, the
wounded were placed on crude litters made of two poles
strapped to horses, and the men moved on down the Concho.
The pack mules were intercepted on the third day and enough
provisions were had for one good meal. A detail was sent out to
kill some beeves, when they reached the Colorado country.
Eighteen head were secured and after some three days devoted
to overtaking the men, despite the lack of a trail which had
been obliterated by additional snow, a good meal was had from
the beef. When the Chisum ranch was reached, more provisions

were secured and, after a night's camping, the men made their way home in scattered groups.

Some comments on the fight and the story of the dreary march home afterward, is concisely but rather vividly narrated in Scrutchfield's diary, thus:

> Made the attack. Got whipped. Twenty men killed and twenty-five wounded. Fell back six miles to Spring Creek, a running creek.
>
> January 9: Stayed in camp; snow fifteen inches deep.
>
> January 10: Marched down the Concho carrying the wounded on litters—snow deep—starvation in the camp. Camped on the Concho.
>
> January 11: March all day.
>
> January 12: Stayed in camp and sold the Indian horses. Two men dead, still carrying corpses on litter.
>
> January 13: March all day and camp at night in bed of a creek.
>
> January 14: Reach settlement on the Concho.
>
> January 15: Bury the dead and cross the Colorado River and camp on Elm Creek.
>
> January 16: Camp on Muke Water.
>
> January 17: Cross Pecan Bayou.
>
> January 18: Cross the mountains.
>
> January 19: Cross the Leon.
>
> January 20: Reach Mills Creek.
>
> January 21: Reach home.

There was little humor in evidence in so serious a conflict at the time it occurred but two or three well known Indian fighters used to tell something of their feelings during the fight. Dr. J. R. Alford of Hico, Texas, who was a lieutenant in Captain Rice's company, was near Captain Culver who was killed almost instantly during the heavy fighting of the first hour of the engagement. As Culver fell he gasped and said, "Oh, Lord!" This remark, coupled with the shock of his friend's sudden end, together with bullets whistling about his ears, caused Alford, so he said, to "feel like I wanted to be away from there." And when the order came to retreat, "I tell you we were not long in getting out of the thicket," the old frontiersman, wryly and modestly, added.

John Anderson of Comanche County had a bit of fun at his own joke concerning the attempt of his friend Ike Richardson and himself to quench their thirst during the fighting. They started up the creek to get to where they thought they could get down on hands and knees to drink and yet escape the murderous rifle fire that had been whistling about their heads. Before quite reaching the place they were going to drink from, John happened to glance into the brush at his left and saw the trunks of the small trees and logs bristling with the rifle barrels of the Indians. He told Ike to look. Then Ike said, "Ha! Ha! I don't want any water either." And they didn't go on after the water, which was plainly exposed to the nearest Indians, although the two friends had not yet been seen by the redskins.

When night descended on the scene of the battle, the Indians built up fires around their encampment, packed up, and marched in a southwesterly direction, as they had been traveling, toward Mexico. They traveled across the Staked Plains in the worst snow storm in the memory of the country's oldest settlers. They no doubt suffered terribly from the cold, as it was afterwards ascertained that they lost more from the march and exposure of their wounded and the children than they had in the battle.

When Totten went back to the battle ground he found and buried the dead whites, with the exception of one man whom he could not find. The dead were unscalped, although they had been stripped of most of their clothing. Wild animals had not molested them and the bodies were in a good state of preservation due to the cold weather. The Indians had left the night after the battle and also abandoned their dead, twenty-three in number, and much of their camp equipage and cooking utensils. Only two Indians were seen and they were gathering up the scattered horses that had been left.

Fossett's report estimated that there were several hundred warriors and that the Indians were from the vicinity of the

Kansas River, Kansas. Perhaps this last opinion was influenced by the finding of a pass on the body of one of the Indians from the Potawatamie Agency in Kansas. There were a few white men with them, and it was supposed by Fossett and others that they were contemplating raids on the settlements.

Later we were to learn that these Indians were a band of Kickapoos who were journeying across Texas to join their tribe in Mexico. Early in the war they had fought under orders from the Federals against the civilized tribes of Indian Territory, who were partisans of the Confederacy. It may have been that they were merely migrating across Texas with no intention of raiding at this time. Certainly they robbed and killed plenty of Texans later, operating from the south side of the Rio Grande. But Indians, with a few well known exceptions, were not supposed to be within the boundaries of Texas since 1859. The long-suffering frontiersmen who were included in this group of attacking militia had appealed to me to help crush or drive out the strange redskins.

Mexico and the United States had agreed to the migration of the Indians, but the emigrants selected a poor time—during the War Between the States—for their crossing. General Throckmorton's information on the possible identity of these Indians was wider than mine and he thought that they were merely in our State for depredations. They had no recognition, and orders from the highest authorities were to treat them accordingly as wild Indians.

CHAPTER XVII

LAST SCOUTING: THE END OF THE WAR

ONE of the grave problems which faced the men of the frontier in the late winter of 1864-65 was an economic one. Families of troops in my detached companies of McCord's Frontier Regiment and those of Bourland's Border Regiment faced starvation. The fall of 1864 was a droughty one and the wheat crop was a failure due to lack of rain at the time of seeding. A severe winter had only made prospects more hopeless. Chances to secure something to eat were certainly gloomy.

Arrival of the latter portion of February reminded us that a crop of corn was perhaps our section's only salvation. Many families had no one at home capable of planting corn and sowing oats. So Colonel Bourland wrote the commanding officer of the North Sub District for permission to grant furloughs to some of the men which would enable them to start a little crop. Many had small boys at home who could cultivate a few acres if it could be planted for them. Only a few of us possessed negroes. Moreover forage was not to be had for the horses and these animals were in poor condition.

General McCulloch replied from his headquarters at Bonham and admitted the necessity of having as much corn planted in the frontier counties as possible. So he ordered that our men be granted furloughs which would allow them fifteen days at home. A maximum of one-third of Bourland's and my command were to be granted this permission. Only men who would be sure to make the best use of their opportunity in the fields were to go, and we were to try to have them again in camp by the full moon in March. The last day of March was to be

the deadline for their answer to roll call in camp. This order
was dated February 18th.

In the meantime, all of the tithe corn at the camps where
troops were under my command, namely, Camp McCord,
Camp Colorado, and Fort Belknap, had been consumed. Some
of the horses died of pure starvation and others were approaching that state. My quartermaster did not have sufficient funds to
purchase feed and the grass in the woods along the Indian
passway had proven insufficient. Hauling of feedstuff was tried
but the distance was great, the weather cold, and the teams
consumed the better half of the loads before it arrived. So I
wrote McCulloch for an order to impress supplies for needs
of my men. At the same time I suggested that if we could be
assured of continuance in that region, that hauling could be
done when the grass came and thus provide for good military
service in the coming winter and spring. In fact, this would
have been my plans for the present had I not been constantly
faced with orders concerning my departure toward Houston,
which eventually came.

As I had been assigned to report to Colonel Bourland for
orders, I received his order attached to General McCulloch's
giving one-third of the men furloughs. The distance from
Gainesville to my men at Camps McCord and Colorado caused
the order to be received some days later. My men were to
be required to report to me for their furloughs properly filled
out and these were to be forwarded through the proper military channels to Colonel Bourland for his approval and return. From Fort Belknap to Camp Colorado was a three days'
ride and two days would be consumed in preparing the furloughs, while it required seven days to go from Colorado to
Gainesville. One day would be devoted to approving the furloughs and seven days would be used in returning them to the
men at Colorado. Bourland's order reached me on March
fourth and a twenty-day consumption of time in executing Mc-
Culloch's order, as demanded by Bourland, would see the

twenty-fifth on the calendar. Thus the men would have only five days which would not be sufficient to more than allow them to reach their homes and return by continuous travel, if they could do it that quickly. On the other hand, Bourland's men, near to their homes and with the order already being executed in their camp, would have the full two weeks benefit of the furlough as intended.

So I wrote General McCulloch that I believed, as he had written, that he wanted all the men to have fifteen days and that I was granting them furloughs in strict accordance with the construction that I had put upon his order, not in disrespect to Bourland's order but because there was no time for it. Thus I was forced, as I saw it, to cut some of the military red tape because of seeing justice done to the men under my command. In the spring, permission to grant men leave to go home and secure their wheat crops, where there was any, was secured more easily. In a few other emergencies in the frontier service I had to assume authority rather than wait for the approval of the General, because of the distance and the time involved. For instance, on one occasion I allowed some of my men to leave to secure remounts and clothe themselves when it could be done in a short time and was obviously a necessity. These men were held strictly accountable to me and realized it and so they respected the order.

This last case was reported to General McCulloch through Bourland and I received a firm rebuke and warning as a result. But an explanation to the General brought a flattering response concerning his opinion of my motives and his personal regard. He hoped that I would find it practical to "comply more fully" with the rules but realized that there were good reasons for many irregularities that I was forced to permit in the interest of the service. I was not careless nor disrespectful of regulations, as I believe my own men knew, but was simply unwilling to allow petty requirements to work grave injury. After all, the frontier service was rather different from that of the regular service of the Confederate armies. Years later, I read from a letter of General McCulloch to the assistant Adjutant General a statement that contained information which helped explain some of Bourland's behavior. One sentence read, "Colonel Bourland is getting old, is in feeble health, and desires to be relieved from the service."

The depletion of the mounts in my command because of starvation forced me to request of the General an order to purchase additional horses and mules. For long scouts, we needed thirty-six pack mules—six to the company—in addition to those we had on hand. These and the post wagon mule teams would allow us about ten to the company. Besides we were greatly in need of pack saddles as those I had were in part abandoned when I was ordered to the southeast in the previous summer. Others had been given to Major Roff and Captain Fossett. But we thought that we could soon fit up the saddles with very little expense to the government.

I made suggestion in the same letter to McCulloch that I recall and record merely because of its nature. I suggested making a requisition for all the camels at Camp Verde which were under the supervision of the quartermaster at San Antonio, if I remember correctly, for the purpose of use in our frontier work in lieu of mules. I had not known of them doing any real service since the opening of the war and thought they might be used instead of buying pack mules. Besides, if I had any knowledge of them, the region of our operations was better adapted to their nature than that where they were. Nearly the whole country we had to scout over was more or less sandy and there were scarcely any rocks or mountains until one came to the plains. There was an abundance of shrubs for them to browse on and when we did not feed them they could be fed cheaper than in their present location. But the idea was never tried and time did not permit its consideration as news was coming over the wires that Lee and Grant were in a death grapple at Appomattox.

The last of March, 1865, saw us attempting to carry on our work as usual despite the news from the eastern theatre of war. The Trans-Mississippi Department sent out, on March 28th, a republication of its orders regulating the Reserves and the Bureau of Conscription. A second order followed this one on the next day relative to enrollment of conscripts within the maximum draft ages, and the next general order directed Commandants of Slave Labor to turn over slave labor in their respective districts to the chief engineers of Texas, West Louisiana, and Arkansas, respectively. Men and officers delivered on parole were notified that they were exchanged and should immediately rejoin their command.

Notwithstanding these fine attempts at maintenance of discipline and organizations there were numerous garrison courts-martial during the last few weeks of the war. These men, if convicted, were generally given rather severe sentences at labor and loss of pay and privileges. Chief among the charges against the accused was over-staying of leave on furlough. Desertion was on the increase, possibly influenced by the news of Lee's surrender and realization of its significance. Still, I remember giving a general order on April 21st to my company officers consisting of my Frontier companies, Fossett's Battalion, and Mosely's company, recently attached to my command, to arrest any deserter or anyone absent without the approval of the Commanding General, that they found in the settlement. I also ordered that loafers and stragglers were likewise to be picked up without awaiting orders from my headquarters. Sharp watch was to be maintained, also, for the appearance of Indians in the settlements.

We prepared to have the quartermaster issue what clothing, pack saddles, buckets, etc., that we needed, in so far as he could supply us, as Colonel Bourland ordered my Command ready for an advance movement as soon as possible. He wanted the preparation made quietly and all of my men save two companies concentrated at Belknap. The occasion for the order was the expected approach of Blount from Fort Gibson on the fifteenth with fifteen thousand cavalry. The order was dated the sixteenth of May and I received it the twentieth. Bourland felt that with General Shelby's Division, other troops, and our own that we could give him a hearty welcome if he crossed Red River. I hastened to execute the order, be it caused by rumor or fact, as we had long guarded our frontier and did not care to see the enemy cross it in our section during the last days of the war.

However, it was about all over. Although General McCulloch wrote on the nineteenth that he had news that General E. Kirby Smith was not going to surrender, he had actually surrendered by the time that I received a copy of the General's letter. Reports that the Yankees had begun a course of oppression east of the Mississippi that was unbearable, caused McCulloch to declare in a letter that he was prepared to fight to the last as death was preferable to submission to such treatment. So we were expected to hold our troops firmly together that we might make the best fight possible.

But ours was indeed a "lost cause." Hardly a week had elapsed since I had received the above mentioned letter of General McCulloch to let the men know that they must fight, when news came of General Smith's surrender, and everything fell into confusion. Seeing that the war was ended, I issued my last special order to the commanding officers at Camps McCord and Colorado that they should discharge the troops at once. I told them that I knew not what better to do in justice to all than to disperse the men. As they had not drawn any pay for fifteen months, I directed that they should make an equal distribution among the men of all the public property at the camp; which was very little, of course. Our regiment, perhaps it is not too immodest to record, had helped hold the frontier along the northern part of the line during the war. To be sure, there had been wavering at times, in a few settlements, but we had done fairly well. In less than two years after these frontier troops had been mustered out, the settlements were pushed back in many places more than one hundred miles.

CHAPTER XVIII

RECONSTRUCTION AND
THE LATER YEARS

ALTHOUGH the frontier had seen less bloody forays during the War Between the States than it would have had it not been for the armed organizations against their invasion, the raiders had by no means been shut out. But the returning of thousands of veterans to their homes from the war theatres across the River would have caused the outsider to think that now the Indians would be forced to behave. However, the opposite proved to be true. The surrender of the Confederate armies seemed to be a signal for not only renewing but increasing in intensity the savage warfare against the State from Red River to the Gulf.

Experienced men were ready to come forward to defend the frontier against these hosts of savages, but "reconstruction" times were beginning and armed forces of ex-Confederates were frowned upon by the Congress which was rapidly falling under the dominance of radical members. Federal troops were not brought forward to the frontier because certain leading members of Congress were so insistent upon their use to protect the rights of the "Freedmen." In this connection, Governor Throckmorton telegraphed President Johnson concerning the falling back of the settlers from the frontier and the fact that the legislators had authorized him to use volunteers on the frontier, but under the control of the Federal government. Then he wrote Stanton, Secretary of War, asking him to take some of the troops from around the cities and place them on the frontier. Throckmorton had been elected governor under the constitution of 1866, adopted as a part of the presidential reconstruction program. Now that returned soldiers made men more plentiful, his plans might have blocked the raids of the Indians which were renewed with new vigor in 1867. But the Federal military authorities would not aid him, and in August, 1867, removed him from office on the ground that he was guilty of blocking reconstruction.

Moreover, General Phil Sheridan, in charge of the Fifth Military District, which included Texas, thought the retiring of the settlers to the interior had been exaggerated and that they were merely moving back to be near markets to trade. It was thought that Stanton might have ordered some assistance but for such reports from Sheridan. Sheridan later learned of his mistake and admitted it. Major Forsyth was sent by Sheridan to the frontier to get first hand information but went no farther than Waco, about sixty-five miles east of my community. The frontier line of settlements was about thirty-five miles west of me by this time, having advanced there during the past few years.

The frontier was in a helpless condition. Governor Throckmorton had a little tiff with Sheridan concerning the seriousness of the frontier needs. In fact, their dispute probably influenced the legislature to pass a defense act in September, 1866. Of course, Sheridan was suspicious of the State's attitude while the Governor was worried by the necessity of doing something while waiting for the reversal of the General's misinformed opinion. Meantime, it was the old, old story. Indian agents and commissioners allowed Indian traders to have permits to sell arms and ammunition to Indians in large quantities. These Indians were on peaceful terms with the United States, in fact, were receiving annuities from the government while they were making depredations on Texas.

It was during this situation that I received some letters from Governor Throckmorton which gave me confirmation of the suspected state of things. Perhaps one or two of them might be regarded here as pertinent. On November 21, 1866, he wrote:

State of Texas, Executive Department,
Austin, November 21st, 1866.

Capt. J. B. Barry,
Meridian, Bosque Co., Texas.

Having heretofore authorized you to raise a company for frontier defense under recent act of the Legislature, and having received information from Major Generals Sheridan and Heintzelman, that the frontier will be amply protected by U. S. troops, and these troops now being *en route* to the frontier, I deem it proper to again advise you, as by previous order, that you will incur no expense in the organization of your company, against the State. I deem it also proper to say, that I apprehend the State will have no immediate occasion to use her frontier forces; yet, I would be gratified if your company was organized in order that its services might be made available in any sudden emergency, arising from Indian invasion or depredation. I would advise this, independent of any ulterior use to be made of the frontier men, by the State, because such an organization might be of great service in assisting as occasion might require, the federal troops. Our own people being much better qualified to follow trails, etc.

Companies of citizens organized with squads in different neighborhoods could frequently be of great service.

Whenever your company is organized and Roll sent up, I will send Commissions to the Officers, so that in the future if service is required, there need be no delay.

Very respectfully,
J. W. THROCKMORTON,
Governor of Texas.

P. S.—Enclosed you will find a commission as Major of the Regiment. I would have consulted you about this at first, but I learned directly I came to Austin that your health was very bad and I tendered the commission to another. It turned out that the person to whom I had proposed it did not wish to engage in the service.

Pete Ross is Colonel; Ed Burleson, Lieutenant Colonel. It will do no hurt for you to hold the commission even though no service is required. But should it be necessary for our folks to take the field I know you will render all the service in your power.

Very truly,
J. W. THROCKMORTON.

The regiment referred to in the Governor's letter was the Frontier Regiment authorized by act of the 11th Legislature, which had been approved on September 21. Added light is thrown on the state of affairs by another letter written the next day by the Governor. It read as follows:

Executive Office,
Austin, November 22, '66.

Dear Major:

Accompanying this you will find circular letter addressed to all the parties authorized to raise Companies.

But for your own private information I will say that if the Indians continue to depredate and the government does not effectually stop them, in the Spring I contemplate a campaign even if it has to be done secretly. But there is not yet a company organized that I know of.

But should a campaign be made, if the frontier companies are not raised, we can get the men.

In the meantime I am trying to induce the Government to have a new Indian treaty and send commissioners from Texas, so that the Indians can be taught to know that Texas is a part of the U. S. If this treaty can be got up we may succeed in getting back our children and women who are prisoners.

The federal cavalry are now going out to Fort Mason, Inge, Camp Verde, Clark, etc. This is the 4th U. S. cavalry. The 6th cavalry, 11 companies, will have their Hd Qrs at Jacksborough. Those of them not gone are to leave here in a few days. I have requested that two companies or more of this force be placed at Camp Colorado—and also 2 companies in the corner of Erath or Comanche—somewhere in that vicinity—and a part of the 11 companies in Montague. I think this will be done—as soon as I learn the facts I will write you.

Truly Yr Friend,

J. W. THROCKMORTON.

P. S.—I have had a pretty broad hint that the State troops had as well not be sent out. This P. S. is private.

T.

In March of the next year, I wrote the Governor tendering suggestions concerning the establishment of a chain of posts and their location. It was my idea to use a similar method to that used by the old Frontier Regiment in the years when it had operated rather effectively and with less hindrance from outside forces—in 1862-63. The Governor replied:

Austin, March 30, 1867.

Maj. J. B. Barry,
Meridian, Bosque Co., Texas.

Dear Sir:

   Yours of March 16th at hand. A copy of portions of your letter with suggestions from me to Genl. Griffin, has been forwarded
to his Hd Qrs. I have been constant in my endeavors to get Posts
established all along the frontier, and have great hopes of success.
I have thought Phantom Hill was most too far out, but I presume
you know best, therefore, I insist on it in my communication.

   Rest assured I shall not weary in my efforts.

Yours truly,

J. W. THROCKMORTON,
Governor of Texas.

The Comanches had raided in Comanche and Parker
Counties in 1866 with some loss of life for the whites as well
as kidnaping of children but met some resistance in both sections. They were defeated in an attack on some wagoners in
Comanche County and were driven off in storming the house
of a man named Millsap in Parker County. But they managed
to kill a few families and take about four children.

The spring of 1867 saw the beginning of raids by the
Comanches, repeated at every full moon, throughout the summer. In one of these raids they came into Bosque County and
stole from me, in day time, thirty-seven head of horses and one
strawberry roan stallion. I had turned the horses on the open
range, feeling somewhat secure, as no raids had come quite to
my vicinity, but the marauders stole past the settlements of the
frontier line and raided a portion of my stock. Of course they
knew from old experience the physical contours of the country
and took advantage of mother nature in getting a good start
on their way out. I valued the horses at fifty dollars each and
the stallion at $250.00.

I had a Mr. Johnson herding the horses but he was evidently not "on the job" and I paid the price. But despite their
cunning and speed the Indians' crime was seen by a neighbor
boy, Ole T. Nystel of Meridian. Another boy, named Helton,

followed the Indians a short distance and then gave the alarm. Neighbors organized a pursuit squad led by a Mr. Helm of Clifton, but none of the horses were recovered. The posse did get sufficiently close to have a sharp brush with the Indians who managed to wound Carl Gueston and capture a fourteen-year-old boy as they rushed out of the county. The boy was taken to the Big Bend Agency later and traded, but he afterwards got away and made his way home.

Bosque County was more fortunate in 1868 but was to witness a final raid in 1869. Counties to the north of us had been invaded in 1868 and so I decided to make a little preparation by way of precaution for 1869. Colonel L. D. Mayman, in command of the state citizen soldiers asked me to raise a company of county militia to operate against any invading hostiles. So in January, I recruited a company of twenty-five men for an indefinite period of enlistment. On the 20th, we made a six-day scout but found no Indians. But while returning we discovered two lurking Indians and chased them into the heavy brush on the Leon River. Here they managed to elude us. This was practically the last of my quarter century's experience in trying to protect the scalps of the helpless and keep my own hair from blowing in the breeze at the top of some Indian brave's wigwam.

The final raid of Indians into my county, mentioned above, was one which threatened, momentarily, to cause a controversy. Indians were seen by some of the citizens, an alarm was given, and a crowd of citizens organized, stole upon them, opened an attack and killed all the redskins—seven in number. It was then learned that these Indians were on a hunt and had a pass from their agent at Fort Sill. The agent was very angry. But the citizens had thought it merely another group of marauders from the Territory and did their duty as they saw it. The Indians were far from home, raids had recently been made, and no one, least of all the Indians, had apprised the people of their presence and their business, until both were accidentally discovered.

It was during one of these last raids in my section of central Texas that an incident occurred which has probably been forgotten except by the immediate relatives and neighbors of the persons involved. The scene of the little adventure was in the upper Duffau Creek country where the prairie was interspersed with timber and settlers were still rather scattered.

The wife of a young farmer named Hurley, decided, in the absence of her husband, that she would take her infant and visit, for two or three days, a neighbor several miles distant. She saddled her horse and led him to the front porch, got her baby, and set out for her acquaintance's. After some two hours, she arrived without mishap. She enjoyed the stay of a couple of days and nights and then suggested to her hostess that the visit now be reciprocated by returning to her home. After some persuasion, during which she emphasized her loneliness in the absence of her husband, the invitation was accepted.

They saddled their ponies, got the baby and a package of food and rode off gaily enough. (They were riding side-saddle, of course.) When the distance had been narrowed to some three miles, and when they had reached the prairie in front of their destination, one of the women happened to glance to the rear. She saw a cloud of dust rising in timber through which they had ridden some minutes before. The dust could not have been caused by their slow passage and she called the attention of her companion to what had excited her curiosity. They paused, gazed for a moment, and caught sight of several figures on horseback riding swiftly through an open space in the timber. It was only too obvious that the leading figure of those who seemed to be following their trail was an Indian, as a flash of color from his war bonnet was plainly visible in the noon-day sunlight.

Wheeling their horses about, they urged them into a run. If any doubt lingered concerning the identity of their pursuers it was dispelled by the dreaded war whoop and shouts from the redskins who were now aware that their expected victims had recognized them. Racing to the house, side by side, each woman was trying to think of some means of escape after they had reached it and yet wondering if they could reach even this temporary refuge. There would be no time for barricading of doors and there was only one rifle and an axe in the house with which they might defend themselves. A raid of the Indians, after some years cessation, had not been expected and, as usual, came at such an unguarded time. Even if they reached the house which offered shelter, the attackers would soon batter down the doors or burn the building over their heads.

By the time the women neared the house the Indians had narrowed the intervening distance to half a mile. The late hostess plied the whip vigorously to her own horse and that of her friend with the infant in her arms. They reached the board fence in front of the house and jerked the ponies to a sliding stop, after almost crashing into the fence. In fact, the woman riding alone fell over her horse's head into the yard. But she was on her feet at once and raced through the gate and took the baby of her friend, who sprang from her mount, and they dashed into the house, slamming the door behind them.

There was only a second's pause, and Mrs. Hurley, whose home they had reached, grabbed the hand of her friend and they went out the back door and into a patch of large weeds. They ziz-zagged some fifty or sixty steps from the house, keeping the house between them and their pursuers, however, and got to where the weeds were rank all around them. Here they dropped to the ground, breathing heavily, and yet almost fearing to breathe.

In the meantime, the Indians had charged directly to the front of the house, dismounted, and entered through the front door. It took only a moment to satisfy them that their victims were not hidden in the house, so they went out the back door and scattered, at their chief's orders, to search through a thicket and a portion of the weeds. The thicket and the weeds yielded nothing and they hurriedly redoubled their efforts to find the women and the infant whom they knew could not have gone far.

The women lay prone and, at times, literally held their breath as some brave stalked near them, parting the thick weeds with his hands in his efforts to be thorough in his search. At times, it seemed that their discovery was certain, and when the infant began to pucker its lips to cry, the mother became almost frantic. Nettles were stinging the baby and the mother was aware that this had caused her child to start crying. But to move the child might shake a weed and betray them while the slightest whimper would assuredly seal their doom. So, the poor mother, to prevent the baby's crying, courageously did a thing that wrung her heart. She took her handkerchief and choked her child until it became limp in her arms and began to turn black in the face.

Perhaps it was due to the Indians' hastily conducted search, inspired by fear that the settlers might have picked up their trail, that the women were not found. Too, the weeds were alive and vigorous and had swayed back into place when the women had passed into them so that no easy trail had been left. Then there was the danger that men were possibly near the premises, and that may have decided the marauders not to make a minute search for tracks or trail of the women.

Anyhow, the Indians returned to the house, ripped open the bed mattresses, and scattered their contents over the floors, smashed a mirror, broke some of the furniture and returned to their horses. As they rode away, they paused to drive arrows through two or three chickens and some hogs. No horses or cattle were about the house save the nags of the women, which they took. They were heard to gallop away and some time was allowed to elapse before the women ventured to raise their heads above the weeds and then to steal quietly, and with many glances about them, back into the house.

On another occasion, but during one of these last raids into my portion of the State, Indians thoroughly frightened some women in Erath County. This story illustrates one piece of strategy used by the wives of frontier settlers to save their scalps and their homes.

One morning at daybreak, two or three men and their families met at the home of an old settler named Collins. The men had come to assist the old gentleman in getting out some new rails for a fence. They had to go several miles to the best timber where they were going to cut down trees and split the rails, so an early start was desired. After a few minutes preparation, the men were ready and set out for the scene of the day's work, leaving the women and small children to enjoy a visit with Grandma Collins and her little grandson, Eddie.

It was a beautiful day. The women had assisted Mrs. Collins in completing tidying up the house and had repaired to the front porch for a welcomed chat. Suddenly, one of the women who was sitting facing toward the prairie, which was widest out in front of the house, uttered an exclamation and pointed toward the object of her attention. After a moment, the object became more clearly defined and was seen to be horsemen. Another brief passage of time showed the horsemen to be coming on the run and it was soon to be discerned, from some of their painted ponies and head dresses, that they were Indians. The children were called from play and all went inside, barricaded the doors and windows, and firearms were taken from their racks.

The Indians charged to almost within shooting range of the house, when their leader threw up his hand as a signal for a halt. They drew up to their chief for a pow-wow and soon evidently decided on a movement, as they began to walk their horses in single file away from the leader. With their varied colored ponies, painted faces, feathered head-dress, and erect posture on their mettlesome ponies, which danced with excitement and yet were so easily sat by their riders, the horsemen presented a colorful but unenjoyable spectacle to witness. At a signal, they raced forward to form a large circle, with intervals between them, around the house. The circle was completed and they raced some two or three times about the house. Then they halted and suddenly faced their ponies toward the house, still retaining their circle formation.

In the meantime, the women had watched these movements with much fear. Apparently, the Indians were preparing for a charge on the house, but had not definitely determined whether its inhabitants were solely women and children, whom they had no doubt seen enter the house while they were some distance away. While the Indians were waiting in their circle formation, sitting their horses, with perhaps their next move a critical one for the women and children, Grandma Collins decided on a bluff which might deter the Indians in making an attack which could only have had one result.

She called her little grandson Eddie to her and talked to him rapidly and earnestly for a few seconds. He was told to go climb on top of the front gate's highest post and perch himself there until told that he might descend. Now, little Eddie had heard Indian stories around the fireside and he saw that these men around his home were real Indians and he was frightened. But obedience to his elders had been instilled into him since infancy and he dared not disobey his grandmother now. So out he went and slowly climbed up the plank gate and on to the top of the large gate post.

The Indians now charged forward toward the house as at the center of a ring, but abruptly checked their ponies after nearly a fifty yard dash, wheeled, and raced back to their former position. Now the chief signaled for the warriors around the circle to again assemble around him. A moment's talk was held and then, with a concerted gobble of their war whoop and shaking high over their heads their rifles, they charged in mass directly toward the boy on the gate post. It appeared that they had decided to make good their first threats and really carry the attack to those in the house. On the other hand, maybe they were going to capture the boy. Or perhaps they were trying to draw the fire of the defenders and thus learn something of the fighting strength of those inside. If men were secreted, they might now show their hand.

But just when the women decided that the redskins were in range and that they must fire, even though it would reveal their weakness and precipitate the attack, the charge halted. The warriors stopped their mounts in their tracks, wheeled them into line and again started on a run for a repetition of their encircling movement. And now, the boy on the post witnessed a display of splendid horsemanship, as the warriors rode first erect and then on the farther side of their ponies clinging with one leg and foot over the mount's back and an arm around his neck, and then erect again, meanwhile firing their arms occasionally, although they were hardly in range and must have known it. And such feats were not common to all the Indians who rode horses.

Their fire was not returned and the racing ponies were again brought to a halt. Led by their chief, the Indians now rode several paces forward, until they evidently thought gun range had been reached, stopped, and indulged in some shouts, gestures, and cat-calls which largely consisted of dares to any paleface present to come out as a champion of his race and offer combat to any warrior present. But, of course, no reply was forthcoming and again they were quiet for a moment. With an earnest and apparently studious gaze toward the house, in which it seemed that they wished they could have an answer to the question in their minds, they shouted a last vituperation and rode away.

Not until the invaders were seen to fade over the distant hills was little Eddie given permission by his grandmother to descend from his precarious position. He had had an experience

not of his own choosing nor for which he could see any necessity, until his elders carefully explained the situation to him
and called him "a little man." But it was something that he
always vividly remembered, and although neither he nor the
others present realized it at the time, he had just witnessed the
last invasion of wild Indians in his community. Grandma Collins' strategy had worked. The Indian was unwilling to fight
that which he could neither see nor comprehend; perhaps the
boy on the gate post was a bold dare to him to come within
range and be knocked from his steed by the bullets from several men secreted and ready in the house. It was hard to tell
whether the boy was being used as a lure or a bluff, and, evidently, the Red Men either decided that they had no more
time to waste in investigation or thought it might prove too
costly.

This story is not told as evidence that the Comanches
would not fight, especially from horseback. The frontiersmen
knew that they were great horsemen, confident of their ability,
and liked to fight out on the prairie where horsemanship was
an asset. However, they were not so anxious to engage in open
combat except when they believed they held or could gain
some advantage. They fought desperately when cornered, but
they seemed to prefer to run away when the opposition appeared equally capable. In flight, however, they sometimes ex-
hibited remarkable and even foolhardy daring and horsemanship. One incident which will illustrate this last statement was
told to me by one of my friends from Erath County, who was
present when the event which he related occurred.

A band of several warriors stole some horses and were
driving them out of the country, when the theft was discovered
and a party of settlers was soon on their trail. The Indians
urged the stolen ponies into a run and as their own mounts
were fresh they hoped to keep their plunder and also make
their escape. But the citizens pressed them and they had to leave
the stolen stock and try to save themselves as they were out-

numbered too heavily to offer serious battle. When the whites ran on to them they were just quitting the stock and plunging out on the open prairie, which extended several miles before them. They were armed with guns and bows and arrows and they hastily fired a few shots and loosed two or three arrows before launching into flight.

One warrior, who rode in the rear of the group, seemed to want to offer resistance. He would slow the pace of his wiry pony, twist about and snap an arrow over his shoulder at his pursuers, and then dash forward to overtake his fellows. Of course the distance was too great and his speed still too fast for accurate shooting. He repeated this maneuver several times. Between shots, he rode, literally, all over his pony. He leaned far to one side then to the other, as he gazed back, and then rode up on his nag's withers to rest him and gain a little distance. Once or twice, he hooked his feet about the animal's neck, sprawled along his back on his own stomach, and seemed to rest his chin on his mount's backbone, while he shot an arrow at the approaching horsemen. He was riding bareback, of course.

This exhibition of riding, accompanied by taunting gestures at his pursuers, continued across the stretch of prairie. Now scattered timber was being neared by the Indians with no appreciable gain by the settlers. A few minutes run would take them to brushy country and ravines where the redskins would scatter and the pursuit would be dropped as hopeless. Apparently not an Indian would fall into the hands of his enemies.

Just at this juncture of the race, the young "buck" who had been having so much fun began to execute a new feat, a repetition of which was to prove fatal to him. He sat his horse properly, but suddenly slapped both hands smartly against the withers of his pony, perhaps to give him a certain leverage, and reversed his position, now facing to the rear. Then he shot an arrow, flipped his body about, and once more faced forward. He repeated this exploit some two or three times.

The last time he was riding backwards, his steed reached the first of the trees at the timber's edge. Under the first tree that the swiftly running pony passed the young warrior was struck by an overhanging limb and swept off. For an instant he lay stunned, and then sprang to his feet and gazed at his fellows, who were evidently unaware of his mishap since he was several yards to their rear, who were now disappearing in the brush. Facing about, he saw the foremost of his pursuers almost upon him and about to ride him down. He skillfully plunged aside and reached for his bow, but his fall had caused him to lose it. He had only an arrow or two left and he grasped one of these to stab at the horseman who had almost trampled him. Swinging his horse around, the settler again approached the warrior and shouted for him to throw down his arrow. His demand was received with a threat of defiance. By this time, another of the citizens had come up, jerking out his pistol as he came, and proceeded to kill the brave with a single well-aimed shot.

But to get back to the story of the visit of the Indians to the Collins home. Grandpa Collins and his two stalwart sons, together with the three neighbors who had been at work when the Indians called, were surprised at the story of Indians in the vicinity. They were told that the marauders only numbered ten and so they decided to trail them to see if they had left the country or were still hovering about awaiting another opportunity to strike at the home. But it was now night, the men were tired, and they decided to guard the house during the night and follow the Indians the next morning as soon as the light of day made the tracks of the Indians' horses visible. After eating supper and posting guard, preparations were made to take the trail early the next morning. Rifles were examined, knives were sharpened, and Sam, one of the Collins brothers, got out the lead and bullet mold and molded an additional supply of bullets. Saddle girths were inspected as well as bridle bits and bridle reins, because an unmanageable horse in a close range fight with the foe might mean a run-away and death inflicted by one of the enemy.

By daylight next morning, the men were up, ate a hurried breakfast, and were off. The trail crossed the stretch of prairie and then turned off at a sharp angle toward the brush and a ravine. For some eight or ten miles the trail led down the ravine. Occasionally, one of the men would dismount and cautiously climb up the side of the little canyon in order to have a look around and especially to try and see ahead for at least a short distance. It was on Ike Collins' turn to take a "spy" about, that he caught a glimpse of some horses about a mile ahead and around a bend in the ravine. He was rather sure that the Indians had camped there and had been careless about making an early departure, although they may not have even contemplated that any pursuit would be made.

Ike scrambled hastily down the bank and reported his discovery. The men decided to continue their advance along the bottom of the ravine and to charge the Indians with pistols in hand and give the Rebel yell as they knew they would be discovered when they rounded the bend. To approach from along the banks would mean that they would be seen even sooner.

They rode forward as cautiously and quietly as possible, and when they had covered a little over half the distance they rode with one hand on the nose of their horses to prevent them from whinnying. But just before they reached the bend, one of the horses stumbled on a small rock and the consequent noise brought one of the redskins to the turn in the ravine. He was afoot and as he turned about toward his comrades, he yelled an alarm. The settlers spurred their mounts and dashed toward the point. When they rounded the bend they began shooting at the Indians, some of whom were already on their ponies and racing away.

While the range was only about fifty yards, the distance was too great for accurate shooting with a pistol from the back of a running horse. So the Indians reached their horses and were instantly away with one exception. This one Indian was a large and rather heavily built fellow. Evidently, he was at the side of the smoldering camp fire nearest his pursuers. His horse was standing tied with a loose knotted rope, to a small tree at the farther side of the group of horses and he thus had a greater distance to run in getting to his pony than his fellows. However, he reached his pony, sprang on him without touching his hands to help, and reached forward and jerked the rope loose. He dug his heels into the pony's flanks, whirled him about, and the animal sprang away. The rider was on the point of throwing himself to one side and riding with his body protected by his mount, when he was overtaken by a shower of lead. One of the bullets struck in the side of his head and he was a "good Indian" before he hit the ground. His pony raced frantically on after the Indians already out of sight down the ravine. As their ponies were fresh and they would scatter in the brush if pressed too closely, Grandpa Collins waved the pursuit to a halt.

Some of the brave's equipment was taken for souvenirs and the men returned to the home of Collins. Had the Indians posted a sentinel the approach of the settlers would have been easily observed and they would have either met with an ambush or found that the redskins had gone. Seldom was the wily Red Man so careless. Of course, one explanation for their headlong flight might be that they were taken by surprise and did not know the size of the force attacking them.

There was plenty of work for good citizens to do in assisting to maintain law and order during the next few years, with the change in the government at Austin after Governor Throckmorton left office. Such men as Captain Jack Cureton, Ed McKezick, and others were outstanding in this work in Bosque County. But it was good to feel that I could again devote some earnest attention to my lands and stock. Besides, enough game

remained in the community to permit me to resume a favorite
sport, the result of which was not bad for the larder.

Politics interested me somewhat in the 'seventies. I remember going back to my old home State, North Carolina, and organizing some local chapters of the Grange. In the 'eighties,
my neighbors saw fit to elect me to the legislature. When I
went to Austin at the opening of the session, in January, 1883,
I found many old soldier friends there. There were Captains
William Pitt, Milton Boggess, and King. Others seemed to
know me but I knew few of them, although it was a pleasure
to greet them. The Senate organized in half a day, but it took
almost two days to organize the House.

As a change from the slow and tiresome organization pro-
cedure of the legislature I attended the Baptist church on the
fifteenth. Three days later came the inauguration ball, which
I enjoyed as a spectator. As the session got under way, I noticed
that we had one Mexican and two negroes as members of our
body. It was soon evident that some members had ridden hobby
horses to the Legislative Hall and could not be induced to dismount and stand on the creed of justice. Personally, I was tre-
mendously interested in getting something on the statute books
concerning the regulation of fence cutting. My bills hardly got
far toward acceptance but perhaps they did call attention to the
necessity of doing something with this matter.

My last efforts in my limited experience in politics were
expended in 1898 when I ran for State Treasurer. I did not
get anywhere, but the race was not uninteresting nor lacking in
its humorous side. Such a defeat in my declining years, I was
able to accept gracefully enough, I trust. One thing that
pleased me after this campaign had ended, was a kind letter
from Dr. George P. Garrison, of the University of Texas,
who notified me that I had been elected a member of the State
Historical Association and requested something from my recol-
lections for publication in the quarterly of the Association. I
appreciated this request but I could not get around to comply

with it. Then, later, there were the notices of meetings, and personal letters frequently accompanied them, from the Secretary of the Texas Veterans Association, who was none other than my old friend, F. R. Lubbock. There were numerous meetings also of the Confederate Veterans. Some of the meetings of the Veterans of the Republic were held at such cities as Houston, Lampasas, and La Grange, and I was so fortunate as to be in attendance at a few of them. The convention at La Grange was held on April 20-21, 1905.

EPILOGUE

ALTHOUGH Colonel Barry has told his own story with characteristic modesty, there remains to the editor the pleasant duty of indicating some of the personal qualities of this frontiersman as viewed by his contemporaries. It seems proper, also, to add a little to the record of his later years.

When Barry settled between the North and the East Bosque Rivers in December, 1855, there was only one house between this new home in Bosque County and Fort Graham on the Brazos in the western part of Hill County. But he was well fitted for this new environment and the experiences awaiting him. He was fairly well educated for the times, experienced in war and public service, of proven courage, ordinarily patient, fair spoken, practical, and energetic. Although only thirty-four years old, he possessed uncommon knowledge of human nature, with unusual ability to understand Indian character. To these qualities were added such characteristics as self-possession and promptness in action so essential to a frontier leader.

A good description of Barry as he appeared during the 'fifties has been left by his contemporaries. He was of medium height, erect and had a small waist and legs; his weight was not over 145 pounds. He had dark, long curling hair (which at death was gray but never white) which he allowed to grow long and fall on his shoulders. His eyes were dark and piercing and his features were firm and regular. His carriage was erect, dignified, and indicated energy, while his manner harmonized with his militant, decisive bearing. His courtesy and interest in public affairs made him popular. He had some enemies but the better class of citizens were his friends. Those who knew him declared him to be fearless.[1] Long after most Texans had forsaken buckskin, Barry chose to wear it.

---

[1]Mrs. W. F. Love, Corsicana, Texas, to the author; interview in the Fort Worth *Star Telegram*, December 15, 1912, with R. W. Aycock, Walnut Springs.

Barry's public service was long, successful, and appreciated
by his contemporaries; but his duties in a place of responsibility
brought him occasionally, even in the army, into periods of em-
barrassment and anxiety, and in a few instances his success produced censorious envy and jealousy, in one or two fellow officers. Nevertheless, he served on the ante-bellum frontier and
through the Civil War with the confidence of his men and his
superiors. For several years after the war the efforts of state
officers to protect the frontier were looked upon with disfavor
by the officers of the U. S. army; but Barry, with other local
leaders quietly carried on against both Indian raiders and white
outlaws.[2]

He could never tolerate theft, or cowardice, or attacks on
the weak, and he believed in upholding the law, even in the
absence of the law. During the days of reconstruction, Barry
and such men as Captain Jack Cureton and Ed. McKezick of
Meridian, Texas, became the Nemesis of organized crime in
their section of the State. A contemporary, Mr. W. M. Bridges,
formerly of Meridian, Bosque County, says that, " 'Buck'
Barry was a typical westerner, and being one of the oldest settlers, was called on many times by newcomers whose horses
had been stolen by the Indians. Colonel Barry had a horror
of outlaws and thieves and did much to put law on top."[3] At
the same time, Mr. Bridges added, "he was kind, jovial, a lover
of horses and of Indian fights."

Colonel Barry had a passion for stock-raising. During the
first years on East Bosque, he had taken great delight in his
rural life with his wife and children,[4] and seemed to find ample
occupation in his absorbing domestic experiences to engage all
of his energies. But repeated raids on his horses by the Indians,

---

[2]Cleburne *Enterprise*, December 31, 1906.
[3]W. M. Bridges, Denton, Texas, to the editor, June 30, 1928.
[4]Barry was married twice. In 1847 he married Sarah A'plis Matticks, daughter of
Wm. Matticks of North Carolina, and had six children, three of whom, Kossuth, Will,
and Gus, lived to maturity. Mrs. Barry died in 1862. On July 14, 1865, he married
Martha Ann Searcy (nee Peveler) at Fort Belknap. To this union were born four children: Sallie, David P., Rachel, and Mattie.

the Civil War with its aftermath of economic depression, and hundreds of dollars trustingly invested in Texas copper mining stock with friends, as organizers, who sank his cash in mysterious and apparently devious manipulations, inflicted financial losses which were ever afterward felt by him and his family. Moreover, at various times he had made small loans to acquaintances which totaled several hundred dollars and his generosity, apparently, prevented their being collected during the following years. Even in his later years, adversity had not hardened him to pressing his small debtors, as is shown by the tenor of personal letters found in his papers.

It is certain that before the war Barry was beginning to prosper. This was true, despite a loss of twenty-eight thousand dollars incurred by going as security on a note for a merchant of Corsicana, who failed in business. A certain physician, a personal friend of Barry, had shared security on the note, but took refuge behind the shield of bankruptcy when the note was called, a maneuver which left Barry to meet the obligation alone. His original motive in coming to Texas was, in part, to acquire a comfortable competence. To make a fortune never could have been more than a distant consideration; to make stable the wavering frontier of central Texas became an obsession with him. He and his wife had acquired twenty negro slaves[5] and those that had been retained as necessary laborers on the ranch, were now freed by the termination of the War Between the States.

These changes in fortune distressed him, coming as they did in rapid succession, at the time of life when he had seen much public service and longed to resume his favorite occupations of stock raising and farming. For years the financial pinch was so great and the outlook so discouraging that when the

---

[5]See list of old notes held by (R. Q.) "Mills & Halbert," Attorneys of Corsicana, placed for collection by Barry after his removal to Bosque County, in the Barry Papers, "Undated and printed" file, in the Archives, University of Texas.

[6]Mrs. Barry had early inherited two negroes, Dick and Edmund, from her father, and one, Sopha, from her grandfather.

Granger movement reached his community, during the panic of 1873, Colonel Barry freely gave his mental energy and his time to the furtherance of its social, economic and educational program. Within the next few years, the political program which grew out of the organization was embraced by this man who for thirty years had supported the Democratic Party.[7] In 1877 he journeyed back to the old home community in North Carolina and organized local chapters of the Grange.

In 1882, Barry was elected to the eighteenth Legislature. Meanwhile, he had been trying to rebuild his shattered fortune by turning his attention again to stock raising, and it is not surprising that his efforts in the session should be centered upon measures related to stock. He introduced bills, in particular, which were aimed to "protect stock" and define the "unlawful fence and affixing a penalty therefor."[8] Although the House Committee on Fence Cutting recommended neither his different bills nor substitutes, his initiative focused attention even more sharply on these issues and ultimately secured much needed action. In fact, fence cutting was rather of common occurrence in Barry's district in the middle of the 'eighties.[9] On one occasion, in January, 1884, Representative Barry, in Austin attending a special "fence cutting" session of the legislature, received a telegram that his fence had been cut for a distance of about a mile. Barry stated that this was the third occurrence of the kind, although gates were properly placed.[10]

Colonel Barry's last active participation in public life was as a nominee of the Peoples Party for State Treasurer in 1898. He was then seventy-six years of age. Just before the election in 1898 some neighbors of Barry issued a signed statement which read in part:

---

[7]"To the People of Texas," a signed political circular published as a *Southern Mercury Supplement,* September 1, 1898.

[8]House Bills No. 66, 41, etc.

[9]The Galveston *News,* December 19, 1883.

[10]The Fort Worth *Daily Gazette,* January 19, 1884.

He has been in more fights and killed more Indians with the same force than any other officer that was ever on the frontier, which the Adjutant General's office will show, and for which the twelfth legislature honored him by presenting to him a gun, which relic he yet possesses.

During his services on the frontier he and his command recovered more than fifteen hundred head of horses from the Indians that they had stolen from the settlers, and he sent them to the settlements, and had them advertised, which enabled the people to get their horses.

The most of us have lived almost neighbors to Colonel Barry for nearly fifty years and some of us were with him in his desperate struggles with the Indians and knowing him as we do, and the many risks he has run of losing his life in protection of the helpless women and children from the inroads of the Indians and outlaws, cause us to feel under many obligations to him; and we believe the people of Texas owe him more than any other man now living in the state.[11] . . .

Although his past life and character were testified to by his friends and his published speeches[12] were rather able efforts, the election returns showed that his was a "lost cause." Once more the greater part of his attention was devoted to his ordinary occupations.

During his last years, Colonel Barry's interest in town, county, and state affairs continued. Wherever he appeared in public he was greeted with evidences of love and esteem. That he was one of her citizens was the pride of Walnut Springs.[13] For the sake of his wife and his daughter, Miss Mattie, he allowed himself to solicit compensation from the federal government for his losses in horses incurred at the hands of the Indians. These women carried on a correspondence extending over several years—even beyond the colonel's death—with depredation claims agents in Washington, but not a penny was ever received.[14] That the effort was hopeless is indicated by the following letter:

---

[11]Walnut Springs *Signal*, October 15, 1898.

[12]Barry's venture into politics late in life is of minor interest and importance and it is unnecessary either to reproduce or to analyze these speeches.

[13]The Dallas *Morning News*, August 26, 1906.

[14]Mr. Koss Barry, to the writer, August 2, 1928.

HOUSE OF REPRESENTATIVES
WASHINGTON

February 20, 1906.

Col. J. B. Barry,
Walnut Springs, Texas.
My dear Colonel:—

Inclose you herewith copy of Bill introduced for your relief because of losses incurred through Indian depredations. Your attorney requested me to mail you copy. I have had an interview with Mr. Stephens who is on the committee on Indian affairs and he tells me that his committee has never reported such a bill since he has been a member of the committee. He says that such bills are referred to one of the Departments here which always reports adversely. I very much regret that this course is pursued because it is an outrage to treat citizens in such a way.

I am doing all I can to secure a favorable report upon your other Bill.

Hoping that your condition is improved and with kindest regards and best wishes, I am

Yours, etc.,

JACK BEALL.

The Colonel lost his eyesight some years before his death, but in his blindness he was buoyant and cheerful. His presence was always demanded at the reunions of his old comrades in arms. This veteran, who had been commissioned by four governors to raise armed forces to protect women and children from the scalping knife, gladly attended these reunions, cheerfully greeted his comrades, and sympathetically listened to their reminiscences. On these occasions he rarely talked of his own experiences.[15] Once, however, he was heard to remark that, "We were perhaps in more fights than any other Confederate regiment." And, with a wry smile, he added, "I served all during the war and never saw a Yankee soldier except three hundred prisoners who were sent up to Camp Cooper on the Clear Fork of the Brazos, so that we could feed them cheap on Buffalo meat, until they were exchanged."[16]

[15] F. M. Peveler, (and others) Granbury, Texas, a contemporary, to the editor, February 12, 1927.
[16] M. B. Davis, Waco, to Miss Mattie Barry, Walnut Springs, (undated), in the Barry Papers, Archives, University of Texas.

Nothing Barry ever did became him more than the manner in which he bore the burden of old age and contemplated the end of his life. Years before he died, he made ready his sepulcher by hewing out a vault in the rock base of a hill a mile to the west of and overlooking his residence. Members of his family had been similarly interred there and he was laid to rest among his own, when he died on his eighty-fifth birthday, December 16, 1906. His last words to his son and companion of many of his adventures, Kossuth, were rational and evidenced a still vigorous mind.[17]

A few comments by contemporaries vividly portray the position occupied by Barry in the estimation of those who knew him best. No doubt many of like nature could have been secured, but a few given below are sufficient to illustrate these opinions. Judge O. L. Lockett, of the 18th Judicial District, wrote from Cleburne, on November 5, 1905:

> Mr. Koss Barry,
> Walnut, Texas.
> Dear Sir and friend:
> I enclose you a clipping from Dallas *News* of this date about your father. I thought it might be of interest to the family. If I might be permitted to make a suggestion, it would be that Colonel Barry write his own biography—it would be very interesting and certainly a very valuable contribution to Texas history. . . .

Following news of his death, the Memorial Committe of the U. C. V. Camp at Cleburne, submitted on December 30, 1906, among other resolutions, the following:

> Pat Cleburne Camp No. 88 U. C. V. has heard with profound sorrow that our old Comrade James Buckner Barry of Walnut Springs, Texas, died on the 16th inst. Col. Barry was not a member of this camp, but he was known to most of us as a true and tried soldier and one that did his whole duty to country, his State and to his fellowman. . . .
> Resolved that there never lived a truer, a braver or a more patriotic man than Col. Buck Barry.[18] . . .

---

[17]Colonel Barry was survived by his wife and six children, Kos, Gus, David, Mrs. Sallie Shelton, Mrs. Rachael Cox, and Mrs. Walter Worley.
[18]Cleburne *Enterprise*, January 5, 1907.

On December 19th, 1906, the following procedings occur in the District Court of Bosque County, in memory of
Colonel James B. Barry:

Mr. C. M. Cureton[19] to the Court: At this time I rise to inform the court in a formal manner of the death of Colonel James
B. Barry, who died at his home Sunday morning at six o'clock, and
at this time move the court stand adjourned out of honor and respect to Colonel Barry for such period of time as to the court may
seem proper. I do this for several reasons; while I know the death
of any good citizen is a matter of regret to the court and to the
administration of the laws of our country; in the death of Colonel
Barry I do believe the county has lost one of its most useful citizens, and the cause of justice a man who stood by it throughout
a long eventful life . . . His ancestors fought in the Revolutionary wars, and from that day to this, there has never been a war in
behalf of humanity in the United States that this great family did
not participate in. Colonel Barry fought in all the wars of Texas
from the time it was a republic down to the present time. He was
commissioned by General Houston when he was governor of the
state. He was commissioned by the Confederate government as
Colonel in the army, and after the death of Colonel Obenchain,
he was in command of the entire Confederate forces in western
Texas; and at that time stood as the defender of all the people
east of that line of forts from the depredations of Indians, and
many were the battles and desperate encounters that he and his
men had. He fought under all the flags that ever waved above this
state. There never lived a braver and more heroic man than Colonel
Barry.

In regard to his later life, we are familiar. He was a man who
always said and did what he thought and believed to be right, and
while on many occasions others differed with him, it may be said
that at the time of his death the great masses of the people had
approved his views on questions which, at the time he first uttered
them, were not accepted by the people at large. He was a great
man for his mentality and great for his courage, and belonged to
a heroic race which gave us our liberty and gave us these great
examples of manhood.

He was the first sheriff of Navarro County while it embraced
a good portion of this state, and while in that position he had
many dangerous men to deal with, and he did it in a manner certainly commendable. He once said to me, without the least show

[19]Now Chief Justice of the State Supreme Court.

of vanity, that in going to arrest a very desperate man he always
went by himself; that he didn't believe that an officer had the
right to endanger the lives of the community at large. He thought
it was an officer's duty first to exercise all of his wits and all of
his intelligence and all of the authority he had under the law
before calling on the citizens to endanger their lives to take a
desperate man. He followed this up by stating who the character
was and how successful he was upon the occasion stated.

For several reasons stated, I make the motion and now introduce to the court the oldest member of the bar here at the present
time, Captain T. C. Alexander.

Captain Alexander, to the court:—I desire to second the motion
and also to make a few remarks upon the character of Colonel
Barry. I have been acquainted with him for forty-eight or forty-
nine years. I was here when he moved to Bosque County, forty-
eight or forty-nine years ago.[19] Mr. Cureton has recited some of
Colonel Barry's experiences as sheriff of Navarro County. In that
day, as Mr. Cureton said, he had desperate men to deal with,
which he succeeded in doing without taking life or having his life
taken. He was successful in his efforts to arrest men who would
be arrested. These were pretty hard times in this country at that
time. His first military service was under the Republic of Texas.
He was on the frontier and I think was stationed at Johnson's
station, about where Fort Worth now stands. I think he called it
the regular army of Texas that was stationed on the frontier of
Texas at that time. He was one of the most successful Indian
fighters I ever knew. Some men, probably the McCullochs and
Jack Hayes, had a reputation before his day, but whether they
were any better Indian fighters, I have my doubts. When he found
Indians he pitched into them. He generally succeeded in killing
some Indians and in capturing the stock they had in charge.

I have been very anxious and have suggested to some of his
family that he would write out or have some one write his experiences on the frontier in fighting Indians. It would be exceedingly
interesting. He had many fights and was out on the frontier with
four or five men at times and would have Indian fights. He was
sometimes without a commission from the government and would
have fights with the Indians. . . .

As a man, Colonel Barry was a man of fixed religious principles. He had a high sense of right and wrong. His religious principles would seem rather peculiar to some of us, but he believed
them and adhered to these principles and acted out his life in accordance with these principles that be held, as an honest man and

---

[19]Fifty years.

a Christian. He once represented this district in the Legislature.
I was at that time living in Waco. I don't know much about his
political history, but he served one or two terms from this district. Everybody who knew Colonel Barry knew where to find
him on any subject of right and wrong.

We have lost a valuable citizen. His life was an example and
one worthy of imitation by the young men of the rising generation, and worthy to be imitated while we live and he ought to
be held in remembrance by all the people on this frontier, for
the services he did in protecting it from the inroads of Indians
for a number of years.

Judge Lockett:—The court is very glad to accede to the request that has been made to adjourn out of respect of Colonel
Barry on account of his death. Of course it is understood that it
would be impossible for the court to adjourn on the death of
every good man, but I do think that when a man has served his
country as long and as well as Col. Barry has, and has undergone
the hardships of frontier life in preparing this great country that
we now enjoy the fruits and privileges of by reason of his labors
and hardships, that it is entirely proper to grant the request as
made. It has been my pleasure to have known Col. Barry very
well ever since I have been in this county. I remember the day
when I first met him in Meridian where they were holding some
kind of a convention. I met him and old Capt. J. J. Cureton together, and they were talking and joking each other as was their
custom. They were strong personal friends and both men of strong,
individual character. I was quite a young man and had just come
to the county and they made quite an impression on me at the
time. They took dinner at old Capt. Fossett's[21] that day. I thought
I could well pitch my destiny and my life in a county the citizenship of which was composed of such men. They were two
representative citizens of the county and I thought I could well
afford to locate among such people as them. I have known of Col.
Barry and his history from that day to this. That was in August
1874. The family into which I married has been so intimate with
Col. Barry's family, that necessarily, if for no other reason, made
me keep up with the history of Col. Barry and his family.

I sometimes think we fail to appreciate the great life work of
these old frontier men, who came here when this was a wilderness and as we might say, blazed out the paths of civilization for
us, and the fruits of whose labors and hardships and toils we now
enjoy. As Captain Alexander has suggested, I am sorry that Col.
Barry has not written his life, giving the details of the important

---

[21]Ex-commander of Fossett's Battalion attached to the Frontier Regiment.

transactions that came under his observation. One of the greatest
histories in the world could be written if the lives and the details
of these old frontier men were written. I think it is a great subject and full of many incidents that have few equals in history.
When we think of a man coming from civilization and bringing
his wife and children many miles out into the frontier that was
threatened by savages, and risking his own life and the lives and
happiness of his wife and children and rearing his children under
these difficulties, and think of the benefits and rewards that we are
reaping today that they didn't get, I think we fail to give them
credit and honor due them and that they are entitled to. Col. Barry
was a man of ideas and thought and, as he thought, the honest
purposes of his life were contended openly and above board. That
kind of a man creates opposition, but always challenges the admiration and love and respect of all honest citizens. I believe Col.
Barry had that. He had it in his lifetime and I believe his name
will go down in history in this state with all honor and respect.

I have known something of his family history, and as Mr.
Cureton remarked, he is from a great family and one of which any
man might feel proud. Col. Barry hasn't always been on the popular side of public questions, but he never hesitated to declare and
contend for what he honestly believed to be right. That not only
challenges the admiration of his friends but of his enemies.

I shall grant the request as made, and the District Court will
now stand adjourned for a period of 24 hours out of respect to the
memory of Col. James B. Barry.[22]

R. W. ("Dad") Aycock, who came to Walnut Springs in
1868, in course of a conversation on Barry, said:

He was one of the best men that ever lived, when he was
treated right, but if a man didn't want to do the right thing, or
wanted a scrap, he could get it out of Buck any time.

Barry was a mighty good citizen. Everybody gave him that
name. They all knew him as an old frontier ranger. That man
gave half he made to people who had been robbed by Indians,
and there were plenty of them. I expect he gave away in his lifetime as many as 200 horses. He was the first sheriff of Navarro
County, which was composed of Hill, Falls, Navarro, Limestone,
and Freestone counties, and so thinly populated that I have heard
him say he did not believe the whole county had over 500 votes.

He used to come into town every day or so up to the time of
his death, and every one knew him and was glad to see him come

and before he died he saw the prairie where he had settled grow to a town of 1,200 people.

Captain Goodnight, of the Plains of Texas who saw service under Colonel Barry during the war, related the following anecdote concerning his commander, which, although it does not contribute to the character sketch, is deemed worthy of reproduction here:

Buck Barry had a very low and pleasant voice. He gave very few orders, all in his gentle manner and easy tone of voice, but when he gave an order we knew he meant it. He was a man of very quick and accurate decision; his coolness in engagements was remarkable.

He had gotten hold of a single barrel shot gun of the cap and ball type, the longest and largest I ever saw, it must have been nearly six feet long and it chambered three, forty-six shooter balls and was a hard hitter, carried a great distance. About October, '62 or '63 the Colonel had to go to Weatherford on some important military business. At that time Indians were quite numerous along our frontier, so when Barry went to leave the post he selected a man named Willett and myself for escorts, only the two of us. I was then ranching on the Keechi near Black Springs, my mother and step-father kept the ranch headquarters there. We rode from Belknap to this ranch the first day and reached Weatherford the next day about two or three o'clock and on our arrival there he asked us to take him to Shirley's office, who held some kind of important confederate office on the west side of the square. After remaining there a while he asked us to take him to Tucker's blacksmith shop.

It happened that after the rebellion had set in, this man Tucker had been making six shooters contrary to law of course. When Barry entered his shop he asked Tucker if he was not making pistols. Tucker shyly answered in the affirmative, then Barry said, "Can't you make me a six cylinder for this shot gun?" Tucker said he could if he could get a piece of steel big enough to make the cylinder. The Colonel seemed to think that this would be easy but Tucker went on to explain that he had no steel except what he could pick up in our own country and he thought it would be very doubtful to ever find a piece that size. The Colonel replied, "Is not that anvil horn steel?" Tucker said it was. He then said, "Well, cut it off and make me a cylinder." But the old blacksmith claimed he could not do that as it would put him out of business. The conversation was rather amusing as they both became quite irritated at each other and the Colonel left the shop very much disgusted.[23]

It would be unprofitable to seek to determine "Buck" Barry's exact rank among the men who converted Texas from a wilderness into a great commonwealth. Obviously, he could by no means be called a great man. But he was one of that indispensable group who made the frontier safe from savage raids and who established law, order, and security. His courage and resourcefulness made him a leader in his section, and he served his people well even to the neglect of his private advantage. He lived bravely, generously, and cleanly; he won the love and respect of the people whom he served; he died poor—as did many of his type and generation—in the midst of a people whose prosperity he had done so much to make possible.

---

[23]Captain Charles Goodnight, Clarendon, Texas, to Mr. Kos Barry, Walnut Springs, Texas, May 11, 1928.

INDEX

A

Accidents, frontier, 83

Africa, 83

Agency, Comanche, 100

Agents, Indian, dissatisfaction of citizens with, 107; see "Reservation War"

Agriculture, see farming and also names of special crops

Alamo, Battle of the, v; "Remember the Alamo . . . ", 44

Alexander, T. C., seconds motion of C. M. Cureton, 230

Alford, J. P., Dr., reminiscence of Dove Creek Fight, 194

Allen, H. M., 81

Alligators, 11; eggs of, used in playing ball, 48; fight of John O'Neil with, 49; drowns bear, 50

Ammunition, 146, 148, 157, 188, 217; scarcity of, 132, 142

Amusements, frontier: barbecues, 33, 82; camp meetings, 82 ff.; fish frys, 88, 107; fishing, 49, 88; of Frontier Regiment, 168; hunting, 49 ff., 85 ff., seining, 88, 95; socials, 81; talking politics, 81; visiting, 82

Anadahkoes, 109, 111, 157; see Indians

Ancestry, Barry's, 1ff.

Anderson, Harry, 103

Anderson, John, 191; reminiscence of Dove Creek Fight, 195

Anderson, Texas, 174

Annexation, Texas, to the United States, 22; undesirable settlers after, 68

Antelope, 87

Antelope Hills, 131

Appomattox (Va.), 200

Arkansas, 29, 49, 60, 61, 130, 201; Bob Tucker, horse thief, flees to, 121

Ash Creek, 29

Ash hoppers, 79

Austin, Stephen F., v, 67; persuades Texans to support Bustamante government, 44

Austin, Texas, 22, 121, 128, 148, 157, 162, 168, 169, 205, 206, 207, 219, 225; capital, Republic of Texas, description of, 1845, 21; secession convention at, 125

Aycock, R. W. (Dad), 222, footnote; on Barry, 232 ff.

B

Bahama Islands, Barry visits, 16

Bankhead, [S. P.] Brigadier General, 160

Bankhead's Brigade, 170

Banks, 180

Baptist church, 220; Pearce, member of, 65; Jacob Elliot, member of, 68

Baptist Association, Barry attends, Waco, 83

Barbecues, honoring Walker's Rangers, 82

Barnes, Captain, in Dove Creek Fight, 189, 191

Barry, A. B. (brother), emigrates to Texas, 47

Barry, Augustus (brother), 67; emigrates to Texas, 47

Barry, Bryant (brother), 94, 95; witnesses death of William Ladd, 64

Barry, Bryant Buckner (grandfather), married a Nobles, 1

Barry, Bryant Buckner (father), 1; death from typhoid fever, 2

Barry, Claudius (brother), emigrates to Texas, 47

Barry, Cora (daughter), death of, 84, 97, 108

Barry, David (uncle), Revolutionary soldier, 1; widow of, moves to Tennessee, 2

Barry, David P. (son), 223, footnote, 228, footnote

Barry, Gus (son), 223, footnote, 228, footnote

Barry, James Buckner (great-grandfather), settled in Cartwright County, N. C., 1

Barry, James Buckner, v, 81; postmaster, vi; reason for writing reminiscences, vii, ix; on religion and politics, ix; ancestry, 1 ff.; brothers and sisters, 2; birthplace, 5; boyhood, 5 ff.; steals watermelons, 6; education, 6; teaches school, 14; emigrates to Texas, 14; experience in a saloon, 15; reaches New Orleans, 16; lands at Jefferson, Texas, 17; lives with Steward and Cherry, 17 ff.; visits outside settlements, 20 ff.; joins Texas Rangers, 22; ascends the Colorado, 23; enlists with Hays' Texas

Cranfill's Gap, 120
Croft, William, 81
Crooks, Jim, Ranger, Mexican War, drummed out for stealing, 41 ff.; Captain Chandler tells story of, 42 ff.
Crops, damaged by deer, coons, hogs, 87; unattended during Indian troubles, 1859-60, 120; men furloughed to plant, 1865, 197; see names of particular crops
Cross Timbers, 29
Crow, Mr., altercation with Ellis, 64 ff.
Cunningham, James, Captain, in Dove Creek Fight, 187, 191
Cureton, Jack, Captain, in Dove Creek fight, 187, 192; assists in maintaining order, Bosque County, during reconstruction days, 219, 223; association with Barry, 231
Cureton, C. M., moves adjournment of Bosque County District Court out of respect to Barry, 229 ff.
Culver, Captain, in Dove Creek Fight, 187, 190, 194
Curt bridles, specified for Texas Mounted Volunteers, 128
Dallas, Texas, 24, 29
Dallas County, 90
Dallas Morning News, 226, footnote; 228; quoted on Indian fight near Willow Springs, 133 ff.
Darnell, Mr., families collected at home of, for protection against Indians, 106
Dashiell, Adjutant General, 157; to Barry, concerning majoralty of Frontier Regiment, 146; suggests undesirable members of Frontier Regiment be transferred to Confederate service, 156

D

Davidson, Mr., 87
Davis, M. B., 227, footnote
Decatur, Texas, 186
Deep Creek, 161
Deer, dried hams, 49; fire hunting for, 58; fights resulting in locked horns, 58 ff.
Defense act, 1866, Texas legislature passes, 204
Delawares, on the Caddo reservation, 111
Democratic party, issues call for secession convention, 125; Barry member of, 225
Denton, Texas, 223, footnote
Denton County, deserters in, 172 ff.
Desert, a, in North Carolina, 10
Deserters, increase in Frontier Regiment, 156; hunted out by Bourland and Barry,

171 ff.; many, in last days of war, 201
Diary, Barry's, partly destroyed, 145, footnote
Dike, a blacksmith, 106
Discipline, attempts to maintain, during last days of war, 201
Dixon, Dr., 96; fire hunting, 58
Dixon, Judge, intimidated by Pearce, threatens to resign, 65; refuses bail to murderers of Wells, 69
Dogs, 53, 56, 59; protect hogs from wild animals, 49; ferocity of, 50; in panther fight, 51 ff.; fight wild hogs, 87
Domestic, price of, 85
Donaldson, R. C., 81
Double Mountains, 189; Barry lost from scout company near, 125
Dove Creek, nature of terrain, 190
Dove Creek Fight, 184 ff.; organization and strength of whites, 187 ff.; white's plan of attack, 190; retreat of whites, 191 ff.; Indians better equipped, 192; casualties, 192, 195; whites return to pack mules following, 193; Indians move off toward Mexico after, 195
Dresden, Texas, 67
Drilling, Texas Frontier Regiment, 174; of little value for frontier fighting, 142
Drought, delays crops, 75; hinders work of Frontier Regiment, 166; winter, 1864-65, 197
Duffau, Texas, road needed to, 80; Indian raids around, 119
Duffau Creek, 118; horses range on, 74, 97; scouting on, 109; Mrs. Hurley's experience with Indians near, 209 ff.
Duncan, Mr., 118

E

East Bosque River, hunting on, 86 ff.; Barry's farm located on, 96, 222; see Bosque River
Eastland County, posse from, pursues Indian horse thieves, 97
E company, Texas Frontier Regiment, 151
Eddie, grandson of Mrs. Collins, helps bluff Indians, 212 ff.
Elliot, Jacob, forged deed to Taylor land, 68; acquitted of murder of Wells, 70
Ellis, Mr., altercation with Crow, 64 ff.
Ellis County, 31; hunting in, 86
Elm Creek, 189, 194; scouting on, 141
Enfield rifles, 175
Erath County, 99, 185, 215; Indian raids in, 96 ff.; ranging company organized in, 1858, 106; dissatisfaction with local

Indian agent, 107; citizens of, attend mass meeting concerning white horse thieves, 122; proposed stationing of federal troops in, 1866, 206; Collins' experience with Indians in, 212 ff.

Erath, George, Captain, 110; interprets Indian charcoal pictures, 94

Ercanbrack, Corporal, 138; fights Indians near Willow Springs, 133 ff.; scalps Indian, 139; wounded, 144

Erkenbrack, see Ercanbrack

Evans, Jack, 81

Explosives, prepared to dislodge Joe Pearce from saloon, 66

F

Falls County, 232

Fannin, "and the fate of Fannin . . . ", San Jacinto, 44

Farming on the frontier, 75 ff.

Federals, aid Indian raiders, 153 ff.; encourage Comanches to attack civilized tribes, 196

Fence cutting, Barry interested in, legislation, 220, 225

Fences, on frontier, 74 ff.

Ferris, Mr. after white horse thieves, 120

Fevers, in Texas Frontier Regiment, 150, 151, 167; Barry sick with yellow, 180

Fifer, Lieutenant, pursues Kiowas, 108

Fifth Military District, Texas in, 204

Firedogs, price of, 84

Fire hunting for deer, in North Carolina, 8; in Texas, 58

First Texas Mounted Rifles, lived on raw green corn during storming of Bishop's Castle, 38; mustered out, 40; scouting, 142; disbanded, 144, 145; see Rangers, Fort Mason, see Rangers, Fort Mason, and also H. E. McCulloch

First Texas Rangers, at Monterey, 38; see First Texas Mounted Rifles and Rangers

Fish Creek, Indian fight between, and Willow Springs, 135 ff.; scouting on, 141

Fish frys, on frontier, 88, 107

Fish hawk, loses prey to eagle, 10

Fishing, in spawning season, 12 ff.; on frontier, 49, 88

Five-shooter, price of, 85

Flag Mountains, Barry stationed at, 1861, 125

Flag Pond, Texas, 104

Flanigan's ranch, 188

Fleming, Rev. 122

Flour, 75

Fodder, 75 ff.

Ford, John S., Colonel, in command of state troops, Rio Grande, 126

Ford, Captain, surprises Comanches, 158

Fort Arbuckle (Ind. T.), 160, 164; taken over by Confederates, 129; report from, of Indian concentration, 168

Fort Belknap, 125, 146, 160, 170, 174, 180, 183, 192, 223, footnote, 233; Indian raids near, 108; scouting near, 126, 141; center of Frontier Regiment's line of defense, 147; Indians' reservation near, 157; Tonkawas located at, 159, 162 ff.; medical officer secured for, 167; four companies, Frontier Regiment, under Confederate service at, 172, 182; "Pin" Indians raid near, 175; scarcity of supplies at, 1864-65, 198; preparations made at, to repel federals, 201; see also Frontier Regiment, Barry, J. B.

Fort Chadbourne, scouting near, 125; taken over by state troops, 127; part of frontier line of defense, 146; troops gather at, preparatory to Dove Creek Fight, 187

Fort Cobb (Ind. T.), Indians moved by government to vicinity of, 117; taken over by Confederate forces, 129; Tonkaway reservation at, 157

Fort Croghan, part of frontier line of defense, 146

Fort Duncan, two companies, Frontier Regiment, stationed at, 172

Fort Gabriel, 121

Fort Gibson (Ind. T.), federal invasion of Texas expected from, 202

Fort Graham, 222

Fort Griffin, Tonkawas at, 165

Fort Inge, two companies, Frontier Regiment, stationed at, 172; Fourth U. S. cavalry stationed at, 1866, 206

Fort McKavett, post of frontier line of defense, 146

Fort Mason, 143; First Texas Mounted Rifles disbanded at, 144; part of frontier line of defense, 147; Fourth U. S. cavalry stationed at, 1866, 206

Fort Murray, Indian fight at 176 ff.

Forts, settlers', plan of, 180 ff.

Fort Phantom Hill, 141, 188, 207; part of frontier line of defense, 146; scouting near, 118, 185

Fort Sill (Ind. T.), 208

Fort Worth, Texas, 24, 230

244   INDEX

H

Hackett, anecdote of bear hunt in North
Carolina, 7

Hackworth, C. K., to Barry, 139 ff.·

Hagler, Captain, buffalo hunter, 20

Halley, Captain, 127

Hamby, in Indian fight at Bragg's picket
house, 176

Hamilton County, Indian raids, 97; militia
of, in Dove Creek Fight, 185, 187

Hamner, Captain, trails slayers of Holden
into Comanche reservation, 111; scouting, 124

Handley, B., 81

Hanna, Captain, minute-man, "Reservation War," 113

Hanna, John, captain of posse after white
horse thieves, 121, 122

Hardee's *Light Infantry Tactics*, used in
drilling First Texas Mounted Rifles, 132

Hardigree, John, 139

Harmonson, Judge, in Fort Murray Indian
fight, 178

Harper's Ferry *Jaeger*, used for hunting
large game, 56

Harrisburg, Texas, 174

Hartzell, D. B., 81

Hauling, on frontier, 75

Hawkins, Thomas G., correspondence with
Barry concerning Indian Agent Neighbors, 104

Hayne's Hotel, Corsicana, Texas, 81

Hays, Jack, 5, 24, 230; keeps spy in
Mexican camp, 22; elected Colonel of
Rangers, '46, 33; challenges colonel of
Mexican lancers to duel, 34; takes Mexi-
can battery across the San Juan, 35 ff.

Headrights, 31

Headrights certificate land, 31

Hébert, P. O., Brigadier General, 174

Heintzelman, Major General, 205

Helm, Mr., 208

Hempstead, Texas, 121; abundant forage
near, 175

Henderson, Nathaniel, sheriff, 64; Pearce
trouble, threatens to resign, 65 ff.

Henry, Patrick, misquoted, 44

Hesters, neighbors of Barry, 82

Hester, Mr., killed in Indian fight, 152

Hicks, William E., 81

Hicks, P. D., 81

Hico, Texas, 194

Hightower, Mr., 99

Hill County, 24, 29, 31, 222, 232

Hilliard, Mr., neighbor of Barry, 96

Hillsboro, Texas, 96

Hitson, William, recaptures horses from
Indians, 102

Hodge, J. B., 81

Hogan, G. M., 81

Hog Creek, Indian raid on, 120

Hogs, butchering of, 76 ff.; range-fattened
on pecan and oak mast, 77; driven to
Bosque County, 96

Holden, Mr., killed by Indians from
Comanche reservation, 111

Holden, F. M., 155

Hood County, Indian fight in, 105

Hood, Major, Minute Company, 1859,
114

Horses, "breaking", 74; raising, on frontier, 73; good saddle, necessary in Indian country, 74; stolen by Indians,
119; insufficient, for needs of Rangers,
131, 147 ff.; suitable, for frontier military service, 128; corporal Ercanbrack's,
carries news of Indian fight to Fish
Creek post, 136; better, of Indians,
153; stolen, recovered and advertised,
153; importance of a well-managed
horse in Indian fights, 218

Horse guard, 183 ff.

Horsemanship, of Kossuth Barry, 73; of
Comanches, 131, 158, 213 ff.; of Francis Peveler, 178 ff.

Horse thieves, white, 120 ff.; mass meetings concerning, 122

Houses, building of, 95, 78 ff.

Houston, Sam, 5, 42, 81, 229; losses, San
Jacinto, 43; reasons for destroying
Vince's bridge, San Jacinto, 44; power-
less to prevent removal of Indians from
Texas, 115; authorizes raising of independent ranging companies, to patrol
frontier, 117; talks with Kossuth Barry,
121; commissions Barry to raise company for frontier defense, 125; deposed by secession convention, 126;
character of, 126

Houston, Texas, 47, 48, 75, 83, 173, 180,
221; nearest market to Bazette Bluff,
56; Frontier Regiment stationed near,
174

Howard, Mr., wounded in Indian fight,
152

Hubbard's Creek, 124, 125, 189; Ranger's
camp on, 106; scouting from, 126

Humphrey, Owen, 50; drove hogs from
Arkansas, 49; hunting with, 55

Hunting, 49 ff.; 85 ff.

Hurley, Mrs., experience of, with Indians,
209 ff.

I

Impressment Laws, 182

Inaugural Ball, Barry attends, 220

Independence Hill, near Monterrey, 36

Indian Agents, dissatisfaction of Texans with, 100; sullen tempers of, 115

Indian ponies, used for food after Dove Creek Fight, 193

Indian Reservations, Brazos River, beef day on, 106; *see* Clear Fork of Brazos River, Fort Arbuckle, Fort Belknap, Fort Cobb, Indians, Indian Territory, Lower Agency, Oakland Reserve, Pattawatomie Agency.

Indians, 25, 47, 82, 124, 127, 160, 171; women and children, 27 ff.; 137, 140; patrols against, ordered by Navarro County Court, 1854, 66; raids delay harvest, 76; attack Norwegian settlers on Gary's Creek, 90 ff.; sign pictures of, 94; chased by Bosqueites, 93; manner of ranging, 94; depredations of, Bosque County, 96 ff.; able to steal much stock, 103; special investigation of Neighbors as agent of, 103 ff.; moved across Red River by U. S., became bitter towards Texans, 117; continue raids from across Red River, 118 ff.; friendly Indians as scouts for Texans, 129; manner of fighting, 133; dressed in U. S. soldier's coat, 138; weapons of, 138; fight on Paint Creek, 151 ff.; use knowledge of terrain to facilitate escape, 154; skirmish with mail express near Murphy's Station, 154 ff.; numbers of, on Texas reservations, 1854-55, 157 ff.; reservations in Texas, extent of, 157; better armed in '64, 168; save John Wooten's life, 177; strength of, Fort Murray fight, 178; sign on Clear Fork, 1864, 185 ff.; manner of fighting at Dove Creek, 190; effect of surrender of Confederate army on, 203; receive ammunition from U. S. while raiding in Texas, 204; secret campaign contemplated against, 1866, 206; final raid into Bosque County, 1869, 208; with pass from agent, killed by Texans, 208; manner of attack on frontier home, 212 ff.; horsemanship of, 131, 158, 213 ff.; careless in posting sentinel, 219; *see* Agents, Anadahkoes, Caddoes, Campo, Castile, Choctaws, Comanches, Delawares, Indian Reservations, Iron Jacket, Jack Harry, Jim Ned, Jim Pockmark, Keechies, Kickapoos, Kiowas, Lipans,

Long Tree, Noconas, Northern Indians, Osage, "Pin" Indians, Placidio, Seminoles, Shawnees, Tahwaccaroes, Tehuacana Creek, Tonkawas, Wacoes, Wichitas, etc.

Indian Territory, 118, 160, 208; U. S. government moves Indians from Texas into, 117; Tonkawas in, 157; Tonkawas placed on Oakland Reserve, 1884, 165; civilized tribes, fought by Kickapoos under federal orders, 196; *see* Forts Arbuckle, Cobb, Gibson, Sill

Iredell, Texas, 87; Peter Johnson and son attacked by Indians near, 97

Iron Creek, 119

Iron Jacket, Comanche chief, v; killed by Tonkawas, 158

Isbell, Y. H., Tonkawa agent, 162 ff.

J

Jack County, Indian raids in, 123; Indians attack mail express in, 154

Jacksboro [also Jacksborough], Texas, Indian depredations near, 125; Sixth U. S. cavalry headquarters at, 206

Jack Harry, Delaware interpreter, 26, 27

Jackson, Andrew, 101

Jacobs, Mr., after white horse thieves, 122

Jail, no, in Navarro County, 64

Jamison's Peak, 188

Jefferson, Texas, Barry landed at, on Red River, 1845, 17

Jim Ned River, 127

Jim Ned, Comanche chief, 168

Jim Pockmark, Comanche chief, 168

Jim Shaw, Delaware interpreter, 112

Johnson, Mr., 207

Johnson, Allen, resigned as sheriff, Navarro County, 62

Johnson, Andrew, president, 203

Johnson, Bill, 139

Johnson, Brit, experience with Indians, 179

Johnson County, citizens, attend mass meeting corncerning horse thieves, 122

Johnson's Peak tragedy, 96 ff.

Johnson's station, 230

Johnston, [A. S.], v

Jones County, Fort Phantom Hill in, 146

Jones, David, on spy to lower reservation, 110

Jurors, moral cowardice of, 70

K

Kansas, 186

Kansas River, 196

250 INDEX

eral Worth, 41; Walker's, 82; qualities requisite in, 131 ff.; duties and regulations, 132; Indian fights, 139 ff.; assisted by Tonkawas, 1858, 158; use Tonkawas as guides, 165; fight, Fort Murray, 176 ff.; *see* First Texas Mounted Rifles, Jack Hays

Rankin boys, hunting, 60

Rats, wood, found in panther's and wildcat's stomach, 5

Reagan, John H. and sister, 48

Reconstruction, east of the Mississippi, effects of, on Texans, 202

Reconstruction problems, 219

Red Oak Creek, 60

Red River, 22, 105, 129, 133, 141, 146, 162; Barry enters Texas by way of, 16; Choctaws cross, to kill buffaloes, 29; Texans want Indians moved across, 112, 115; Indians moved across, 117, 118; McCulloch commands five companies from, to the Colorado, 128; Texas Mounted Rifles defend frontier from, to the Rio Grande, 130; Tonkawas escorted to, 135; Seminoles escorted to, 142; Barry in command of frontier forces from Camp Cooper to, 143; hostile Indians across, 147; scouting above, 150; "Pin" Indians pursued to, 179; federal advance by way of, 180; Kickapoos below, 186; suspected advance of Blunt across, 202; Indian depredations from, to the Gulf, reconstruction days, 203

Red River Station, 155, 169; citizens near, fear Indian raids, 149; Indian sign near, 160; scouting from, 167

Religion, 47; Barry on, ix; frontier, 83

Resaca de la Palma, Texas, 33

"Reservation War", 106 ff.

Revolutionary War, 1, 229; payment of soldiers in wild lands, 2

Rice, price of, 85

Rice, Captain, in Dove Creek Fight, 187, 194

Riggs, J. M., 81

Richland Creek, 67; buffalo hunters on, 21; scouting on, 24

Richardson, Ike, anecdote, Dove Creek Fight, 195

Richmond (Va.), 143

Rio Grande, 42, 105, 115; Mexicans cross, for San Antonio, 22; Mexican army surrounded near mouth of, 33; Santa Anna driven across, 43; Texans patrol frontier from, to Red River, 117; Colonel John S. Ford in command of posts

on, 126; Texas Mounted Rifles defend frontier from, to Red River, 130; Kickapoos raid Texans from south of, 196

Road building, frontier, 80

Roberts, Chandler, 113, 119

Roberts, Lieutenant, finds Confederate money unacceptable, 147

Roberts, O. M., president Texas secession convention, 126

Robertson County, buffaloes in, 20; Barry surveys in, 31

Robertson, Doctor, 107

Robertson, Mr., 95

Robinson, W. H., Dr., medical officer, Fort Belknap, 167

Rockey community, turkey hunt in, 87

Roff, Major, 200

Rogers, Texas, 121

Romance, on the frontier, 84

Ross, Captain, 158; Indian agent, 1859, 104, 114

Ross, Hal, kills Pearce, Waco, 66

Ross, Pete, Colonel, reconstruction Frontier Regiment, 205

Ross, Sul, Captain, 114, 125; ex-governor, 66

Rough, Mr., 99

Root, E. H., 81

Rowland, Captain, Company H, Texas Frontier Regiment, 172; scouting, 150, 167, 174; reports Indian signs near post, 160; drouth hinders effectiveness of, 166; Bourland's accusation against company of, 169

Runnels County, on Frontier, 1861, 146

Runnels [H. R.], Governor, investigates difficulties between frontiersmen and reserve Indians, 116

Rush Creek, fire hunting on, 58; Indians steal horses from, 119

Rye, 75

S

Sabine River, 20, 44

Saddle blanket, price of, 84

Saline road, 19

Salt, 140

Saltillo, Mexico, 34

Salt meat, 76 ff.

San Antonio, Texas, 22, 42, 142, 148, 200; Rangers guard archives between Austin and, 21; siege of, 32; Colonel Ben McCulloch in command of post at, 126; headquarters, Military Department of Texas, 143

San Antonio road, to Santa Fé, 31; to the Yeguas, 121